# Pearls of Love

# Pearls of Love

## How To Write
## Love Letters and Love Poems

By
# Ara John Movsesian

Cover Design By
**Lightbourne Images**

Interior Illustrations By
**Suzanne Raus**

**The Electric Press**

Fresno, California

*Library of Congress Cataloging in Publication Data*

Movsesian, Ara John 1949-
      Pearls of Love: How To Write Love Letters and Love Poems (A Complete Handbook on Love Letters and Love Poems)/by Ara John Movsesian; interior illustrations by Suzanne Raus. - Fresno, Calif.: Electric Press © 1983-1993.

ix, 310p: ill 22cm.

Bibliography: p301-302
Index: p303-307

1. Love Letters. 2. Letter-Writing. 3. Love Poetry.
I. Title

ID: CFCG84-B948   CC: 9116   DCF: a

Library of Congress Cataloging in Publication No. 84-147625

CALL: 808.6M869p

ISBN 0-916919-00-5

Printed in the United States of America
First Printing, December 1983
Second Printing, June 1987
Third Printing, February 1991
Fourth Printing, September 1993

The Electric Press, P.O. Box 6025, Fresno, CA 93703

## Pearls Of Love

Words that fit your heart's intent;
    Words that seem so Heaven sent;
Words that flow with feelings true,
    Are found within to be used by you.

These letters, poems, quotes and such,
    Are here for you to add your touch.
Transform them well to suit your needs;
    These words of love will do good deeds.

So when the words are hard to find,
    And you have really wracked your mind;
Use these "Pearls of Love" to say,
    "I love you" in a special way.

*Dedicated With Love To
My Natural Mother:
Nevarte Movsesian
My Adoptive Mother:
Helen Movsesian
And My Father:
John Movsesian*

# PREFACE

Love is one of the most powerful of human drives, thus many of us spend a major portion of our lives in its pursuit. In fact, were it not for love, life would be quite a dismal experience.

The expression of one's love for another is as old as human existence. Of course, today, a club on the head would not achieve the same results as it might have at the Dawn of Man. Indeed, the expression of love has evolved greatly since the creation of verbal and written language.

Verbal language has enabled individuals to personally express their love in a more refined manner than was earlier possible. Written language has provided lover's a very potent tool which, in turn, has given rise to two forms of Romantic Communication: The Love Letter and Love Poem.

Both of these forms have been used by literate people everywhere for centuries to communicate their innermost passions, desires and emotions. Even Henry VIII and Napoleon wrote love letters to their sweethearts. The most famous legendary writer of love letters was Cyrano De Berjerac who wrote countless love letters, not for himself, but on behalf of his close friends.

Today, in this age of telecommunications, the telephone, and mass-produced greeting card have largely replaced the letter as a viable form of personal communication. Consequently, many of us have lost or failed to develop our ability to competently write letters of any type, especially love letters.

The primary purpose of Pearls Of Love is twofold: 1) to help you develop your writing skills in the areas of love letters and love poems, and 2) to serve as a modern day version of Cyrano De Bergerac by helping you express yourself when the words are hard to find.

Pearls Of Love contains sections on basic instruction as well as various types of pre-written material. It is a complete guidebook which will help you say "I love you" in a very special and unforgettable way.

Ara John Movsesian

## Acknowledgements

Acknowledgement is made to Alfred A. Knopf,
Inc. for providing a source through which I
obtained the five historic love letters from
the greats of the past.

My sincere appreciation goes to Theodora
Ebrahim, Judith Farrington, Gene Garabedian
and Alberta Melkonian for reviewing and
proof-reading the manuscript.

Also many thanks go to Rod Mazman and the
Bedrosian and Garabedian families for their
encouragement and moral support.

# TABLE OF CONTENTS

**PART I:**  **LOVE LETTERS**

**PART II:**  **LOVE POEMS**

# APPENDICES

# Part I:
# THE LOVE LETTER

# THE LOVE LETTER

The first part of this book concerns itself with the *Love Letter*, the first of the two major forms of romantic communication. A love letter is more than just correspondence; it is, in effect, a bridge which links two people - the most intimate form of written communication. If a love letter is composed well, it has the ability to touch the reader's innermost heartstrings.

This portion has been divided into five sections which contain the following: 1) several original love letters from the greats of the past along with more than forty selected love quotes, 2) a general overview of the basics of good love letter composition along with a short technique which is designed to help you organize your thoughts in preparation to writing a love letter, 3) twenty-five complete, original love letters which you can modify or use as is, 4) over sixty original love paragraphs which address a variety of sentiments and which you may use in the composition of your own love letters, and 5) more than six hundred love sentences which you may utilize to create your own love paragraphs.

Whether you need a finished love letter or merely some instructional help to get started, you will find it here along with everything else inbetween.

# SECTION 1 / LOVE LETTERS AND QUOTES FROM THE PAST

Love letters have been written for centuries. Some have survived through the years and offer us a glimpse into the romantic lives of those who have come before us. This first section contains five *Historic Love Letters* and a variety of selected *Love Quotes* from some of the great personalities of the past.

The love letters should provide you with examples of various expressive styles. You may be able to incorporate some of these in your own writing. Even if you don't, the five letters should prove enjoyable to read.

The love quotes have been gathered from world literature for you to use within your own love letters. They include excerpts from famous works of prose and poetry from greats such as Longfellow, Shakespeare and Shelley.

# LOVE LETTERS
# FROM THE PAST

## Napoleon Bonaparte
## To
## Josephine De Beauharnais
### (Paris, December 1795)

*I wake filled with thoughts of you. Your portrait and the intoxicating evening which we spent yesterday have left my senses in turmoil. Sweet, incomparable Josephine, what a strange effect you have on my heart! Are you angry? Do I see you looking sad? Are you worried?...My soul aches with sorrow, and there can be no rest for your lover; but is there still more in store for me when, yielding to the profound feelings which overwhelm me, I draw from your lips, from your heart a love which consumes me with fire? Ah! it was last night that I fully realized how false an image of you your portrait gives!*

*You are leaving at noon; I shall see you in three hours.*

*Until then, mio dolce amor, a thousand kisses; but give me none in return, for they set my blood on fire.*

# Napoleon Bonaparte
## To
## Josephine Bonaparte
(Nice, 1796)

*I have not spent a day without loving you; I have not spent a night without embracing you; I have not so much as drunk a single cup of tea without cursing the pride and ambition which force me to remain separated from the moving spirit of my life. In the midst of my duties, whether I am at the head of my army or inspecting the camps, my beloved Josephine stands alone in my heart, occupies my mind, fills my thoughts. If I am moving away from you with the speed of the Rhône torrent, it is only that I may see you again more quickly. If I rise to work in the middle of the night, it is because this may hasten by a matter of days the arrival of my sweet love. Yet in your letter of the 23rd. and 26th. Ventôse, you call me vous[1]. Vous yourself! Ah! wretch, how could you have written this letter? How cold it is! And then there are those four days between the 23rd. and the 26th.; what were you doing that you failed to write to your husband? ... Ah, my love, that vous, those four days make me long for my former indifference. Woe to the person responsible! May he as punishment and penalty, experience what my convictions and the evidence (which is in your friend's favor) would make me experience! Hell has no torments great enough! Nor do the Furies have serpents enough! Vous! Vous! Ah! how will things stand in two weeks? ... My spirit is heavy; my heart is fettered and I am terrified by my fantasies....You love me less; but you will get over the loss. One day you will love me no longer; at least tell me; then I shall know how I have come to deserve this misfortune. ...Farewell, my wife: the torment, joy, hope and moving spirit of my life; whom I love, whom I fear, who fills me with tender feelings which draw me close to Nature, and with violent impulses as tumultuous as thunder. I ask of you neither eternal love, nor fidelity, but simply...truth, unlimited honesty. The day when you say "I love you less", will mark the end of my love and the last day of my life. If my heart were base enough to love without being loved in return I would tear it to pieces. Josephine! Josephine!*

*Remember what I have sometimes said to you: Nature has endowed me with a virile and decisive character. It has built yours out of lace and gossamer. Have you ceased to love me? Forgive me, love of my life, my soul is racked by conflicting forces.*

*My heart obsessed by you, is full of fears which prostrate me with misery....I am distressed not to be calling you by name. I shall wait for you to write it.*

*Farewell! Ah! if you love me less you can never have loved me. In that case I shall truly be pitiable.*

*Bonaparte*

*P.S. - The war this year has changed beyond recognition. I have had meat, bread and fodder distributed; my armed cavalry will soon be on the march. My soldiers are showing inexpressible confidence in me; you alone are a source of chagrin to me; you alone are the joy and torment of my life. I send a kiss to your children, whom you do not mention. By God! If you did, your letters would be half as long again. Then visitors at ten o'clock in the morning would not have the pleasure of seeing you. Woman!!!*

---

[1]   **Vous** is the formal pronoun, **You,** in French. Napoleon expected to see **Tu** which is the informal (*more romantic*) pronoun. To him, **Vous** could only mean that his wife, Josephine, did not love him as much as she once did.

# John Keats To Fanny Brawne
(March 1820)

*Sweetest Fanny,*

*You fear, sometimes, I do not love you so much as you wish? My dear Girl I love you ever and ever and without reserve. The more I have known you the more have I lov'd. In every way - even my jealousies have been agonies of Love, in the hottest fit I ever had I would have died for you. I have vex'd you too much. But for Love! Can I help it? You are always new. The last of your kisses was ever the sweetest; the last smile the brightest; the last movement the gracefullest. When you pass'd my window home yesterday, I was fill'd with as much admiration as if I had then seen you for the first time. You uttered a half complaint once that I only lov'd your Beauty. Have I nothing else then to love you but that? Do not I see a heart naturally furnish'd with wings imprison itself with me? No ill prospect has been able to turn your thoughts a moment from me. This perhaps should be as much a subject of sorrow as joy - but I will not talk of that. Even if you did not love me I could not help an entire devotion to you: how much more deeply then must I feel for you knowing you love me. My Mind has been the most discontented and restless one that ever was put into a body too small for it. I never felt my Mind repose upon anything with complete and undistracted enjoyment - upon no person but you. When you are in the room my thoughts never fly out of the window: you always concentrate my whole senses. The anxiety shown about our Loves in your last note is an immense pleasure to me: however you must not suffer such speculations to molest you anymore: nor will I any more believe you can have the least pique against me. Brown is gone out - but here is Mrs. Wylie - when she is gone I shall be awake for you - Remembrances to your Mother.*

*Your affectionate*

*J. Keats*

## Juliette Drouet To Victor Hugo
### (1833)

*To my beloved,*

*I have left you, my beloved. May the memory of my love follow and comfort you during our separation. If you only knew how much I love you, how essential you are to my life, you would not dare stay away for an instant, you would always remain by my side, your heart pressed close to my heart, your soul to my soul.*

*It is now eleven o'clock in the evening. I have not seen you. I am waiting for you with great impatience, as I will wait for you always. It seems a whole century since I last saw you, since I last looked upon your features and became intoxicated with your gaze. Given my ill-luck, I shall probably not see you tonight.*

*Oh! come back, my love, my life, come back.*

*If you knew how I long for you, how the memory of last night leaves me delirious with joy and full of desire. How I long to give myself up in ecstacy to your sweet breath and to those kisses from your lips which fill me with delight!*

*My Victor, forgive me all my extravagances. They are a further token of my love. Love me. I need your love as a touchstone of my existence. It is the sun which breathes life into me.*

*I am going to bed. I shall fall asleep praying for you. My need to see you happy gives me faith.*

*My last waking thoughts, and all my dreams, are of you.*

*Juliette*

## Franz Liszt To Marie D'Agoult

(Thursday Morning, 1834)

*My heart overflows with emotion and joy! I do not know what heavenly languor, what infinite pleasure permeates it and burns me up. It is as if I had never loved!!! Tell me whence these uncanny disturbances spring, these inexpressible foretastes of delight, these divine tremors of love. Oh! all this can only spring from you, sister, angel, woman, Marie!...All this can only be, is surely nothing less than a gentle ray streaming from your fiery soul, or else some secret poignant teardrop which you have long since left in my breast.*

*My God, my God, never force us apart, take pity on us! But what am I saying? Forgive my weakness, how couldst Thou divide us! Thou wouldst have nothing but pity for us...No, no! ... It is not in vain that our flesh and our souls quicken and become mortal through Thy Word, which cries out deep within us Father, Father ... it is not in vain that Thou callest us, that Thou reachest out Thine hand to us, that our broken hearts seek their refuge in Thee ... O! we think, bless and praise Thee, O God, for all that Thou hast given us, and all that Thou hast prepared for us. ...*

*This is to be - to be!*


*Marie! Marie!*

*Oh let me repeat that name a hundred times, a thousand times over; for three days now it has lived within me, oppressed me, set me afire. I am not writing to you, no, I am close beside you. I see you, I hear you. ...Eternity in your arms. ...Oh! Leave me free to rave in my delirium.*

# LOVE QUOTES
# FROM THE PAST

## Love is...

Love is a smoke raised with the fume of sighs;
Being purged, a fire sparkling in lover's eyes;
Being vex'd, a sea nourish'd with lover's tears:
What is it else? A madness most discreet,
A choking gall and a preserving sweet.
> - Shakespeare, *"Romeo And Juliet"*

♡ ♡ ♡

Love is the magician, the enchanter, that
Changes worthless things to joy, and makes
right-royal kings and queens of common clay.
It is the perfume of that wondrous flower,
the heart, and without that sacred passion,
that divine swoon, we are less than beasts:
but with it, Earth is Heaven and we are
Gods.
> - R.G. Ingersoll, *"Works"*

♡ ♡ ♡

Love is a canvas furnished by nature and
embroidered by imagination.
> - Voltaire

♡ ♡ ♡

Love is space and time measured by the
heart.
> - Marcel Proust

## The Beginings Of Love...

Amid the gloom and travail of existence
suddenly to behold a beautiful being, and as
instantaneously to feel an overwhelming
conviction that with that fair form forever
our destiny must be entwined ... This is
love!

- Benjamin Disraeli

♡ ♡ ♡

O, there is nothing holier, in this life of
ours, than the first consciousness of love,
- the first fluttering of its silken wings.

- Longfellow, *"Hyperion"*

♡ ♡ ♡

It is difficult to know at what moment love
begins; it is less difficult to know that it
has begun.

- Longfellow, *"Hyperion"*

♡ ♡ ♡

Few people dare now to say that two beings
have fallen in love because they have looked
at each other. Yet it is in this way that
love begins, and in this way only. The rest
is only the rest, and comes afterwards.
Nothing is more real than these great shocks
which two souls give each other in
exchanging this spark.

- Victor Hugo, *"Les Misérables"*

## I Love Thee...

I love thee - I love thee!
    'Tis all that I can say;
It is my vision in the night,
    My dreaming in the day.
                    - Thomas Hood, *"I Love Thee"*

♡ ♡ ♡

The fountains mingle with the river,
    And the rivers with the ocean;
The winds of Heaven mix forever
    With a sweet emotion;
Nothing in the world is single;
    All things, by a law divine,
In one another's being mingle -
    Why not I with thine?
                    - Shelly, *"Love's Philosophy"*

♡ ♡ ♡

For soft the hours repeat one story,
    Sings the sea one strain divine,
My clouds arise all flushed with glory;
    I love, and the World is mine!
                    - Florence E Coates, *"The World Is Mine"*

♡ ♡ ♡

I love thee with the breath,
Smiles, tears, of all my life! - and, if God
Choose,
I shall but love thee better after death.
                    - Elizabeth Barrett Browning

## True Love...

True love cannot be created by mortal beings
but it can be destroyed by such, for it is a
divine gift from Heaven which is subject to
the failings of the human spirit.

> - J. A. Moses

♡ ♡ ♡

The night has a thousand eyes,
    And the day but one;
Yet the light of the bright world dies
    With the dying Sun.

The mind has a thousand eyes;
    And the heart but one;
Yet the light of a whole life dies
    When love is done.

> - Francis W. Bourdillon, *"Light"*

♡ ♡ ♡

True love is born of despair and nurtured by
one crises after another. It is the child
of adversity who thrives on and triumphs
over all earthly threats to its existence.

> - A. John Hovannes

♡ ♡ ♡

There is only one kind of love, but there
are a thousand imitations.

> - La Rochefoucauld, *"Maximes No. 74"*

## A Potpourri Of Love Thoughts...

A boat at midnight sent alone
   To drift upon the moonless sea,
A lute, whose leading, chord is gone,
   A wounded bird, that hath but one
Imperfect wing to soar upon,
   Are like what I am, without thee.
       - Moore, *"Loves Of The Angels"*

♡ ♡ ♡

The hours I spent with thee, dear heart,
   Are as a string of Pearls to me;
I count them over, every one apart,
   My rosary, my rosary.
       - Robert C. Rogers, *"My Rosary"*

♡ ♡ ♡

And blessings on the falling out
   That all the more endears,
When we fall out with those we love,
   And kiss again with tears!
       - Tennyson, *"The Princess"*

♡ ♡ ♡

Love scarce is love that never knows the
sweetness of forgiving.
       - Whittier, *"Among The Hills"*

♡ ♡ ♡

The quarrels of lovers are the renewal of
love.
       - Terence, *"Andria"*

Tho' near the gates of Paradise,
Gladly I'd turn away,
Just to hear you say, "I love you!"
Sometime, somewhere, some day.
- Rida J. Young, *"Sometime"*

♡ ♡ ♡

But ah! in vain from Fate I fly,
For first, or last, as all must die,
So 'tis as much decreed above,
That first, or last, we all must love.
- George Granville, *"To Myrna"*

♡ ♡ ♡

To fear love is to fear life, and those who
fear life are already three parts dead.
- Bertrand Russell, *"Marriage And Morals"*

♡ ♡ ♡

Not from the whole wide world I chose thee,
Sweetheart, light of the land and the sea!
The wide, wide world could not inclose thee,
For thou art the whole wide world to me.
- R.W. Gilder, *"Song"*

♡ ♡ ♡

The course of true love never did run
smooth.
- Shakespeare, *"A Midsummer Night's Dream"*

I have heard of reasons manifold
   Why love must needs be blind,
But this the best of all I hold -
   His eyes are in his mind.

What outward form and feature are
   He guesseth but in part,
But that within is good and fair
   He seeth with the heart.
- Samuel T. Coleridge, "Reason For Love's<br>Blindness"

♡ ♡ ♡

My heart I fain would ask thee
What then is love? say on.
"Two souls with one thought only,
Two hearts that beat as one."
- Friedrich Halm, "Der Sohn Der Wildniss<br>(Charlton, trans.)

♡ ♡ ♡

The greatest happiness of life is the
conviction that we are loved, loved for
ourselves, or rather loved in spite of
ourselves.
- Victor Hugo

♡ ♡ ♡

Love reckons hours for months, and days for
years; and every little absence is an age.
- John Dryden

Yes, loving is a painful thrill,
And not to love more painful still;
But oh, it is the worst of pain,
To love and not be lov'd again.

         - Anacreon, *"Odes No. 29"*

♡ ♡ ♡

I hold it true, whate'er befall;
I feel it when I sorrow most;
Tis better to have loved and lost
Than never to have loved at all.

         - Tennyson, *"In Memoriam"*

♡ ♡ ♡

I seek for one as fair and gay,
But find none to remind me,
How blest the hours pass'd away
With the girl I left behind me.

         - Unknown

♡ ♡ ♡

Like Dian's kiss, unasked, unsought,
Love gives itself, but is not bought.

         - Longfellow, *"Endymion"*

♡ ♡ ♡

Two human loves make one divine.

         - Elizabeth Barrett Browning, *"Isobel's Child"*

# SECTION 2 / THE BASICS OF LOVE LETTER WRITING

In Section One you had the opportunity to read five actual love letters from several of the great personalities of the past. As you can see, there is a lot to the writing of a good love letter. If you were to analyze all the great love letters of the past, you would almost always find the presence of 1) *strong emotions* and 2) *good writing ability*.

You, no doubt, also possess the strong emotions needed to write such passionate love letters. But do you have the writing ability? The answer is, most likely, *yes*. What you probably need is some guidance to develop it.

This section will help you in this respect, for it deals with *Words*, *Love Sentences* and *Love Paragraphs* - the building blocks of a love letter. It also contains a discussion on *writing styles* and a step-by-step *technique* for writing a love letter.

# BASICS

## Words

Words are the vehicles of your thoughts. A good love letter requires that you choose your words carefully. In order to assure proper word choice, you should bear in mind the following:

1. **Use words which are familiar to you.**

The problems unfamiliar words may cause are:

a) Confusing one word for another because they sound alike:

*Wrong:*    Yesterday, I went to the hair **saloon** and got a perm.

*Correct:*    Yesterday, I went to the hair **salon** and got a perm.

b) Spelling errors, especially if two different words exist which have identical pronunciations:

*Wrong:*    I hope you didn't get **board** yesterday?

*Correct:*    I hope you didn't get **bored** yesterday?

2. **Use words which are fitting to the occasion.**

Stay away from:

a) Uncommon words which have a tendency to give the love sentence an artificial flavor:

*Bad:*    I love it when your lips **impinge** upon mine.

*Good:*    I love it when your lips **touch** mine.

b) Too many large words which prevent the love sentence from flowing smoothly:

*Bad:*      Your **provocatively sensuous** smile is
            a **sensorial** feast **appropriate** for
            a **monarch.**

*Good:*     Your **provocative** smile is a **sensual** feast
            fit for a King.

## 3. Do not use too many *trite* words or phrases.

These are overused and outworn figures of speech, quotations and expressions (*Cliches*). If you utilize them too often, they will lower the overall quality of your love letter:

| | | |
|---|---|---|
| Father Time | Mother Nature | better half |
| macho man | foxy lady | troubled times |
| food for thought | Till death do us part | fit for a King |

## 4. Use watered down words or phrases sparingly.

Such expressions are called *Euphemisms* and, at present, are not considered desirable or appropriate:

*Wrong:*    My love for you **passed away** when you left me.

*Correct:*  My love for you **died** when you left me.

## 5. Use alternate words to create variety within a love letter.

These alternate words are called *Synonyms* and possess the same basic meaning as the original word:

*Original:*   You are a **beautiful** woman.      You are **wonderful.**

*Synonyms:*   You are an **attractive** woman.     You are **magnificent.**
              You are a **good-looking** woman.   You are **terrific.**
              You are a **lovely** woman.          You are **divine.**

If you have any doubt as to a synonym's appropriateness, you should look it up in a dictionary or thesaurus. In Appendix C, you will find a listing of *Love Terms*. In effect, this is a dictionary of over 3,000 synonyms which you can consult when writing your own love letters.

# The Love Sentence

The *Love Sentence* is the basic unit of all thought expression and its importance cannot be overstated. Indeed, the success of any love letter depends greatly upon how well you can write the love sentence.

## Form

Every complete love sentence has two distinct parts: *The Subject* and *The Predicate.* The Subject usually comes first within the love sentence and may be composed of a single Noun, Pronoun, Infinitive, Gerund or a group of words (*phrase*) which acts as a noun (see Appendix A: *Parts Of Speech* for further information):

| | |
|---|---|
| *Pronoun As Subject:* | **I** love you. |
| *Noun As Subject:* | **Love** is an irresistible force. |
| *Infinitive As Subject:* | **To love** is my greatest need. |
| *Gerund As Subject:* | **Kissing** is one of the joys of life. |
| *Noun Phrase As Subject:* | **The beauty of your smile** is truly captivating. |

The Predicate usually follows the Subject and must contain a Verb which describes the *action of, action upon* or *state of being* of the Subject. In addition to the Verb, the Predicate may contain other elements:

| | |
|---|---|
| *Verb Only:* | He **smiled.** |
| *Verb + Adverb:* | You **kiss passionately.** |
| *Verb + Object:* | I **love you.**<br>You **love John.**<br>She **kissed him.** |
| *Linking Verb + Adj.:* | You **are handsome.** |
| *Linking Verb + Noun:* | My name **is John.** |

## Love Sentence Rules

There are several do's and don'ts which you should bear in mind when writing love sentences:

### 1. Love sentences should vary in length.

If you make too many sentences the same length, the letter will become monotonous, and the reader will get bored:

> *Hello, my love. How is everything? I feel fine.*
> *What about you? Let's get together. It's been ages.*
> *Write me soon.*
>
> *I Love You,*
>
> *John*

### 2. Love sentences should vary in the order of their elements.

This will help create variety of rhythm, and make the total love letter more enjoyable to read:

*Standard Order:*    **[Subject] + [Verb] + [Object] + [Verb Modifier]**

I + cherish + our love + more than anything else.

*Variation:*    **[Verb Modifier] + [Subject] + [verb] + [Object]**

More than anything else, + I + cherish + our love.

If you include a question or two in your love letter, you will achieve similar results:

When will I see you again?

### 3. Love Sentences should not have their flow interrupted.

Long descriptive phrases between the Subject and Verb are not desirable:

*Wrong:* Since I arrived here last December, I, **like many of my buddies in the Fifth Infantry,** have been restless.

*Right:* **Like many of my buddies in the Fifth Infantry,** I have been restless since I arrived here last December.

Short phrases which describe in some way the Subject are acceptable:

Our love, **boundless and eternal,** is the only thing that makes life worth living.

4. **Love sentences should always be direct and to the point.**

You can say it better and with more impact if you don't beat around the bush:

> *Wrong:* During our last meeting in a romantic setting, you were a perfect gentleman, and I enjoyed your company very much.

> *Right:* Our last romantic meeting was very enjoyable because you were a perfect gentleman.

5. **Love sentences should not contain repeated words.**

Repeated words and redundant phrases can become very tiresome if used indiscriminately. They should be utilized only to add poetic color:

> *Wrong:*    Our **love** is a boundless and eternal **love.**

> *Right:*    Our **love** is boundless and eternal.

> *Poetic:*    Our **love** is a **love** born of despair and nurtured by adversity.

# The Love Paragraph

The *Love Paragraph* is the main unit of thought organization. It may be of any length, that is, it can contain any number of Love Sentences. Love paragraphs, in general, tend to be shorter at the beginning and end of love letters because thoughts expressed there are more intense and condensed (*Greetings and Good-byes*). Love paragraphs located in the middle of a love letter tend to be longer because they usually express: 1) *accounts of events*, 2) *detailed descriptions* and 3) *facts, interpretations and opinions*.

## Form

The Love Paragraph is a distinctive grouping of related Love Sentences. It is very easy to identify because its first sentence is usually *indented* or *set in* from the margin. This suggests to the reader that a change of thought is about to take place. The end of a Love Paragraph is likewise easy to determine since the beginning of the following Love Paragraph is also indented.

## Thought Flow

The thoughts within a Love Paragraph should flow effortlessly. Logic rules here. If an idea changes too abruptly within the paragraph, you lose thought flow:

> *John, I love you very much. I need you now more than ever before. When can we go to the Tea Dance? I always enjoy myself there and the people are so friendly. I know you'll have a good time too.*

In the above Love Paragraph, two distinct thoughts are being expressed. First, *she loves John* and second, *she wants to go to the Tea Dance with him.* One group of Love Sentences does not flow into the other. Only one of the two thoughts should have been introduced and developed throughout this paragraph:

> *John, I love you very much and I need you now more than ever before. Yet, you and I are so far apart. When will our separation end? When will I hold you again in my arms? If only you could answer my questions with certainty.*

By including only one primary thought or topic within each paragraph, you will create better flow and make a more powerful statement.

## Style

Your choice of words and the way you use those words to create Love Sentences and Love Paragraphs determines the *Style* of your writing. In other words, your style depends upon the *Language* you use.

## Types

There are several basic styles of writing; however, we will discuss only the three most important: The *Plain, Formal* and *Casual:*

## The Plain Style

The *Plain style* is very common and requires that you use clear, straight-forward language. To achieve this, you must:

1. **Avoid twenty-five cent words.**

   These are uncommon words which the letter-reader may not understand:

   > *Wrong:*     I am **desirous** of you.
   >
   > *Right:*      I **desire** you.

2. **Avoid inappropriate words.**

   These are words which are too general in nature:

   > *Wrong:*     You have a **good** personality.
   >
   > *Right:*      You have a **charming** personality.

3. **Avoid Figurative words.**

   These are words which refer to *Historical Events, People, Places* or *Objects*. If you use them, you are assuming that the letter-reader knows the history behind them. In the Plain style, such risks are undesirable:

   > You are my **Tyché.**

   *Tyché* is the Greek *Goddess of luck.* If the letter-reader does not know this, the love sentence will be meaningless.

4. **Avoid overly elaborate descriptions.**

   Usually, these can be replaced by a common word and are totally unnecessary:

   > *Wrong:*     The **mental images of past experiences** with you will never fade.
   >
   > *Right:*      My **memories** of you will never fade.

5. **Use only Simple, Complex or Compound sentences.**

   These are the clearest of all and the easiest to understand:

   > *Simple Sentence:*      I am very depressed.
   >
   > *Complex Sentence:*      I am very depressed because you are not with me.
   >
   > *Compound Sentence:*      I am very depressed, but I will get over it.

In a compound sentence such as the last one, make sure that the two clauses relate to one another properly. To accomplish this, you must use the correct type of *Connective* word:

a) When one clause is used to qualify the other, you must use connective words or phrases such as *However, Nevertheless* and *Of course:*

> You hurt me very much; **nevertheless,** I still love you.

b) When one clause is a logical consequence of another, you must use words such as *Hence, Consequently, For* and *Therefore:*

> I cannot bear the thought of losing you, **for** you are the only joy of my life.

c) When one clause follows another and adds to it similar information, you must use connective words and phrases such as *Also, In addition to* and *Furthermore:*

> I will call you as soon as I reach my destination; **furthermore,** I will write you a letter.

6. **Use Love Sentences which contain the standard order of elements:**

**[Subject] + [Verb] + [Object/Modifier]**

I + love + you.                    (*you* as Object)

You + look + handsome.        (*handsome* as Modifier)

Any changes from this order tend to make a sentence more complicated thus reducing clarity.

## The Formal Style

The *Formal Style* accepts many of the rules of the Plain style. Its goal, however, is the expression of thoughts and ideas in a more refined and poetic manner. In the Formal style:

1. **Words may be fancier.**

Twenty-five cent words and Figurative words are permitted as long as they are appropriate to the thought expressed. Such words, if used correctly, have the power to give the Love Sentence a poetic quality:

| | |
|---|---|
| *Plain:* | You are a **pretty lady.** |
| *Formal:* | You are a **ravishing woman.** |
| *Figurative:* | You are my **Venus.** |

## 2. The Love Sentence may be more complicated.

Longer modifying phrases may be used in the Predicate to make the love sentence more expressive. Some elements may even be doubled for extra effect:

> Only I know **the pain and torment, agony and despair** of a love deprived.

Secondary clauses may be added to the Predicate:

> Your suggestive body language has aroused passions within me **which I did not know existed.**

## 3. The Love Sentence may be made Compound-Complex.

Such a sentence is composed of one secondary clause and two primary clauses. In this way, several thoughts can be expressed as a unit:

> *When you kiss me,* **my heart skips a beat,** and **my passions soar to heights undreamt.**

## The Casual Style

The *Casual Style* tries to imitate the conversation between friends. It is very informal and contains phrases which can be found in everyday talk. Often there are *slang words, incomplete sentences, exclamations* and *side remarks*:

> *Wow! What a great day! You know, it was one of the nicest ones I've had in a long time, and I owe it all to you. Thanks a million, Dave! I hope we can do it again, real soon.*
> *Till then,*
>
> *Love Ya,*
> *Jennifer*

## Style And The Love Letter

A Love Letter is a very important document. Often, it could mean the difference between happiness and despair. The style you use in writing it must feel comfortable to you. If it is forced, the result will sound artificial.

All three styles which were discussed have their good points. The Plain style with its emphasis on clarity can serve as an excellent foundation. The Formal style can provide a poetic quality to your writing. Finally, the Casual style can create a more intimate atmosphere, tempering the other two. Indeed, a writing style which blends elements of all three basic styles can make a Love Letter, not just correspondence, but, in effect, a work of "romantic art" scaled for intimacy.

# Love Letter Writing Technique

An expert love letter requires preparation. Just how much, of course, depends upon your ability to write well spontaneously. If you have found through past experience that you have trouble putting your thoughts down in writing, you may benefit from such preparation.

The following is a *technique* for writing a love letter. It is a guide to help you organize your thoughts. By following it closely, you will be able to write clear, well-organized and effective love letters.

1. **Determine the subject matter.**

   List everything you want to say in your love letter. Use a sentence for each idea:

   a)   *I like the sound of your name.*
   b)   *You are constantly on my mind.*
   c)   *I wish you were here.*
   d)   *My greatest wish is for your safe return.*
   e)   *Your letters keep me going.*
   f)   *Without them, I would be in bad shape.*
   g)   *I crave them because they link me to you.*
   h)   *I pray that your health remains good.*
   i)   *I want to be held by you and kiss you.*
   j)   *I'm very depressed and lonely without you.*
   k)   *I saw someone who looked like you.*
   l)   *For a minute I thought it was really you.*
   m)   *I wish that it had been you and not someone else.*

## 2. Determine the order of presentation.

A love letter should have a logical order of progress. To achieve this, you should develop an outline using the love sentences from *Step No. 1* as the topic headings for each love paragraph. Bear in mind that some of your love sentences may be related and should, therefore, be combined within a single love paragraph. You may use the following general outline as a guide:

**I. Opening Love Paragraph**
A. Greeting, or
B. Opening Remark

**II. Developing Love Paragraphs**
A. Declarations Of Love
B. Stories Or Happenings

**III. Concluding Love Paragraphs**

**IV. Closing Love Paragraph**

The love sentences from Step No. 1 can now be organized in the following manner:

**I.** *I like the sound of your name.*

**II.** *You are constantly on my mind.*
**A.** *I wish you were here.*
**B.** *I want to be held by you and kiss you.*

**III.** *I am very depressed and lonely without you.*

**IV.** *I saw someone who looked like you.*
**A.** *For a minute I thought it was you.*
**B.** *I wish it had been you and not someone else.*

**V.** *Your letters keep me going.*
**A.** *Without them, I would be totally devastated.*
**B.** *I crave them because they link me to you.*

**VI.** *I hope your health remains good.*
**A.** *My greatest wish is for your safe return.*

Now that you have determined your subject matter and its order of presentation, you are ready to begin the actual writing of your love letter. Before you do, however, there are a few more rules of preparation you should bear in mind:

### 3. Point Of View

A personal letter calls for a personal point of view. Your letter should, therefore, be written in the *First Person (I)*:

>   I love you.

>   My heart yearns for your caress.

### 4. Voice Type

You should always write in a strong and direct way. This means you should use what is called the *Active voice* and not the *Passive voice*. When a sentence is made in the Active voice, it usually becomes less wordy and more direct:

>   *Passive Voice (weak):*      It is my belief that you are telling the truth.

>   *Active Voice (strong):*      I believe you are telling the truth.

### 5. Language

The statements you make in a love letter should be positive and assertive. They should not be weak, meek, cautious or unsure.

### 6. Scale

The length of your love sentences and love paragraphs is an important consideration. Keep in mind the do's and don'ts of good love sentence structure. Also, do not overpad your love paragraphs with unnecessary love sentences.

### 7. Punctuation

Be sure you punctuate your sentences correctly. If you come upon a situation which you are not sure of, consult Appendix B: *Punctuation* or a textbook on English for the Solution.

If you recall, in *Step No. 2* we developed an outline. If you turn to Section 3: *Original Love Letters* and find love letter No. 3: *Declarations*, you will see the outline in its final letter form.

A well-written love letter can be considered a "work of art". This technique is only a guideline and cannot assure that every one of your letters will be a masterpiece. That comes with familiarity and practice. It is our hope that this technique will serve as a foundation on which you can further develop your abilities.

ORIGINAL LOVE
# LETTERS

The following twenty-five original love letters have been composed for you to use in any way you desire. You may utilize them as they are or you may change them to suit your own particular needs and stylistic requirements.

Each original love letter is listed alphabetically by its topic or main sentiment. You will find love letters of all types including several addressed to Mother and Father. You will also notice several others which contain a section where you can insert a love poem or quotation.

Many love letters contain word options, that is, opportunities for you to choose the word or words which best fit the need or occassion:

> (Name), *you are the most* (handsome/attractive)
> (boy/girl/man/woman) *I have ever known.*

These original love letters will offer you a wealth of ideas. Use them without hesitation if they express, in any way, your innermost feelings and emotions.

# ORIGINAL LOVE LETTERS

## LOVE LETTER No. 1: *Attraction*

*Dear* (Name),

*How are you? I hope this letter finds you healthy and in good spirits. Everything has been going smoothly for me, and I've been keeping quite busy with* (school/work).

(Name), *the last time I was with You, I enjoyed myself more than you can ever imagine. I really felt great with you by my side because I'm attracted to you far more than I have ever been to any other* (guy/gal). *It's as though we are the two remaining pieces of a puzzle, which, when joined together, complete the total picture.*

*To tell you the truth, I've been thinking about you constantly. I see your* (handsome/beautiful) *face smiling at me and your* (strong, muscular/delightfully curvaceous), *body standing near me. I hear your sexy voice calling my name and feel your warm embrace. As I relive these times, my body trembles with anticipation, and I get butterflies in my stomach.*

(Name), *dreaming of the past with you is not enough to satisfy my passions. I need to be with you again. I need to experience those special feelings which I get only when I am* (at your side/in your arms). *So please, write me quick and tell me when I can expect our next* (rendezvous/ encounter). *Until I hear from you, take very good care of yourself.*

*Love,*

(Name)

## LOVE LETTER No. 2: *Belated Reply*

*Dear* (Name),

*I know it has been quite some time since I last wrote you. Believe me, it is not because I did not think of you these past* (two/three/four/five) *weeks, but because I could not find the proper words to express my true feelings for you.*

(Name), *I realize that a long-distance romance can be quite difficult to maintain, but I know in my heart that you are well worth the effort. To me, you are a very special person, and I am deeply and undeniably attracted to you.*

(Name), *you are the most* (handsome/attractive) (boy/girl/man/ woman) *I have ever known. Everytime we are together, your eyes melt me into submission, and your gentle caress makes my body* (quiver/tremble) *with excitement. Your* (alluring/captivating/vibrant) *smile and cheerful, loving nature always lift my spirits and bring joy into my life.*

*Hopefully, if all goes well, I may be able to come up and see you in* (one/two/three) *week(s). To be honest, I can hardly wait to be with you again. I hope you feel the same. For now, take care of yourself and write me. I promise to reply faster the next time.*

*With deep and sincere affection, I remain*

*Your Loving Friend,*

(Name)

## LOVE LETTER No. 3: *Declarations*

(Name),(Name),(Name),

*Your name is pure music to my ears. Truly, I could call it out loud a million times and never tire of its sound.*

(Name), *believe me when I say that not a minute passes without my thoughts turning to you. At this very moment, I wish you were here holding me in your arms and kissing me on my lips - I would not tire of that either.*

*Surely you must know how difficult it is for me to pretend as though all is well when you are so far away. In all honesty, I am very depressed these days and lack my usual sense of humor. All my friends tell me to lighten up, but then, they can't understand the torment of my loneliness. How can I lighten up when my heart is torn hopelessly between two* (worlds/ continents/countries/states/cities)?

*Yesterday, I saw someone who reminded me of you, and I had to look twice. You know, something deep down in my heart was hoping against all hope that, by some miracle, it was really you standing on the corner and not some stranger. Truthfully, this has been happening to me a lot lately, and each time my disappointment increases. Sometimes I wonder just how I'm going to last another* (No. of days/weeks/months).

(Name), *the fact is, if it weren't for your letters, my loneliness would be totally devastating. They really keep me going and are a source of great comfort and joy. In truth, I crave them with a passion and whenever one arrives at my mailbox, my heart races with anticipation, for the words which lie within are my only direct bridge to you.*

(Name), *I pray that the Lord will keep you well, so that someday soon, you can come safely back to me. This is my greatest wish.*

*Until that day is a reality, I remain*

*Your Eternal Love,*

(Name)

## LOVE LETTER No. 4: *Desire*

*Dearest* (Name),

*Each day - each hour - each minute we are apart is* (an eternity/a lifetime). *Thoughts of you flood my mind with desire, and, at times, I cannot bear our separation. My love, it feels as if a part of me is missing, and that is very distressing.*

*I know that, in time, we will be together again, and this knowledge consoles me to a small degree. However, it can never take away the pain and anguish of the moment. Only your presence can do that.*

(Name), *you are the light of my life, the nourishment of my soul, the essence of my being and you, my love, give me the strength to carry on. Until that wonderful day when we are reunited, I remain totally yours in thought and spirit.*

*Love Always,*

(Name)

## LOVE LETTER No. 5: *Destiny*

*My dear* (Name),

*There are things in life which are inevitable; I am powerless to control them. The Sun will rise and set, the tide will come in and go out, the seasons will change, the birds will fly South for the winter and return in the spring and the Caterpillar will transform itself into a* (beautiful/handsome) *butterfly. Somehow, I feel reassured by this because many other things in life are so transient - so momentary.*

(Name), *from the first moment we met, I knew that our friendship would develop into something lasting and precious just as I am sure that the Caterpillar will one day become a* (beautiful/handsome) *butterfly.*

*Dearest, I believe that our love is* (blessed/ordained) *by God. It is a union of two spirits destined for everlasting happiness. Thus, you have become the star of my life which brings me light in this dark world and warmth when I need it. You offer me the promise of renewal, the joy of living, the peace of mind which comes from sharing and caring and that shoulder to lean on in times of stress. You are my Swallow from Capistrano - my precious butterfly, and I will cherish you and love you forever.*

(Name)

## LOVE LETTER No. 6: *Excitement*

*Dear* (Name),

I had to write you as soon as I could to express just how much I enjoyed being with you last (night/day of week). I really had a great time! To be honest, I have never felt as happy, as content or as excited about being with someone as I was with you. The whole (evening/night/day) was a joy to experience.

Truthfully, (Name), you are a class act. Even though I met you only recently, I feel as though I've known you for a long time. I consider myself a good judge of character, and from what I've seen, you are a one-in-a-million (guy/gal). You're so unpredictable and exciting yet so stable in that you seem to know what you want out of life. You're so strong (physically/ emotionally) yet you seem to have a gentle and compassionate nature. You are so intelligent yet so humble and down to earth. Last but not least, you are so (good-looking/handsome/beautiful) yet not in the least bit conceited. All these are endearing qualities which attract me very much.

(Name), whenever I think of you, my heart skips a beat, and my senses swirl in anticipation of seeing you once again. You have become the Ambrosia of my heart, and I am drawn to you as a bee is to honey.

*Your Loving Friend,*

(Name)

## LOVE LETTER No. 7: *First Encounter*

*Hi* (Name),

*Just thought I'd write you a short note to tell you how much I enjoyed meeting you at* (place). *I can't recall when I had a more pleasant time. Everything felt so natural, and you were very easy to talk to. It's hard for me to identify what it is about you that attracts me so. I suppose it might be the combination of your great sense of humor, your charming personality and your good-looks. Whatever it is, I can sense its presence. You could call it chemistry or, better yet, the possibility that we're on the same wavelength.*

(Name), *I really hope that our first* (encounter/meeting) *was not our last because I felt very special when I was with you. I truly want to give our friendship a chance to grow.*

*Well, I guess I've said enough for the time being.* (Name), *have a wonderful* (week/day) *and, hopefully, I'll see you again real soon. If you get a chance,* (write/call) *me and tell me your thoughts. Until I hear from you, take good care of yourself.*

*Always,*

(Name)

## LOVE LETTER No. 8: *Hugs And Kisses*

*Dear* (Name),

How are you, Babe? I want you to know that I miss you tremendously. Lately, I've felt an obsessive urge to send you all the hugs and kisses I've saved up all these months since our parting. So, Honey, I'm going to take this opportunity to do just that. Are you ready? Well, here they come! xoxoxoxoxoxoxoxoxo xoxoxoxoxoxoxoxoxo xoxoxoxoxoxoxoxox oxoxoxox xoxoxoxoxoxoxoxoxo xoxoxoxoxoxoxoxoxo xoxoxoxoxoxox oxoxoxoxox xoxoxoxoxoxoxoxoxoxoxoxo I need to catch my breath. xoxoxoxoxox xoxoxoxoxoxoxoxoxoxoxo xoxoxoxoxoxoxoxoxo xoxoxoxoxoxox oxoxoxox xoxoxoxoxoxoxoxoxo xoxoxoxoxoxoxoxoxo xoxoxoxoxoxoxox oxoxoxoxox xoxoxox Whew! This is hard work, but I love it! xoxoxoxox oxoxoxoxoxox xoxoxo xoxoxoxoxoxoxoxo xoxoxoxoxoxoxoxoxo xoxoxoxoxoxoxoxoxox xoxoxoxoxoxoxoxoxoxoxoxoxoxoxo Are you enjoying it? xox oxoxoxox xoxoxoxoxoxoxoxoxo xoxoxoxoxoxoxoxoxo xoxoxoxoxoxoxox oxoxox xoxoxox This is Heaven! xoxoxoxoxoxoxoxoxoxoxoxoxoxoxox oxoxoxox xoxoxoxoxoxoxoxoxo xoxoxoxoxoxoxoxoxoxo xoxoxoxoxoxoxox oxoxox xoxoxoxoxoxoxoxoxoxoxoxoxoxoxoxoxox There's more! xox oxoxoxox xoxoxoxoxoxoxoxo xoxoxoxoxoxoxoxo xoxoxoxoxoxoxoxox oxoxox xoxoxoxo I'm having a great time! xoxoxoxoxoxoxoxoxoxoxox oxoxoxox xoxoxoxoxoxoxoxo xoxoxoxoxoxoxoxo xoxoxoxoxox xoxoxoxoxox xoxoxoxoxoxoxox xoxoxoxoxoxoxoxoxo xoxoxoxoxoxoxoxox oxoxox xoxoxoxoxoxoxoxoxoxoxox I'm running out of space!! xoxox oxoxoxox xoxoxoxoxoxoxox xoxoxoxoxoxoxoxoxo xoxoxoxoxoxoxoxoxox oxox xoxoxoxox I just realized that there is no end to this! xoxoxox oxoxox xoxoxoxoxoxo xoxoxoxoxoxoxo xoxoxoxoxoxoxoxo xoxoxoxoxoxoxox xoxoxoxoxoxoxoxoxoxoxox Oh! well, until next time....xoxoxoxoxoxox xoxoxoxoxoxoxoxoxoxoxoxo xoxoxoxoxoxoxoxoxoxo xoxoxoxoxox oxox

## LOVE LETTER No. 9: *Longing*

*Dearest* (Name),

*How can I express the longing I have to be with you? Words are very hard to find. It is as though I am a compass needle, and you are the North Pole. Constantly, my thoughts are drawn to you, my love, for your influence on me is absolute.*

(Name), *my life so far away from you is empty of all substance, and my existence on this lonely planet is two-dimensional at best. I anxiously count the days until we, at last, will be together again to share the divine love that God has created between us.*

*Until that day is a reality, I remain*

*Your True Love,*

(Name)

## LOVE LETTER No. 10: *Love*

*Dearest* (Name),

*I love you.*

*I love you. - I love you. - I love you.*
*Love you - love you - love you - love you*
*You - you - you - you*
*You are. - you are. - you are. - you are.*
*My love - my love - my love - my love*
*Love - love - love - love*
*Is sharing - sharing - sharing - sharing*
*Is caring - caring - caring - caring*
*Is bearing - bearing - bearing - bearing*
*Each other's faults that keep on tearing*
*Tearing - tearing - tearing - tearing*
*At bonds of*
*Love - love - love - love*
*Love you - love you - love you - love you*
*I love you. - I love you. - I love you. -*

*I love you!*

(Name)

## LOVE LETTER No. 11: *Love*

*Dearest* (Name),

    *Once again, I send you a letter with the hope that it finds you well and in good spirits. In all honesty, whenever you are gone, the emptiness of my situation becomes unbearable, and I turn to corresponding with you as an* (activity/passtime) *which helps dampen the* (desperation/loneliness) *of the moment.*

    (Name), *my love for you can only be measured in exponential form, and that in itself falls far short of its true magnitude. For you are the nourishment of my spirit; consequently, you are my strength. When we are together, you provide that electric potential which gives my life that spark of vitality. When we are apart such as now, I get butterflies in my stomach as if in anticipation of our reuniting - that "Opening Night" which is sure to come.*

    (Name), *each time I gaze into your eyes, I am drawn into the farthest reaches of your mind's inner world. There, I find a land of compassion, of understanding and of love and, by some good fortune, I also find myself as one of its inhabitants. For this, I am very grateful.*

    *Until we are together again in each others embrace, I remain*

*Your Eternal Love,*

(Name)

## LOVE LETTER No. 12: *My Goddess*

*Dear* (Name),

*I know that it disturbs you that I don't write you as often as I should, but you must know by now how difficult it is for me to compose a letter. For some people it is easy, but I have the hardest time expressing myself. Even though my feelings for you are strong, at times, I cannot for the life of me, find the proper words to describe them. It really is frustrating because I love you very much.* (Name/Babe/Honey/Sweetheart/Pet Name), *you are the only love of my life, and I need you to realize that.*

*Yesterday, I found a book on Mythology - you know, Gods and Goddesses. I couldn't believe my eyes! The descriptions of several Goddesses fit you perfectly. I must be one of the luckiest men on Earth! To think, that I'm in love with a woman who possesses the beauty of Venus, the wisdom of Athena and the poise and stature of Juno.*

(Name), *being so far away from your loving arms is pure torture. It's as if you are a powerful transmitter, and I am a receiver. You are on all of my frequencies; nothing else can get through, and my days are spent endlessly under your universal influence.*

(Name), *I can't believe all these words are coming to me as easily as they are. Could it be that I'm finally getting the hang of it, or is it that you inspire me so? I think it's the latter. How can I help but not be inspired by your all-encompassing beauty and charm?*

*My love, I want you to know that I can hardly wait for the day when I return home to your waiting arms. That truly will be one of the happiest moments of my life.*

*Until that day is a reality, I remain*

*Your Eternal Love,*

(Name)

## LOVE LETTER No. 13: *Original Poem Insert*

*Dearest* (Name),

*How can I properly express the joy I derived from reading your last letter? I must tell you that it lifted my spirits to heights undreamt - a very welcome change from where they had been for so long. The fact is, your letters have always worked miracles, and I pray that you will not stop writing them.*

*My love, I want you to know that I am well, and that my situation here is comfortable. In all honesty though, it could never compete with home, for boredom and loneliness are my constant companions. But enough of this kind of talk for now! I hope you are well and in good spirits because if you are not, I could never hope to be. Right now, I truly wish I could hold you in my arms and kiss your soft, supple lips. What a heavenly thought, if only but a daydream.*

*(Name), you mean the world to me! I can't imagine life without you. How empty it would be! In truth, only a love poem of classic dimensions could express my love for you. Although I am not a poet, I have always wanted to write you such a poem. Unfortunately, in the past, I lacked the discipline to attempt it. Lately though, I've had a lot of time on my hands, and in my own inadequate way, I finally gave it a try. I think you'll find that the thought is there even though the poem may be lacking in technique. So, here it is! I hope you like it.*

(Insert Poem)

*Dearest, I can't think of anything more to add at this time. So, until I hear from you, I wish you the best of health and send you my deep and everlasting love.*

*Yours Eternally,*

(Name)

## LOVE LETTER No. 14: *Pleasant Memories*

*Dear* (Name),

Greetings from (Name of City/Country)! *I hope this letter finds you well. Since last I saw you, I've been very busy with* (school/work/my duties). *I've wanted to write you for quite sometime now, but it seems as though every time I got started something would come up, and I'd have to stop. I'm sure you can understand that.*

(Name), *I often think of that wonderful evening when we first met - the first time I saw you - the first time we spoke to each other - the first time we touched - the first time we kissed. It seems just like yesterday because I keep such precious memories constantly alive in the pages of my mind.*

(Name), *I just haven't felt the same since I met you. Knowing that you are in this world excites me and makes my body tingle all over. I get butterflies in my stomach, and my heart skips a beat.*

*I guess what I'm trying to say is that I miss your smile, I miss your soft caress, I miss your tender kiss and most of all I miss the thrill of just being* (at your side/with you).

(Name), *please write me and tell me how you're doing even if it's just a small note. Until I hear from you, or better yet, until we meet again, my thoughts are with you.*

*Your Loving Friend,*

(Name)

## LOVE LETTER No. 15: *Poem Insert*

*Dearest* (Name),

I pray that this letter finds you healthy and in good spirits because your well-being has been and will always be my foremost concern. My love, I am as well as can be expected, even though at this point in time, my life is far from ideal. Our separation has cast a cloud of loneliness and despair over me, and only your safe return will bring with it the winds which can blow it away.

(Name), there are many things I desire to tell you and I have many passions yearning for expression. Yet it seems as though I'm always at a loss for words. This inability of mine is (truly/very) frustrating.

Yesterday, I was reading a book of poetry to help me subdue my loneliness when I came across a love poem which, to my (surprise/ amazement), expresses to perfection all my inner thoughts, desires and feelings. Truthfully, I couldn't believe my eyes, for it was written (some/ many) years ago by (Name of Poet).

My love, as you read it, try to think not of the poet but of me, for its verses express the sentiments of my heart.

(Insert Poem)

Example:

*You Are*

*You are my brave Centurion;*
    *You are my learned historian;*
*You are my Knight in shining armor;*
    *You are my handsome, courtly charmer.*

*You are my personal troubadour;*
    *You are a man I can't ignore.*
*You are my loyal Samurai;*
    *You are one dynamic, hell of a guy!*

With eternal love and devotion, I send you my most passionate kiss and remain

*Yours Forever,*

(Name)

## LOVE LETTER No. 16: *Proclamation*

*Dearest* (Name),

*Just as a poet needs inspiration to write a masterpiece,*
   *I need you...*

*Just as an artist needs a subject for his work of art,*
   *I need you...*

*Just as a teacher needs a pupil to mold into greatness,*
   *I need you...*

*Just as a composer needs a theme to create a timeless melody,*
   *I need you...*

*For without you, (Name), my life will be empty of all inspiration. There will be no work of art for me to gaze at; no person of greatness before me; no timeless melody to listen to. My life will exist in shades of gray instead of vibrant colors, and I will be less than whole.*

*In the past, the proper words have escaped me, and my innermost feelings have been kept locked away in the depths of my heart. No more, for through this letter, I proclaim to you, (Name), my undying love and eternal devotion.*

*Yours Forever,*

(Name)

## LOVE LETTER No. 17: *Quote Insert*

*Dearest* (Name),

*I write you this letter with mixed emotions. In all honesty, I do not know where I stand with you, and the torment of my uncertainty is fast becoming unbearable.*

*It's hard to believe that only a short time ago we had such a loving relationship. To me, it is even more difficult to comprehend why you would throw all that away with one blink of an eye. If I had said or done something to hurt you deeply, then I could accept such a reaction, but I haven't. So what could be the cause of this sudden cooling of emotions?*

*(Name), I love you very much, but I am confused and bewildered by your unreasonable behavior. If there is something that is bothering you, tell me about it. I am confident that our love will enable us to work things out. But if you let your emotions get the best of you, all hope will be lost. If you only knew how much you mean to me, and how much this situation hurts me!*

*(Name), in closing, I would like to leave you with this thought. It pretty much sums up the way I feel at this moment:*

(Insert Quote)

Example:

*Yes, loving is a painful thrill,*
*And not to love more painful still;*
*But oh, it is the worst of pain,*
*To love and not be lov'd again.*
*-Anacreon: "Odes No. 29"*

*With hope for a brighter future, I remain*

*Eternally Yours,*

(Name)

## LOVE LETTER No. 18: *Reminiscing*

*Dearest* (Name),

*Tonight, I sit alone vividly reliving all those pleasant moments we shared only yesterday. It's hard to believe that we were together just hours ago, and now we are worlds apart, I in my corner of the Universe and you in yours. Why is it that the good times don't last? It just doesn't seem fair especially to two people such as we who are so in love with each other.*

(Name), *even though our physical separation is a fact of life which we cannot change, we are still united in spirit because the love we share knows no bounds. It is universal poetry and with its durability, it shall continue endlessly bringing us strength, patience and hope for a bright and fulfilling future.*

*Truthfully,* (Name), *the excitement of our last* (meeting/encounter) *will not easily fade from my memory, and my pulse will always quicken with anticipation at the thought of our next rendezvous.*

*My love, until that joyous moment arrives, take good care of yourself and please keep those letters coming. They help me make it through the lonely times. For now, I want to close this letter with these few words: I love you! - I love you! - I love you! - sincerely, passionately, absolutely!*

*I Love You!*

(Name)

## LOVE LETTER No. 19: *To Dad*

*Dear Dad,*

*How's the expert fisherman doing? Have you caught any trophys lately? You can't imagine how much I miss going after the big ones with you. We really used to have some great times out there on the boat, didn't we? A lot has happened since those days. My present life feels a million light years removed from the life I once shared with you and Mom. Truthfully, I miss it very much, for it was a life full of love, affection, sincerity and understanding.*

*Dad, it saddens me when I realize how far away I am from you. If only I was closer, then, once in a while, we could relive all the good times. But for the present, this is impossible, thus I must accept my situation and learn to bear its shortcomings. Someday soon, I hope it will change and I will be able to move closer to home.*

*At present, I am well physically as well as emotionally. There are times when I am quite busy and then there are times when I die of boredom. I guess they cancel each other out.*

*Dad, I really enjoy receiving your letters. They boost my spirits because they are the closest thing to being home. I appreciate you taking the time to write them.*

*Well, it's getting late, and tomorrow promises to be a very busy day. I hope this letter finds you healthy and in good spirits. With it, I send to you my warmest wishes and deepest affection.*

*Until I hear from you again, I remain*

*Your Loving* (Son/Daughter),

(Name)

## LOVE LETTER No. 20: *To Mom*

*Dear Mother,*

*Greetings from the end of the World. All is terrific here in this Paradise of Paradises. The weather is great, and the night life is* (fantastic/ exciting). *I'm healthy and I'm having a ball! So, why do I feel so lousy? I know! It's because I really miss home, and most of all, Mom, I miss you.*

*I've had a difficult time adjusting to my new life. It's so different from what I had before! Sometimes, I feel like a fish out of water, and sometimes, I feel as though I'm in total control. Truthfully, my feelings are mixed, my emotions are unstable, and my life is in transition. You, dear Mother, are the only stabilizing influence I have. You give my life perspective and remind me of my roots. For this, I am truly thankful.*

*Mom, the cuisine here is quite unique. Unfortunately, no matter how hard I try, I can't make myself appreciate it. I guess I'm sort of spoiled after being exposed to your great cooking. In all honesty, I dream of it each time I sit down to eat. Perhaps, you'll give me a thrill by sending me some assorted samples of your art. It would make me very, very happy.*

*I still don't know when I'll have the opportunity to come home for a visit. If I had my way, I'd catch the next flight out of here. But I'm not that fortunate, so I guess I'll have to wait until my time comes up. In the meantime, I want you to know that you are always in my thoughts and prayers.*

*Until I hear from you, I wish you good health and much happiness and send to you my most sincere and everlasting love.*

*Your Loving* (Son/Daughter)

(Name)

## LOVE LETTER No. 21: *To Mom*

*Dear Mother,*

*I hope this letter finds you well. It truly has been a long time since I last wrote you, and I feel somewhat ashamed at my laziness. I trust you will forgive me.*

*Mom, the character of my life has changed drastically since I left home. I find myself no longer surrounded by familiar faces and places. In truth, I am in another world. I feel an emptiness now which I know I must learn to live with. This emptiness, dear Mother, is caused by your absence. It has taken time, but I have come to realize that our parting was inevitable, and that I must accept and adapt to the changes it has brought on. But, Mom, this is most difficult to do, for we live in such an impersonal world.*

*Although, I cannot be with you physically, rest assured that I will always be with you in my thoughts, for you occupy a very special place in my heart. Your positive influence will always guide my actions, and the memories of your motherly love will sustain me.*

*May God give you health, happiness and a long, fruitful life on this earth. Thank you for being such a wonderful, caring mother!*

*With Deepest Love,*

(Name)

## LOVE LETTER No. 22: *To Mom And Dad*

*Dear Mom and Dad,*

*How are you both doing? I trust all is well. I really enjoyed reading your last letter because it made me feel very special. I am truly fortunate to have two loving parents such as you. Believe me when I say that there are many here who are not as lucky as I in this respect.*

*Please give my love to (Name) and (Name) and my warmest regards to all of my friends should you see any of them. I miss them all. You know, I didn't realize how much "Home" really meant to me until I left. Truthfully, there is nothing on Earth that can replace it.*

*At present, I am fine and impatiently waiting for the end of my time here. A change will do me a world of good. I have to say that your letters gave me the needed strength to get me through the toughest moments. For this, I thank you from the bottom of my heart.*

*There is a chance that I may be able to come home for a short visit within a month or two. I hope I can swing it! In any case, I'll keep you informed. For now, there isn't very much more to say other than life here is quite unique. I know I'll never forget the experience nor will I miss it either.*

*Time is getting short, so I better close for now. I want you both to know that you occupy a very special place in my heart. Thank you for being so caring.*

*With the deepest respect and affection, I remain*

*Your Loving* (Son/Daughter),

(Name)

## LOVE LETTER No. 23: *True Love* ✓

*Dearest* (Name),

*It is very important for me to express to you how much you really mean to me. I wish I could do this in person while holding you in my arms and gazing into your eyes. But since we are physically separated by miles of emptiness, this expression must come in the form of letters such as this.*

(Name), *I know it is difficult for you, as it is for me, to be separated for so long. Life seems to be full of trials of this type which test our inner strength, and more importantly, our devotion and love for one another. After all, it is said that "True Love" is boundless and immeasurable and overcomes all forms of adversity. In truth, if it is genuine, it will grow stronger with each assault upon its existence.*

(Name), *our love has been assaulted many times, and I am convinced that it is true because the longer I am away from you, the greater is my yearning to be with you again. You are my* (enchanted Princess/ charming Prince), *and I am your devoted* (consort/Prince/Princess). *I cherish any thought of you, prize any memory of you which rises from the depths of my mind and live for the day when our physical separation will no longer be.*

*Until that moment arrives, I send to you across the miles, my tender love, my warm embrace and my most passionate kiss.*

*Love Always,*

(Name)

# LOVE LETTER No. 24: *Yearning*

*Dear* (Name),

    *Greetings from* (city/state/country)! *I sincerely hope that all is well with you and yours. I am fine. Surprisingly, I've been keeping myself quite busy since I last saw you. Which reminds me, the last time we were together I had a* (ball/blast/great time), *and you were so* (charming/crazy/funny/ hilarious) *I couldn't get over it. In fact, I still haven't.*

    (Name), *I think of you every day - I can't help myself! Memories of pleasant times with you are hard to suppress, and my being so far away from you doesn't help matters either because it makes me wish I could be with you even more. Truthfully, knowing that you are alive and I can't be with you is an unbearable torment.*

    (Name), *when will I see you again? I can't stand the pain and anguish of our separation much longer. I yearn to gaze into your captivating eyes. I crave your tender touch, your warm embrace and your passionate kiss. I yearn for the day when I can be with you again.*

    *Until that* (fateful/wonderful) *day arrives, I wish you the best life has to offer.* (Name), *please take good care of yourself and write me as soon as you can.*

*Love,*

(Name)

## LOVE LETTER No. 25: *Wholeness*

*Dearest* (Name),

*I have lived for a long time* (responsible for/dependent upon) *no one, answering to no one and commited to no one except myself. During this period of my life, I considered the World mine for the taking and truly believed that I was living life to the fullest. Then, you came into the picture, and all of a sudden, I realized that I was deceiving myself.*

(Name), *I am an incomplete* (man/woman) *in need of wholeness. I find that my life is not all that I thought it was. In fact, it is terribly lacking in many things, the foremost being love. Now, through some great fortune, I have found that love and along with it the one person who can make my life truly complete.*

*(Name), you are that person, and I have somehow fallen hopelessly and undeniably in love with you. To be honest, I never thought I would ever utter those words, but now, they come forth effortlessly and with great sincerity. I'll be forever grateful to you for showing me just how shallow my life was. At last, I have a chance to give it depth and purpose.*

*I wanted to tell you all this in person, but I knew that the proper words would escape me. I wrote you this letter instead. Please call me after you read it, and we'll talk.*

*Until I hear from you, I remain totally yours in thought and spirit.*

*Love,*

*(Name)*

/**LOVE PARAGRAPHS**

The *Love Paragraph* is the main unit of composition within a love letter. Each love paragraph is made up of several love sentences which are arranged in a somewhat logical sequence. Often, the first sentence of the love paragraph suggests the topic or helps make the transition from the previous paragraph.

This section contains over 60 *Love Paragraphs.* Each has been identified by its topic or main sentiment. You can combine one or more of these with an opening and closing paragraph, pre-written or original, to form a complete love letter or you can pick out certain love sentences and create from them your own personalized love paragraphs suited to your own specific needs.

# LOVE PARAGRAPHS

## Openings I

*Dearest (Name),*

I was thrilled to receive your letter today. To be honest, I didn't think you would write. I'm so happy you proved me wrong. Nowadays, it's so much easier to phone than to take the time to write. But, in truth, a phone call isn't as romantic. Take your letter for example. I savored every word and read and reread every line. It's sweetness will always be there whenever I get the urge to partake of it. You can't do that with a phone call!

*Dearest (Name),*

I thought I'd write you immediately after receiving your letter. That way, my letter will reach you faster so that you can respond with another more rapidly. My love, you must realize by now that I live each day for your letter. To me, it is a part of you - a part which I can physically touch. Without it, the emptiness of your absence would prove unbearable.

*Dearest (Name),*

I cannot contain the joy which I feel at this moment. Thank you for your letter! It was truly a godsend. You can't imagine how impatiently I had waited for it to arrive. In fact, I had almost given up, and my spirits were at an all-time low. Now I'm feeling great, and my spirits are soaring!

# Openings II

*Dear* (Name),

*Je t'aime! Je t'aime! Je t'aime! No matter what language I use, I love you, I love you, I love you, Babe, completely! totally! absolutely! You inspire me, and your sweet love is my greatest joy in life. Since you left, I've been so miserable without you. I hope you don't mind me writing you every day. To me, it is a much needed therapy which, somehow, soothes the pains of our separation.*

*Dear* (Name),

*At last, I finally got some time to myself to write you the type of letter my heart requires me to write. To me, (Name), just any letter would not be enough, for you are the most important person in my life. I hope you will understand and not be too (annoyed/mad) at me for being so late in writing.*

*Dearest* (Name),

*I just had to write you as soon as possible to tell you how I felt. In truth, a moment does not pass without my thoughts turning to you. Your vision floods my senses with (beauty/delight/anticipation), and my heart is filled with a divine inspiration. (Name), you are the fulfillment of all my dreams, hopes and desires and you have given me a renewed optimism towards life.*

## Anguish And Despair

*For weeks, I have lived with little else but your name on my lips and your vision in my thoughts. I am consumed with anguish and wracked with despair at the realization that our separation is still in its infancy. How could fate be so cruel as to keep apart two people who so deserve to be together? It is truly unbearable! Yet, I cannot change the present; therefore, I must live for the future. I know that I must overcome my anguish and subdue my feelings of despair. This, I will* (attempt/try) *to do with the help of the love which binds* (our hearts/the two of us) *across the miles that separate.*

*I am an optimistic person by nature yet I too have my limits. At first, your silence was not unusual. As a result of our petty squabbles, I have come to expect a week without hearing from you. But this time, it has stretched out twice that long. My concern has grown into alarm. The anguish of my uncertainty and my despair at the thought of having lost you are fast becoming unbearable. Why do you torment me so? Please call me, write me or better yet, come and see me. You have punished me long enough!*

*I know that you are finally doing what you have worked so long and hard to prepare for. I am sincerely happy for you. To realize a dream such as yours is a great achievement which I am sure gives you much satisfaction and fulfillment. Thank you, (Name), for making me a part of your life during the long road to your goal. It was a joy for me to give you my love, understanding and emotional support. I also knew that someday I would probably lose you to your dream. I thought I could handle that reality if it came, but, alas, I've found that I can't. I have grown too attached to you and now I suffer the anguish of withdrawal and the despair of loneliness. In truth, I yearn to be with you as* (a viable/an important) *part of your present life, not just a pleasant memory which surfaces now and then.*

## Anniversaries

*Believe me when I say that, of all my acquaintances, you are the dearest. Ever since we met one year ago today, our friendship has evolved into a satisfying emotional partnership, and my life has changed for the better. (Name), I must tell you that you possess many (rare/unique) qualities which I find absolutely irresistible. In all honesty, I've never felt this way before. I guess what I'm trying to say is that I've fallen hopelessly in love with you.*

*I can't believe that our Anniversary is almost upon us again. Time sure flies when one is as happy and content with one's situation as I am. Dearest, you have made my life a joy to live, and your love is ever so sweet. You are the ultimate life partner, and I am truly fortunate to have you as my very own. I sincerely hope you share my sentiments because I want you to be as happy as me. To this end, I will work as hard as I can, for you are worthy of the best life has to offer.*

*Do you remember the first time we met? I do. It was two years ago tomorrow. I'll never forget it! If there ever were two people who hit it off badly, we were they. It was almost comical. To this day, I don't know which one of us was more irate. Luckily, we were able to resolve our dispute, and the rest is history. My sweet, even though our beginnings were turbulent, our life together has been great. Sure, we've had our storms, but they could never sink our ship. It was built too well for that. On this special Anniversary, I look forward to our future with optimism, for a love such as ours, based on mutual respect, trust and forgiveness can never falter.*

# Christmas And Hanukkah

*Christmas is a very special holiday. For me, it is a time during which families come together, worship and share in the joys of our Lord's birth. In truth, some of my fondest memories are of the two of us together during Christmas. My love, I am saddened by the thought that I will not be home with you this year during this special time. It is very hard for me to accept this reality, and my heart cries out in despair. I want you to know that were it in my power, I would fly home to you at a moment's notice. But unfortunately, it isn't. So, in lieu of my physical presence, I send to you by way of this letter my deepest love and warmest wishes for a safe, healthy and merry Christmas.*

*You'll never know how much I yearn to be with you this Christmas. It has become an obsession which I cannot subdue, for I love you deeply. My love, it seems as though I feel the loneliness of our separation more during holidays than at any other time, and Christmas is the ultimate one. During this special time, I will (truly/really) miss exchanging gifts, singing carols and attending midnight Mass with you. I will miss your warmth and humor. Most of all, I will miss your loving arms. (Name), my greatest wish is that by next Christmas we will be reunited so that we may, once again, share, hand in hand, the promise of Christ's birth.*

*My love, Hanukkah will not be the same this year. For me, eight days of dedication will be eight days of heightened loneliness without you at my side. This joyous holiday will take on a somber cast, for I know that the light of the candles on your Menorah will not reach me so far away. Our separation is already difficult to bear, and holidays such as this which are commemorated by the family make it all the more difficult. I can only hope that my boundless and everlasting love for you will help me overcome my depression. With that hope, I send to you across the miles that separate us, my deepest love and warmest wishes for a healthy and joyous Hanukkah.*

## Easter And Passover

*For some reason, it doesn't seem like Easter time. I guess that's because my past Easters were spent among family and friends. Here, I am alone, and my acquaintances do not project the same warmth and affection. I truly wish that I could be home with you this Easter, but as you know, circumstances will not permit it. So when you go to Easter services, say a little prayer for me, and, maybe, if the Lord is willing, I will be with you again next year in body as well as in mind to commemorate His resurrection.*

*Easter eggs and chocolate rabbits - colorful clothes and Easter Mass - these are but a few of the happy memories I have of Easter. The Easter meal shared with the loving members of my family is still another. At this moment, all these visions flood my mind, and I am all the more saddened by the fact that I am so far away from you. Easter will not be the same this year, and the loneliness of my situation will swell to greater proportions during this holiest of holidays.*

*If I had but a single wish, I would ask that I be allowed to come home to share the Seder with you. The celebration of Passover is not a solitary occasion but requires the participation of the entire family. Thus, it is times like this which make me wish I was closer to home. Alone, I can never fully partake in a meaningful commemoration of this holiday. So when you sit down to eat your Matzoth and each time you drink of your four cups of wine, think of me, for I will be thinking of you with the deepest love and affection.*

# Forgiveness And Understanding

*As usual, my emotions got the best of me. What can I say or do on my behalf to express the regret that I feel at this moment? I am so ashamed of the way I acted and the things that I said. If only I could turn back the clock and prevent my emotions from affecting my behavior. But I know that's impossible and sadly realize that I have hurt the one person whom I love most in this world. (Name), I am disconsolate at the thought of losing you. How can I expect you to understand my actions; moreover, how can I ask you to forgive me? I feel hopelessly lost. My one prayer is that, somehow, somewhere within your heart, you will find the last ounce of love which I (hope/pray) still exists and use it to heal the grave wound I inflicted by my thoughtless and impulsive behavior. Then and only then will I be able to find my way from the dark pit of despair back to your loving arms.*

*At first I thought I could change you. But now I know that is impossible. You are too quick to judge and too slow to forgive. Yet, you are the one I love; therefore, I must accept you as you are. This, I will do with all the forgiveness and understanding in my heart, for I am certain that my future happiness as well as yours depends on it.*

*Forgiveness and understanding are essential for true love to exist. If you are unable to forgive me for some thoughtless action, (shortcoming/ habit) or indiscretion, it will haunt you until it destroys our love. If you cannot understand what (makes me tick/motivates me), you will not be able to tolerate me. Without forgiveness and understanding, you can never enjoy peace of mind which is, after all, the prerequisite to happiness and fulfillment: the fruits of true love.*

# Happiness And Joy

*Ever since you uttered,* ("Will you marry me?"/"I love you.") *I have been in a constant state of bliss floating through a cloudless Heaven. You cannot imagine how long I had been waiting to hear you say those* (four/ three) *precious words. I had almost given up on you. Now, I keep praying that I am not dreaming. My dearest, the magnitude of my happiness, at this moment, is immeasurable. In truth, no word can justly describe the way I feel, for it is a feeling which rises above all earthly joys.*

*When I read your letter telling me that you would be coming home, I could not contain my joy. You would have laughed at my* (antics/ behavior). *Truthfully, I didn't care how crazy I was acting. All I knew was that you would soon be coming home to me. My sweet, you can't imagine how much I've longed to hold you in my arms. Honestly, your homecoming will be the nicest present you could ever hope to give me. The joy and happiness I feel at this moment is beyond compare. It is truly a wonderful change from the loneliness and despair which I have felt for so long.*

*To be honest, I never thought that I would ever find a* (woman/man) *like you. When we first met, I couldn't believe my senses. I really thought that they were deceiving me, for you seemed too good to be true. Now, I realize that you are all that you appear to be, and that excites me greatly. My love, you have changed my whole outlook on life. Your inspiration and love have truly worked miracles. Moreover, I have never before felt such happiness nor experienced such spiritual joy. I feel very, very lucky. After all, how many* (men/women) *can say that they are in love with a real* (Angel from Heaven/Knight in shining armor)?

## Jealousy And Possessiveness

*It is very difficult for me to describe just what I am feeling at this moment. It is as if my insides are about to explode outward under the pressure of my emotions. You are probably wondering what I am talking about, but then, you should know, for you are the cause of my* (distress/ despair). *To think, all these weeks you have been seeing another behind my back and acting as if all was well between us. I feel so betrayed; so wronged. You cannot imagine the* (torment/mental anguish) *of this revelation. The worst thing of it is that I feel so jealous of the other, who, somehow, has succeeded in taking part of you away from me. That, in itself, is the hardest realization of all.* (Name), *even though I love you very much, the ultimate outcome will depend upon your future actions and my ability to forgive you.*

*Lately, you have become a different person, and I am saddened by the transformation. No matter what I do - no matter what I say, I can't seem to stop your consuming jealousy and stifling possessiveness. My only hope is that before it's too late, you will, somehow, regain your senses and curb your jealous and possessive behavior so that trust and love can once again prevail in our relationship.*

*When you told me you wanted to break up, I didn't believe you. I really thought you were just upset and that you really didn't mean what you were saying. I finally realized you weren't when you told me you were going out with* (Name). *I can't begin to explain to you how much that hurt nor can I accurately describe the extent of my jealousy. Even now, no matter how hard I try, I cannot calm my emotions, and the shock of losing you is still a cause of great torment and mental anguish. Whether you know it or not,* (Name), *you were the focus of all my dreams and hopes for a brighter future.*

## Love And Affection

    *I am neither a seasoned writer of prose nor am I a poet skilled in verse, thus it is very difficult for me to express to you in writing the depth of my love. Yet love flows through my veins, and poetry is in my heart. My love, I must show you the depth of this love which burns within me. I will do so, not by the written word, but if you permit, by the poetry of actions symbolized by a tender kiss, a gentle caress and a warm embrace. These are my words, and together they will form the poetic expression of my deep and sincere love for you.*

    *No one can love you more completely nor give you more affection than I. You are the focus of my world, and I am totally committed to your well-being. When you are happy; I am happy. When you are sad; I am sad. My fate is entwined with yours. This is what makes my life so exciting, so meaningful and so fulfilling.*

    *Your love and affection nourish my spirit and sustain my body. Take either away and I will wither into nothingness. Take both away and I will surely die. My love, I cannot bear the thought of even a short separation. Such (a deprivation/an absence) would surely be damaging in many ways. So please, reassure me once more that you will always stay here by my side to provide me with that spark which makes my life worth living.*

## Love And Trust

*You disappoint me each time you (profess/proclaim) your love and then turn around and accuse me falsely of being unfaithful or disloyal. First of all, your accusations have no substance whatsoever, and secondly, they are so childish that I'm amazed they would even merit any attention. You should know by now how much I love you. I would never jeopardize my relationship with you for anything or anyone else in the world. I'm beginning to wonder though whether or not you really love me. To exist, true love requires the presence of trust. From your actions, I don't think you possess that quality, although I pray that I'm wrong. (Name), you and I are perfect for each other. That's why you must try to curb your insecurities and (cultivate/develop) tolerance, understanding and forgiveness. Only then will you be able to fully trust and love me with peace of mind.*

*I truly believe that our love is boundless and eternal. It has made my life meaningful and fulfilling and it has enabled me to attain happiness and contentment. It is a love composed of mutual understanding, tolerance, forgiveness, loyalty and sincerity - all bound together by trust. Without these qualities, I am certain our love could not exist.*

*If I didn't love you, why would I give you a shoulder to lean on in times of despair? If I didn't love you, why would I tolerate your bothersome shortcomings or forgive your many indiscretions? If I didn't love you, why would I be so faithful or so caring? If I didn't love you, why would I trust you so completely?*

## Loyalty And Devotion

*Everyone needs a cause to which they can devote themselves. (Name), you are mine. Always, you can count on me to protect your best interests. You can be certain that I will never leave your side through the good times and bad. You can rest assured that I will cherish you and love you faithfully forever. By giving you such devotion, loyalty and love, I find purpose and meaning to life, and that is what gives me the ultimate satisfaction.*

*You say that you sincerely love me. Yet, all I hear are empty words without actions to give them substance. True love requires loyalty. You like your freedom too much and enjoy flitting from one enticing flower to another. True love needs the presence of devotion. The only thing you are devoted to is the pursuit of (pleasure/good times). How can you tell me that you truly love me when I am just a "pit stop" in your life? You ask too much of me. Only when I detect the existence of faithfulness and sincerity in your actions, will I be able to take your words seriously.*

*Many people go through life without ever experiencing a truly loving relationship. They dream about such happiness, but it always seems to elude them. I, on the other hand, consider myself one of the lucky few who have been blessed with a love which is based on mutual trust, loyalty and deep devotion. I bask in its warmth and delight in the divine pleasures which are the fruits of its existence. Thank you, (Name).*

# New Years

*I can't believe that the year is almost at an end. It seems as though it took forever. Each day felt like an eternity with you so far away from me. But now, my heart beats with anticipation at the thought of the new year bringing with it an end to our separation and the beginning of a new life together. This realization heartens me greatly, for I love you above all else on this earth. This New Year's Eve will certainly be lonely without you, but I will not despair because it will mean that I am another day closer to your loving arms.*

*Another year is about to pass, and once again, I find myself apart from the love of my life. The pain of this separation is overwhelming, and the realization that this is to be for many more New Years is almost unbearable. Dearest, no physical torture can match the mental torment of my situation. The yearnings I have to embrace you, to kiss you and to love you are overpowering. The only thing that keeps me from going mad is your all-encompassing love and my dreams and hopes for a brighter future with you.*

*You can't imagine how disappointed I was when I found out that I will not be able to spend New Year's Eve with you. I was looking forward to it very, very much. (Name), you are (truly/very) special to me, and I am hopelessly in love with you. Although I will not be with you to bring in the new year, I know that throughout the evening my thoughts will, and my heart will feel the emptiness of your absence.*

## Parent's Love: *Mother*

*I'm ashamed to say that I took you for granted when I was living at home. Many times, in return for your love and affection, I paid you back with anger and ungrateful behavior. Mother, I was blind to your special qualities. Worse yet, I was stubborn, uncompromising, selfish and tactless while you were always tolerant, understanding, compassionate, unselfish and forgiving. It took this separation to put things into perspective. I now realize just how much you really mean to me. I only hope and pray that you will accept my deepest regrets at my past thoughtlessness. You were and are, now more than ever, the best thing in my life. May God bless you and keep you healthy and happy.*

*I often dream of home. Even though it is so far away, my memories of it are vivid and heartwarming, and you, Mother, are always present. I feel very lucky to have been raised by a mother like you, for with patience and understanding, you nurtured me. You sacrificed much on my behalf. You forgave me for my (indiscretions/bad behavior). You tolerated my short-comings. Most importantly, you taught me my values, you molded my character and you showed me the true meaning of love. With such a solid foundation, I am confident that I will be able to face and overcome all of life's trials and tribulations. For this, I am eternally grateful.*

*Mom, I left home only a short time ago yet I miss you very much. I didn't (realize/know) how much you really meant to me. I thought going away would be easy. It is proving very difficult. Hopefully, with God's help, I will overcome my insecurities. Even so, I will always cherish the memories of my life at home, and never will I lose the deep and sincere love I have for you.*

## Parent's Love: *Father*

*When I lived at home, it seemed as though you and I were always at odds with each other. I don't know what caused such friction between us. All I know is that from my perspective, I was always right, and you were always wrong. Unfortunately, our confrontations led to a growing lack of communication, and , consequently, a cooling of affections. Now I look back from a different perspective - a perspective tempered by time, distance and maturity. I now regret my behavior and am saddened by the realization that I missed out on what could have been a loving relationship between father and son. Although much has come between us, Dad, I hope and pray that you will be able to forgive me, for I love you and respect you deeply and sincerely. I truly want to be your son in life as well as in name.*

*I miss you very much, Dad, for you have been such a good friend to me. Now that I am on my own, I feel an emptiness in my heart. In time, I will most likely get over the initial effects of our separation, but never will I forget the love and friendship you gave me during my childhood and adolescence. Nor will I ever forget your wisdom and sensible advice. Dad, I send to you across the miles, my sincere love and affection and wish you good health and much happiness.*

*Thank you for being such a good father to me. Were it not for you, I never would have been exposed to the values of honesty, sincerity, loyalty, trust and love. I never would have learned the qualities of perseverance, tolerance, compassion and forgiveness. You introduced me to all of these not by words alone but by example, and I am proud to be my father's (Son/ Daughter). Dad, I want you to know that I will cherish you and love you always.*

## Passions And Desires

*A moment does not pass without my thoughts turning to you, for my mind is linked directly to my heart where my passions burn out of control. The truth is, your captivating beauty, exciting personality and intelligence attract me so much that, at times, I cannot bear the thought of even the shortest separation for fear that my desires will overwhelm me.*

*(Name), you are ever present in my thoughts even though we are so very far apart. Each day, your hold on me gets stronger, and my emotions swell to even greater heights. I crave your honeyed kiss. I yearn for your gentle touch. I desire your impassioned love. (Name), during these long months of separation, you have become my greatest passion, and I need you now more than ever before.*

*Sometimes I wonder whether your feelings for me are as intense as mine are for you. Although you express your profound love, at times, your behavior does not reflect this. You must realize that I have wants and desires which need fulfillment. Often you ignore these in favor of your own pleasures. Your inconsiderateness disappoints me. Furthermore, I have passions which cry out for satisfaction. Many times, you close your eyes to them. Your thoughtlessness hurts me a great deal. If you were truly in love with me, you would not be so uncaring. You would acknowledge my needs and do your best to fill them even if it means a bit of sacrifice.*

## Silence An Uncertainty

*You do not realize how much I yearn to hear your golden voice over the telephone or read your honeyed words in a letter. These are the only joys of my present life, for through them I am reborn in spirit. Unfortunately, the periods between such contact are full of silence and uncertainty. They are dark and desperate times filled with the torment of loneliness and the despair of a long separation. During these periods, my salvation rests solely with the hope that, once again very soon, I will be hearing your voice or reading your words. This is what makes the inbetween times bearable.*

*The silence of your anger is fast becoming unbearable. Why must you hurt me so? Is it because you can't accept the fact that what I said is true? By lashing out at me, you will not solve the problem nor will you be able to sweep it under the rug. I still love you very much, but if you continue this form of* (deprivation/mental torture), *you will heighten my doubts and uncertainties. What you will succeed in doing is alienate me, and that will be a great loss for both of us. You must realize that silence is a childish reaction. What we both need now is to sit down together and talk, as adults, with an open mind and understanding heart.*

*It seems as though I have not heard from you for ages. (Name), each day gets longer and more difficult to bear. Over and over again, I wonder to myself why you have not called or, at least, written. I think back at all that I said or did in your presence to determine if I annoyed you in any way. I always draw a blank. Your silence is killing me! Uncertainty and self-doubt are swelling up within me, and I am wracked with despair. I crave your voice - your letter - anything that shows me that there is still hope for us.*

# Thanksgiving

My Thanksgiving dinner this year will be just another meal without you here at my side to share it with me. It certainly won't taste as good as your cooking nor will it have the same significance. After all, it is hard to give thanks when fate has cast us apart. (Name), this separation is truly hard to bear, and my spirits are at a very low ebb. My passions burn deep within my heart, and my loneliness torments me without reprieve. My only salvation is the thought of returning home to your waiting arms. Hopefully, this will happen soon so that next Thanksgiving might, once again, be a time of appreciation and thankfulness.

No matter how hard I wish, I know that you will not be able to come home for Thanksgiving. This thought is very depressing because a holiday is always a very lonely time when you are gone. In truth, I know that the day will pass ever so slowly, and the emptiness in my heart will be overwhelming. Dearest love, my thoughts and prayers will be with you on this occassion, for you are the most important thing in my life. Always, with unreserved sincerity, you give me your deepest love and affection, and that is what makes my life so meaningful. For this, I am truly thankful.

I've got it all planned out. A tremendous Turkey! - scrumptious stuffing! - yummy yams! - vibrant vegetables! - colorful Cranberry sauce! - delicious deserts! - A Thanksgiving feast fit for a (king/queen)! All I need is you here with me to enjoy it. (Name), I sincerely hope you will accept my invitation to come spend Thanksgiving with me. I haven't seen you in a very long time and I miss you very much. I'll be waiting impatiently for your answer. Please don't disappoint me!

## Valentine's Day

For me, Valentine's Day this year will be a day of loneliness and despair. How can it be otherwise with you so far away? While other lovers are embracing, I will be sitting here alone dreaming of you. How unfair it is for us to be apart on such a romantic occasion. (Name), were it in my power, I would conjure up some special (incantation/spell) and transport you into my arms. Unfortunately, that is just another dream, and somehow, I must resolve myself to the reality of our situation. So, in lieu of a warm embrace, I send to you through this note, my deepest and most sincere Valentine's Day love.

Today, I looked at my calendar and noticed Valentine's Day fast approaching. My thoughts immediately turned to you, and I was saddened by the realization that I would not be home on this romantic day to show you just how much I love you. It is truly a tragedy that I am caught in a world so far away from yours. If I had a choice, it would not be so. But since I don't, I must accept what is and try to subdue the loneliness and despair associated with it. This, I know I can do by looking forward to my future with you. It will come, and we will, once again, share a life filled with love and affection. For the time being, my dearest, I reaffirm to you my eternal love and send to you across the vast distance which separates us, my most passionate Valentine's Day kiss.

An exquisite Valentine such as you is a rarity in this world. I have found no other that can come close to matching your looks, personality and intelligence. Truthfully, (Name), I feel very fortunate to have you as my very own. More than anything else, I wish I could be with you this coming Valentine's Day. But since I can't, I want to take this opportunity to send you my deepest love along with my most sensual Valentine's Day kiss.

# Warmth And Friendship

*Our chance meeting was a miracle conceived in Heaven. It signaled the beginning of a true friendship which has provided me with a foundation on which to build a more meaningful life for myself. (Name), you'll never know how much that really means to me. I only hope and pray that our relationship will last for a long, long time to come, for it provides me with a warmth I've never experienced before.*

*Your friendship provides me with more than just companionship; it gives to me a sense of belonging I've never felt before. It lights my path through the darkness which surrounds me and gives me hope for a brighter future. Such a friendship instills within me a warmth which overcomes the biting chill of an impersonal world and kindles the fires of love.*

*How lucky I am to have a friend like you who demands nothing of me except my friendship. It is comforting to know that you exist as a stabilizing influence in my life. What would I do without you? How would I survive? I pray that I never have to cross that bridge. Truly, words cannot express my feelings toward you nor the extent of my love. Suffice it to say that my life would be an empty shell without you around to fill it with purpose, companionship and understanding.*

# Closings

*Even though I have much more to say, I guess I should conclude this letter. It's getting quite late, and tomorrow promises to be a very long day. Tonight, as I lie in bed, I will be thinking of you, and as I drift off to sleep, your (lovely/handsome) face will be the last wonderful image of the day. My dear (Name), until next time, I send to you all the love I possess along with ten thousand times ten thousand kisses.*

*Your eternal love,*

(Name)

*In closing, I want you to know that I consider myself a very lucky person to have you as my very own. In all honesty, I don't know if I could make it without you. My emotional well-being depends, to a great degree, upon your warm, sustaining love, and luckily, letters such as the one I just received are its messengers. So, (dearest/Honey/Babe/Name), keep the letters coming, for they bring me strength to meet the (loneliness/ challenges) of our separation. Until I hear from you again, I send to you with this note my deepest and most sincere love along with my most passionate kiss.*

*Eternally,*

(Name)

*It has been difficult without you, my love. Time has passed very slowly. Ever since we parted, you have been the focal point of all my thoughts. Fortunately, corresponding with you has given me something to do in my spare time so that the loneliness I feel does not overwhelm me. Besides, it excites me to think that my letter will soon find its way into your warm, loving hands, and that your eyes will feast on my words. (Name), please don't delay your reply - I too need to feast. Until I hear from you once again, take very good care of yourself. I love you very much and wait impatiently for the day of your return. For now, I remain*

*Your devoted love,*

(Name)

# SECTION 5 / LOVE SENTENCES

You will find over 600 *Love Sentences* in this section. Many thoughts and sentiments are expressed and a great number of emotions are addressed. You may use these love sentences as *topic* or *idea* sentences for love paragraphs or you may combine several of them in a flowing sequence to create a complete love paragraph.

Each love sentence contains one *Key Word*:

### HEART

- You reside in the innermost recesses of my *heart*.

- Whenever I think of you, my *heart* burns with passion.

For clarity and convenience, each key word along with its love sentences has been alphabetically placed into one of four catagories which correspond to four of the major parts of speech: *Nouns*, *Adjectives*, *Verbs* and *Adverbs*.

### NOUN KEY WORDS

#### ABSENCE

- Your *absence* causes me great torment.

- My love for you grows stronger with each *absence*.

#### ACTUALITY

- Such an *actuality* is hard to imagine.

- The *actuality* of my loneliness is devastating.

### ADMIRATION

- My *admiration* for you is sincere and heartfelt.

- I have absolute *admiration* for you.

In effect, the catagory describes the function of the key word within the sentence. This should help you develop your grammatical skills.

These love sentences, like the love letters and love paragraphs of the preceeding sections, have been composed for you to use in any way you desire. When the words are hard to find, they will help you to express your innermost feelings.

# LOVE SENTENCES

## Noun Key Words

### A

**ABSENCE**
- Your *absence* causes me great torment.
- My love for you grows stronger with each *absence*.

**ACTUALITY**
- Such an *actuality* is hard to imagine.
- The *actuality* of my loneliness is devastating.

**ADMIRATION**
- My *admiration* for you is sincere and heartfelt.
- I have absolute *admiration* for you.

**ADORATION**
- The *adoration* I have for you is reinforced each time we meet.
- My *adoration* for you is constant and complete.

**AFFECTION**
- Your sincere love and *affection* is a dream come true.
- Your loving *affections* spell the difference between happiness and despair.
- My *affection* for you is boundless.

**AGONY**
- Every moment we're apart causes me infinite *agony*.
- The *agony* of your silence torments my spirit.

**ANGUISH**
- *Anguish*, despair and misery have been my constant companions ever since you left.
- The *anguish* of a love deprived is hard to bear.

**ANSWER**
- You are the *answer* to all my dreams.
- I yearn to hear "yes" as your *answer*.

## ANTICIPATION
- I tremble with *anticipation* each time you smile at me.
- I'm thrilled with *anticipation* at the thought of seeing you again.
- The *anticipation* of your homecoming is truly exciting.

## ANXIETY
- The *anxiety* which torments me will only clear with your safe return.
- *Anxiety* and loneliness are my constant companions.
- The *anxiety* of our separation is a torment I cannot shake.

## ATTACHMENT
- Why can't you develop an *attachment* to me?
- An *attachment* born of love is hard to break.

# B

## BEAUTY
- You possess an unrivaled *beauty*.
- Your *beauty* is inspiring.
- Your stunning *beauty* melts me into submission.
- I love you not just for your outward looks but also for your inner *beauty* as well.
- You have a *beauty* which is divinely inspired.
- Your *beauty* overwhelms me with desire.

## BODY
- Your heavenly *body* makes my passions soar.
- Your *body* must have been sculpted in Heaven.
- In my eyes, your *body* is a poetic masterpiece.

## BOND
- The *bonds* of our love are truly strong.
- The *bond* between you and me was born of adversity and will continue nurtured by love.

## BUILD
- Your fantastic *build* is a sensual feast.
- A *build* such as yours is one-in-a-million.

# C

## CARESS
- I cherish your heavenly *caress*.
- Your *caress* is a delight to experience.
- I dream of your *caress*.
- I crave your passionate *caress*.

## CHARM
- You have a unique and overwhelming *charm*.
- Your manly *charm* excites my passions.

## CHEEKS
- Your tender *cheeks* are a pleasure to kiss and squeeze.
- I love to nuzzle your blushing *cheeks*.

## CLOSENESS
- The *closeness* I feel for you increases with each passing day.
- I thank the Lord that you and I share a *closeness* others only dream about.

## COMMITMENT
- I need *commitment* from the man I love.
- It seems as though, to you, *commitment* is a dirty word.
- My *commitment* to you is made with sincere love and devotion.
- True love means *commitment*.

## CONFIDENCE
- I love you for instilling *confidence* within me.
- The *confidence* which you gave me has proven invaluable.
- Thank you for having *confidence* in me.
- You must have *confidence* in my judgement.

## CONSTANCY
- The *constancy* of your love is all that I desire.
- *Constancy* is difficult in this transient world.

## CREDIBILITY
- Your *credibility* has gone down the drain.
- How can I believe you when you have lost your *credibility*?

# D

## DARKNESS
- The *darkness* brings on a devouring loneliness.
- The *darkness* of our separation floods me with despair.

## DEDICATION
- I will love you with enthusiasm and *dedication*.
- Your *dedication* and devotion to our loving relationship can only strengthen it.

## DELIGHT
- You are a constant source of surprise and *delight*.
- Your sensual kiss is a *delight* to experience.
- You are a fountain of flowing *delight* and wonder.
- You are a *delight* to behold.

## DEPARTURE
- Your *departure* from my world has left me devastated.
- Your *departure* has left an overwhelming emptiness in my heart.

## DEPRESSION
- *Depression* has set in since you left.
- *Depression* and loneliness torment me.
- The knowledge of an impending long-term separation has caused within me an overwhelming *depression*.

## DESIRE
- Your safe return is my foremost *desire*.
- You are the total fulfillment of all my *desires*.
- A thousand *desires* flood my senses.
- Your love is my greatest *desire*.

## DESPAIR
- I find myself hopelessly imprisoned in the darkest pit of *despair*.
- Each moment apart from you is a moment of sadness and *despair*.

## DESPERATION
- I cannot endure another lonely night of silent *desperation*.
- My *desperation* is a result of our untimely separation.

## DEVOTION
- I give to you my unwavering loyalty and *devotion*.
- My *devotion* to you is immeasurable.
- Your love and *devotion* are the miracles of my life.
- Your *devotion*, respect, loyalty and love are the cornerstones of my happiness.

## DIGNITY
- You project an image of serene *dignity*.
- You move with *dignity* and grace.

## DISTANCE
- The vast *distance* which separates us cannot destroy our love.
- The greater the *distance* between us, the stronger is our love.

## DISTRUST
- *Distrust* is the catalyst of jealousy and hate.
- Your *distrust* wounds my faithful heart.

## DOUBT
- I have no *doubt* that our love is true and enduring.
- You have dispelled any *doubt* which I may have had concerning our relationship.

## E

## EARS
- Your sweet melodic voice is music to my *ears*.
- Your *ears* are a joy to nibble on.

## ECSTACY
- You give to me an *ecstacy* which is not of this earth.
- The *ecstacy* of your love is what I need.

## EMBRACE
- Your divine *embrace* is my safe refuge from the outside world.
- Your loving *embrace* gives me contentment.
- I dream of your *embrace* each lonely night.
- I yearn for your *embrace*.

## ENVY
- *Envy* can cause either creativity or destruction; never both.
- *Envy*, if not controlled, can destroy a friendship.

## ESSENCE
- You are the *essence* of my being.
- Your love is the *essence* of my happiness.

## EXQUISITENESS
- The *exquisiteness* of your luring smile floods me with desire.
- The *exquisiteness* of your body inflames my deepest passions.

## EYES
- Your dark, dreamy *eyes* enchant and entrance me.
- I love to gaze into your *eyes* and feel their sensual charm.
- Your sparkling *eyes* stir my emotions and heighten my anticipation.
- *Eyes* can say a lot.

## EYELASHES
- Your fluttering *eyelashes* attract and disarm me.
- Such gorgeous *eyelashes* as yours are weapons of love.

## F

## FAITH
- My *faith* in your ability to overcome your personal problems is unshakable.
- Have *faith*, for our boundless love will help us get through these troubled times.

## FATHER/DAD
- *Father*, I sure could have used some of your sensible advice.
- *Father*, although we never could see eye to eye, I still want you to know that, to this day, I truly respect you.
- *Father*, I realize how wrong I've been and want you to know that I love you.
- *Dad*, my leaving home has made me realize just how much you and Mom really mean to me.
- *Dad*, I want to thank you for all the advice you gave me through the years and the values you instilled within me.

- *Dad*, I miss you very much and send my sincere love.
- *Dad*, thank you for all the good times.
- *Dad*, a father such as you is a one-in-a-million happening.

## FIGURE
- Your fabulous *figure* had to be made in Heaven.
- You've got the *figure* of a Greek goddess.

## FONDNESS
- My *fondness* for you is difficult to hide.
- I pray that your *fondness* for me will someday grow into love.

## FORGIVENESS
- I ask only for your *forgiveness* and understanding.
- Your *forgiveness* means more to me than any earthly pleasure.
- *Forgiveness* is a quality you do not seem to possess.
- How can I ask for your *forgiveness* after what I have done?

## FORM
- Your supple *form* is a delight to behold.
- Love can assume many *forms*.

## FRIENDSHIP
- Your *friendship* means the world to me.
- My *friendship* with you is the best thing I've got going.

## FULFILLMENT
- Your love gives my life a divine *fulfillment*.
- You are the ultimate *fulfillment* of all my desires.

# G-K

## GENTLENESS
- You possess grace and a *gentleness* of manner.
- The *gentleness* of your caress is delightfully sensuous.
- Your *gentleness* and warmth are qualities which I cherish.

## GOODNESS
- I love you for all the *goodness* you embody.
- You possess a *goodness* which brings happiness to all those whose lives you touch.

## HAIR
- The vision of your silken *hair* shimmering under the Moon's soft light is exciting.
- I love to stroke your long, silken *hair*.

## HEART
- You reside in the innermost recesses of my *heart*.
- Whenever I think of you, my *heart* burns with passion.
- Love of my *heart*, when will I see you again?
- My *heart* soars at the slightest thought of you.
- My *heart* aches for your radiant love.

- My *heart* weakens the longer I am away from you.
- You arouse great passions from deep within my *heart*.
- My *heart* is lonely without your love.
- Only you can heal my broken *heart*.
- My *heart* yearns for your precious love.
- A boundless love resides within my *heart*.
- Only you can soothe my aching *heart*.

## HEARTACHE
- The *heartache* of our separation is hard to endure.
- Why do you cause me such *heartache*?

## HEARTBREAK
- The *heartbreak* of our separation desolates my very soul.
- My *heartbreak* is total.

## HEARTSTRINGS
- Your inspiring love vibrates my *heartstrings*.
- Only you can touch the *heartstrings* of my love.

## HEAVEN
- You are a gift to me from *Heaven*.
- You are an Angel from *Heaven*.

## HOPE
- It is my *hope* and prayer that I become worthy of your love.
- Each day brings me renewed *hope* that you will soon come back to me.

## HUG
- Your affectionate *hug* is all I need to chase the blues away.
- An enthusiastic *hug* is always appreciated.

## HUSBAND
- A *husband* with your qualities is a once-in-a-million find.
- A woman is fortunate if she can find a *husband* as exciting as you.
- The ideal *husband* is restlessly content, excitingly dull and handsomely homely.

## INNOCENCE
- You captivate me with your delightful *innocence*.
- An *innocence* such as yours is refreshing.

## INTIMACY
- The *intimacy* we share is joyous and fulfilling.
- The *intimacy* of our love is glorious.
- I yearn for more *intimacy* in our relationship.

## JEALOUSY
- The *jealousy* I feel consumes me with a gnawing restlessness.
- Your *jealousy* is difficult to comprehend.
- What have I done to cause such an outburst of *jealousy*?
- *Jealousy* is an undesirable quality which turns me off.
- A bit of *jealousy* is good if it promotes positive reactions.

- *Jealousy* is not your style.
- Your destructive *jealousy* has made a shambles of what was once a loving relationship.
- Such *jealousy* is unbecoming of you.
- Your *jealousy* will destroy our love if you cannot control it.

## L-O

### LEGS
- Your slender *legs* always excite me.
- I adore a woman with lovely *legs*.
- I love to feel your muscular *legs*.
- Your sexy *legs* are a sight to behold.

### LIPS
- I yearn to kiss your tender *lips*.
- Your honeyed *lips* are warm and sweet.
- I crave the feel of your passionate *lips*.
- I love the thought of your manly *lips* next to mine.
- Your luscious *lips* are a feast for kings.

### LOCKS
- I love to fondle your curly *locks*.
- I love to run my hands through your golden *locks*.

### LOVE
- My *love* for you is boundless and everlasting.
- Our *love* will never die.
- A *love* such as ours is indestructable.
- *Love* is the greatest joy in life.
- Your *love* is my salvation.
- *Love* is not a one-way street.
- True *love* can move mountains.
- Your *love* and affection have healed my wounds.

### LOVELINESS
- You possess a fresh and disarming *loveliness*.
- You have a *loveliness* which is beyond all description.

### MARRIAGE
- The best move of my life was my *marriage* to you.
- A *marriage* born of love and nurtured by friendship will last forever.

## MEMORY
- The *memory* of our first encounter still floods me with excitement.
- That delirious night when first we met provides me with my most cherished *memory*.
- The *memory* of our parting kiss sustains me through these lonely times.
- A pleasant *memory* cannot satisfy the passion which burns within my heart.

## MERCY
- Have *mercy* upon this tormented soul who loves you so deeply and undeniably.
- The *mercy* of your love has saved my sanity.

## MIND
- Your exquisite face is ingrained in my *mind*.
- My *mind* is filled with a frantic desire to love you.
- Your handsome face is etched in my *mind*.
- Each night, my *mind* is flooded with your beauty.

## MISTRUST
- Why is *mistrust* a way of life for you?
- Suspicion and *mistrust* are the enemies of love.

## MOTHER/MOM
- *Mother*, I miss your gentle touch and loving guidance.
- *Mother*, I will cherish you in my heart forever.
- *Mother*, thank you for raising me as you did.
- *Mother*, I think the world of you and miss you very much.
- *Mom*, I sure wish I could savor some of your good cooking.
- *Mom*, I love you deeply for all the sacrifices you made for me.
- *Mom*, I send you my deepest love and affection.

## NECK
- A *neck* like yours was made to be kissed.
- An elegant *neck* such as yours is hard to resist.

## NIGHT
- Each *night*, my dreams are filled with blissful memories of you.
- The *night* is infinitely long without you here to hold me.
- Each *night* is a time of lonely desperation.
- The thought of you waiting for me gives me the strength to make it through each long, lonely *night*.

## NOSE
- Your handsome *nose* has a noble air.
- You have the cutest little *nose* this side of Heaven.

## OPTIMISM
- Love brings with it a soaring *optimism*.
- Each day begins with *optimism* at the thought of hearing from you.

## P-Q

### PARTING
* The pain of our *parting* is unbearable.
* Our *parting* may be the beginning of a closer relationship.

### PASSION
* My deepest *passions* are aroused each time I see your lovely face.
* You fire up my *passions* and stir my emotions.
* You are the greatest *passion* of my life.
* Your unbridled love is my ultimate *passion*.

### PERFECTION
* You, my love, are the embodiment of *perfection*.
* The *perfection* of your beauty is a divine gift.

### PHYSIQUE
* I yearn to embrace your ripling *physique*.
* My heart skips a beat each time I see your *physique*.

### POEM
* You are a *poem* of classic dimensions.
* You are a delightful *poem* which fills my senses with beauty.

### PRINCE
* You are my charming *Prince,* and I am your devoted consort.
* *Prince* of my heart, you are the focus of my world.

### PRINCESS
* A lovely *Princess* such as you is worthy of only the best life has to offer.
* You are the *Princess* of my heart's kingdom.

## R

### RADIANCE
* The *radiance* of your smile warms my heart.
* You possess a *radiance* which captivates me.

### REALITY
* The *reality* of our love brings purpose to my life.
* Your sustaining love makes the gloomy *reality* of this world bearable.

### RELATIONSHIP
* Our *relationship* will endure because it is based on trust and mutual respect.
* A special *relationship* such as ours can overcome all obstacles on the road to happiness.

**REMOTENESS**
- I sense a *remoteness* in your behavior which is very alarming.
- My *remoteness* has absolutely nothing to do with you or my feelings towards you.

**RESPECT**
- My *respect* for you is absolute.
- It does not seem as though you have any *respect* for me anymore.
- *Respect* goes hand in hand with love.
- I need your *respect* or else our relationship will surely suffer.

# S

**SACRIFICE**
- Each *sacrifice* I made, I made willingly for you.
- True love requires *sacrifices* on both sides.

**SADNESS**
- The *sadness* of our parting is surpassed only by the torment of our separation.
- *Sadness* overwhelms me at the thought of losing you.

**SECURITY**
- Some nights, I do not want to leave the *security* of your warm embrace.
- *Security* and friendship are the two most precious gifts you have given me.

**SENSES**
- The sparkle of your eyes dazzles my *senses*.
- Your sweet kisses flood my *senses* with delight.

**SENSITIVITY**
- Your *sensitivity* is all out of proportion.
- I adore a man who possesses the qualities of thoughtfulness and *sensitivity*.

**SEPARATION**
- This sudden *separation* causes me great despair.
- When will this tormenting *separation* come to an end?
- Our trial *separation* has proven how much you really mean to me.
- My love, I cannot bear this *separation* much longer.
- The pain and anguish of our *separation* is hard to endure.

**SHAPE**
- A *shape* like yours is truly rare.
- You have a Heavenly *shape* which I find deliciously seductive.

**SILENCE**
- The torment of your *silence* engulfs me with despair.
- *Silence* is golden unless one is in love.
- The anguish of your *silence* hurts me more than could any form of

physical torture.
- The deafening *silence* of a day without your voice is unbearable.
- Why have you chosen to punish me with your *silence*?
- Does your *silence* mean the end of our loving interlude?
- What have I said or done to deserve the wrath of your *silence*?
- The *silence* of your anger devastates me.

## SOUL
- You are the ambrosia of my *soul*.
- I would sell my *soul* for your radiant love.
- My *soul* needs the nourishment of your love.
- My *soul* hungers for a companion.

## SPIRIT
- Whenever my thoughts turn to you, my *spirits* soar to heights undreamt.
- You lift my *spirits* each time you kiss me.
- My *spirit* needs you for inspiration.
- You are the Doctor of my *spirit*.

## SUSPICION
- Your *suspicions* concerning my loyalty are groundless.
- I am afraid of the outcome if my *suspicions* are proven correct.

## T

## TENDERNESS
- You possess a loving *tenderness* which can heal the soul.
- You give to me a love full of *tenderness*, warmth and understanding.

## TORMENT
- Since you departed, each day has been full of *torment* and despair.
- The *torment* of our long-distance courtship is a small price to pay for your eternal love.

## TRUST
- Your unquestioning *trust* is surely a sign of true love.
- Why is it so difficult for you to have *trust* in me?
- *Trust* is one of the cornerstones of our relationship.
- You have destroyed my *trust* in you.

## TRUTH
- Love is the ultimate *truth* - all else is a lie.
- The *truth* of the matter is that I'm hopelessly in love with you.
- Love is beauty and *truth* combined.
- Our love is the only *truth* of my life.
- *Truth*, sincerity, loyalty and self-sacrifice are the cornerstones of our precious love.
- Sooner or later, the ultimate *truth* will out.

## TRUTHFULNESS
- Your *truthfulness* is sincerely appreciated.
- *Truthfulness* is not your greatest virtue.

# U-Z

## UNCERTAINTY
- The *uncertainty* of our separation is frightening.
- Each passing day without a word from you ends in *uncertainty*.

## UNION
- Our loving *union* was conceived in Heaven.
- The *union* of our hearts is a wondrous happening.

## VACUUM
- Only you, my love, can fill the *vacuum* of my loneliness.
- Our separation has created a *vacuum* in my heart which only you can fill.

## WARMTH
- You project a *warmth* which can melt a frigid heart.
- Your sympathetic *warmth* has healed my broken spirit.

## WEAKNESS
- At times, my *weakness* for beauty gets me into trouble.
- A *weakness* overcomes me whenever I am in your presence.

## WIFE
- A wonderful *wife* like you is as rare as the rarest orchid.
- A man is blessed with good fortune if he has a *wife* who understands, tolerates and loves.

## WISH
- My greatest *wish* in life is to be loved by you.
- You are the answer to my every *wish*.

## WORD
- A loving *word* from you is all I crave.
- Your *word* is as good as gold to me.

# Adjective Key Words

## A-B

**ABANDONED**
- Why have you got such an *abandoned* look?
- Your heartless behavior leaves me feeling cheated and *abandoned*.

**ADORABLE**
- Your *adorable* personality and charming ways are difficult to resist.
- You are the most *adorable* guy I've ever met.

**AFFECTIONATE**
- I was stunned by your *affectionate* kiss.
- I love an *affectionate* man.

**ALONE**
- I feel utterly *alone* and starved for affection.
- I suddenly find myself *alone* and frightened without you by my side.

**ANGELIC**
- Your *angelic* face is a divine poem.
- Is your *angelic* behavior sincere or made up?
- Your *angelic* face is truly heavenly.

**ATTRACTIVE**
- You are the most *attractive* woman I've ever had the pleasure of meeting.
- Could it be that you find me *attractive*?
- You looked so *attractive* the other night.
- Your *attractive* smile is a pleasurable sight.

## C-D

**CARING**
- You are the most *caring* and compassionate man I've ever known.
- Your *caring* love is the key to my happiness.

**CHARMING**
- Your *charming* voice is matched by your alluring beauty.
- You have a very *charming* sense of humor.
- I love your *charming* personality.

**COMPASSIONATE**
- You are a loving and *compassionate* woman.
- I adore you because you are so strong yet *compassionte*.

**DELIGHTFUL**
- Your *delightful* kiss is sorely missed.
- You provide me with the most *delightful* sensations.

**DELIRIOUS**
- I am *delirious* with desire and in desperate need of your calming love.
- The thought of our upcoming rendezvous makes me *delirious* with anticipation.

**DESIRABLE**
- You become more *desirable* with each passing day.
- Your *desirable* body is very distracting.
- You are the most *desirable* man in the world.
- I am fortunate to be in love with a *desirable* woman.

**DESOLATE**
- A life without love is a life of *desolate* desperation.
- My life is a *desolate* desert when you are not around to fill it with love.
- I feel *desolate* within and empty of inspiration.
- Ever since you left, my soul has been wracked by a *desolate* emptiness.

**DISTRUSTFUL**
- If you had true love in your heart, you would not be so *distrustful*.
- *Distrustful* people are very difficult to love.

**DIVINE**
- You possess a *divine* elegance rarely seen.
- Your passionate kiss is truly *divine*.
- I need your *divine* inspiration.
- The poetry of your *divine* beauty is inspiring.

**E-F**

**ECSTATIC**
- You have made me the most *ecstatic* woman on the face of this earth.
- Your *ecstatic* love is a welcome treat.

**EMPTY**
- My days are *empty* without you.
- Only you can give my *empty* existence purpose.
- My life is an *empty*, barren waste without you to give it beauty.
- My life has become an *empty* pit without you to fill it with love.

**ENVIOUS**
- I know girls who are *envious* of your stunning beauty.
- Many people are *envious* of our romantic relationship.

**ETERNAL**
- True love springs *eternal.*
- Ours is an *eternal* love.
- I give to you my *eternal* devotion.
- True love will bring *eternal* happiness.

**FORLORN**
- How can I help but be *forlorn* with you so far away?
- Our separation has caused within me a *forlorn* resignation.

**FRANTIC**
- Each night without you is a night of *frantic* desperation.
- I've been *frantic* with despair ever since the day you left.

## G-H

**GORGEOUS**
- You have a *gorgeous* face and a splendid figure.
- You're a *gorgeous* hunk of a man.
- I thought you were *gorgeous* the first time I saw you.
- You are a *gorgeous* woman inside and out.

**GRACIOUS**
- You are a charming and *gracious* lady with whom I've hopelessly fallen in love.
- Your charm and *gracious* personality are qualities which attract me.

**HANDSOME**
- I can't resist a *handsome* man especially if he is as charming and witty as you.
- Your *handsome* face is a joy to gaze at.
- A *handsome* guy like you is hard to find.
- I can't believe how *handsome* you are.

**HEAVENLY**
- Your *heavenly* body makes me delirious with desire.
- Your *heavenly* kisses destroy my defenses.

**HOPEFUL**
- I am *hopeful* that we will reconcile our petty differences and begin anew.
- This *hopeful* soul yearns to bask in the radiance of your love.

**HYPNOTIC**
- Your *hypnotic* eyes are formidable weapons.
- I cannot help gazing into your *hypnotic* eyes.
- Your *hypnotic* smile is very seductive.
- I am captivated by your *hypnotic* charm.

# I-K

## IMPETUOUS
- You are truly the most *impetuous* and exciting woman I've ever known.
- Your *impetuous* behavior is difficult to understand.

## INFINITE
- My love for you is *infinite* and everlasting.
- I cherish your *infinite* wisdom and all-encompassing love.

## INSATIABLE
- I'm obsessed with an *insatiable* desire to love you.
- Love is an *insatiable* urge which is hard to cure.

## INSENSITIVE
- Why are you so *insensitive* to my needs?
- An *insensitive* person can never truly love another.

## INSINCERE
- I cannot fall in love with an *insincere* person.
- I can see right through your *insincere* declaration of love.

## INTIMATE
- The *intimate* love which we share is divinely inspired.
- People who are truly in love usually share their most *intimate* feelings.

## INTOLERABLE
- Your playboy behavior is *intolerable*.
- The hurt you have caused is *intolerable*.

## IRRESISTIBLE
- You are extremely *irresistible* and alluring.
- Love is an *irresistible* force.
- Your kisses are truly *irresistible*.
- Your lovely smile is *irresistible*.

## JEALOUS
- Your *jealous* blindness is disappointing.
- A *jealous* love is doomed from the start.
- Your *jealous* attitude is uncalled for.
- Your *jealous* behavior is unbearable.

# L-O

## LONELY
- I am very *lonely* without your reassuring presence.
- The days of *lonely* desperation will end only with your return.
- My *lonely* heart needs a friend like you.
- Each *lonely* day seems like an eternity.

## LONESOME
- The *lonesome* road to your love was well worth it.
- I'm a *lonesome* guy in need of your friendship.
- I feel so *lonesome* without you near.
- I am a *lonesome* woman in need of love.

## LOVABLE
- I yearn to kiss your *lovable* lips.
- I am lucky to have such a charming and *lovable* friend like you.

## LOVELIEST
- You are the *loveliest* creature in the world.
- You have the *loveliest* face I've ever seen.

## MAD
- I am simply *mad* about you.
- I am *mad* with desire.

## MADDENED
- I am *maddened* by your love.
- You are *maddened* by a jealous hate.

## MADDENING
- The combination of your tempting smile and cool detachment is *maddening*.
- The thought that you exist yet I cannot hold you in my arms is *maddening*.

## MARVELOUS
- You have a *marvelous* sense of humor.
- You are a *marvelous* girl, and I love you dearly.
- You have a *marvelous* figure and a lovely personality.
- My love, you have a *marvelous* physique.

## P-R

## PASSIONATE
- I *didn't* know you were such a *passionate* man.
- I crave your *passionate* kiss.
- A *passionate* woman like me needs someone nice to love.
- Our *passionate* love will never die.

## POETIC
- You are my *poetic* masterpiece.
- Your *poetic* love is a sensory delight.

## POSSESSED
- I am *possessed* by your alluring beauty and charming personality.
- I am *possessed* by your captivating love.
- A *possessed* man like me is beyond help.
- Why are you *possessed* by such jealousy?

**POWERLESS**
- I am *powerless* under your captivating influence.
- A beautiful woman is never *powerless*.

**PROVOCATIVE**
- You are a delightfully *provocative* lady.
- Your *provocative* smile tempts and tantalizes.
- You are by far the most exciting and *provocative* man I've ever met.
- Your *provocative* behavior is very hard to resist.

**RAGING**
- My *raging* passions need your calming touch.
- Only you can quench the *raging* love which burns within my heart.

**RAVISHING**
- To me, you are the most *ravishing* woman on Earth.
- You have a *ravishing* body which is a delight to behold.

# S

**SEDUCTIVE**
- Your *seductive* eyes captivate me each time I gaze into them.
- Your *seductive* voice is music to my ears.
- I cannot resist your *seductive* ways.
- Your *seductive* smile is your most potent weapon.

**SENSUAL**
- I crave the *sensual* pleasures of your love.
- You are the *sensual* man of my dreams.

**SERENE**
- Your *serene* beauty calms the rage within me.
- Your *serene* composure has a soothing affect upon me.

**SEPARATED**
- Although we are *separated* by miles of emptiness, our hearts are still united by the bond of our universal love.
- I feel an overwhelming loneliness whenever I am *separated* from you.

**SOLITARY**
- Each day without you is a day of *solitary* anguish.
- Even a *solitary* man like me needs love.

**SPLENDID**
- You are a *splendid* specimen of a male.
- Your *splendid* smile warms my heart.

**STARVED**
- I am *starved* for your passionate love.
- It is hard for me to admit that I am *starved* for affection.

## SUGGESTIVE
- Your alluring body is marvelously *suggestive* and inspiring.
- Your *suggestive* body language has aroused passions within me I did not know existed.
- It is difficult for me to ignore your *suggestive* eyes.
- Someday, I will succumb to your *suggestive* ways.

## SUPPLE
- Your *supple* thighs are but one part of a wondrous work of living art.
- I can't ignore your *supple* body.

## SUSCEPTIBLE
- I am *susceptible* to your every whim.
- Someday, you may find me in a very *susceptible* frame of mind.

## SUSPICIOUS
- Why must you be so *suspicious* all the time?
- A *suspicious* person will never know true happiness.

## SWEET
- I don't want to hurt a *sweet* and charming girl like you.
- Your *sweet*, winning ways are irresistible.
- The *sweet* sound of your voice is what I dream of each night.
- I yearn for fragrant, balmy nights and your *sweet* caress.

# T

## TEMPTING
- Your *tempting* words are music to my ears.
- A *tempting* woman like you is my greatest weakness.

## TENDER
- Your *tender* words, last night, were true poems of the heart.
- Your *tender* kiss is what I need to chase the blues away.
- You are a *tender*, loving guy who makes me feel vibrantly alive.
- Your *tender* love is inspiring.

## THRILLING
- Just talking to you over the phone is a *thrilling* experience.
- Your kisses were as *thrilling* last night as they were the very first night.

## TOKEN
- Dear heart, I have sent you a lock of my hair as a *token* of my unwavering love.
- Your *token* embrace and shallow words indicate to me a change of sentiments.

**TORMENTED**
- My *tormented* soul and tortured flesh cry out for your soothing love.
- I am a *tormented* man all because of your indifference towards my affections.

**TOTAL**
- My love for you is *total* and absolute.
- I need a *total* man like you to make my life complete.

**TREMBLING**
- When I first met you, I prayed that you would not hear my *trembling* knees.
- My *trembling* heart needs reassurance.

**TROUBLED**
- You must have faith in the strength of our love to get us through these *troubled* times.
- I am *troubled* by the thought of being separated from you.

# U

**UNBEARABLE**
- Our separation is fast becoming *unbearable*.
- Your *unbearable* behavior is jeopardizing our friendship.
- Your haunting silence is *unbearable*.
- My yearning for your loving caress is reaching *unbearable* proportions.

**UNCONTROLLABLE**
- My actions are *uncontrollable* - my love undeniable.
- I am driven by an *uncontrollable* urge to love you.

**UNIQUE**
- You are an incredibly *unique* woman.
- You have a *unique* way of displaying your love.
- Our love is *unique* in many ways.
- You have a *unique* personality.

**UNSELFISH**
- An *unselfish* love such as yours is rare indeed.
- Your *unselfish* love and devotion have made my life worth living.

## V-Z

### VIBRANT
- You are as *vibrant* as the Sun.
- Your *vibrant* personality and compelling beauty fill me with excitement.

### VIVACIOUS
- I love your *vivacious* personality.
- I cannot resist a *vivacious* lady with romantic inclinations.

### WINNING
- Your *winning* ways charm me and disarm me.
- Your *winning* smile warms my heart.

### WONDROUS
- Life with you is a *wondrous* experience.
- You are a *wondrous* woman and a loving companion.

### YEARNING
- Your seductive smile ignites great passions from deep within my *yearning* heart.
- My *yearning* heart will die if you do not reply.

# Verb Key Words

## A-B

**ABANDONED**
- Why have you *abandoned* the one person who loves you more than anything else in the world?
- I cannot believe you *abandoned* my love for the love of another.

**ADMIRE**
- I *admire* the way you carry yourself.
- I *admire* an honorable man.
- I *admire* a lady who knows what she wants.
- I *admire* a man who is strong yet capable of compassion.
- I *admire* you for your high principles and honest nature.
- I *admire* you for your dauntless determination.

**ADMIT**
- I *admit* that I was wrong, and you were right.
- Why is it so difficult for you to *admit* that you love me?

**ADORE**
- My love, I *adore* you in a thousand ways.
- I *adore* you for loving me as you do.

**AFFIRM**
- I *affirm* to you the existence of a love which will overcome all earthly threats.
- I *affirm* to you that my love is sincere and everlasting.

## C-D

**CARESS**
- I become feverish with desire each time you *caress* me.
- I love to *caress* you tenderly.

**CHERISH**
- I *cherish* you above all else.
- I *cherish* the love you give me more than you'll ever know.
- I *cherish* the very thought of you.
- Do you *cherish* our loving relationship?

**DEPEND**
- I *depend* upon your loving support to get me through these stressful times.
- You can *depend* on me to fill your life with love and affection.

**DEPRIVED**
- Fate has *deprived* me of your fiery kiss.
- You *deprived* me of peace of mind when you left without a word.
- Why must I be *deprived* of your exhilarating love?
- How can you say that I *deprived* you of your freedom?

**DESERTED**
- Why have you *deserted* me for another?
- I have not *deserted* you; I have merely withdrawn myself in order to re-evaluate our relationship.

**DESIRE**
- Tell me truly if you *desire* me.
- I *desire* the ecstacy of your passionate kiss.
- I *desire* your love and devotion.
- I *desire* the sensual pleasures of your love.

**DISTRACT**
- You *distract* me with your extremely good looks and superb physique.
- You *distract* me with your loveliness and charm.

### E-F

**EMBRACE**
- I want to *embrace* you with my loving arms.
- Why won't you *embrace* me lovingly?
- I passionately *embrace* your lovely vision each lonely night.
- I yearn to *embrace* you tenderly.

**ENVY**
- I *envy* the woman who possesses your affections.
- I *envy* your strength and determination.

**EXPRESS**
- It is hard for me to *express* in words the magnitude of my love.
- I must *express* to you how incredibly happy you have made me.

**FORGIVE**
- Can you find it in your heart to *forgive* me for my thoughtless behavior?
- Can you *forgive* a man who realizes he made a terrible mistake?
- I will *forgive* you for your indiscretions only because I am hopelessly in love with you.
- My absolute love compels me to *forgive* you.

**FORSAKEN**
- Why have you *forsaken* me for someone who obviously cannot give you the love you deserve?
- I have not *forsaken* you for another but merely need time to sort things out.

## G-H

**GRASP**
- I *grasp* you every night and pull you into my dreams.
- I want to *grasp* you around your waist and smother you with kisses.

**HOLD**
- I need to *hold* you in my lonely arms.
- I *hold* you above all other earthly delights.

**HUG**
- I love to *hug* you with unbridled enthusiasm.
- Why don't you *hug* me as lovingly as you once did?

## I-L

**INSPIRE**
- You *inspire* me in countless ways.
- How can I *inspire* you to love me?

**KEEP**
- I always *keep* you in the forefront of my thoughts.
- May the good Lord *keep* you healthy, happy and strong.

**LOVE**
- I *love* your exquisite taste.
- I *love* you completely and without reservation.
- I *love* to hear your seductive voice.
- I wonder if you *love* me as much as I *love* you?
- How can I *love* a man who is inconsiderate?
- If you *love* me, don't keep it a secret.

## M-Q

### MISTRUST
- I *mistrust* your intentions because you are known for your insincerity.
- Why do you always *mistrust* my most noble intentions?

### PROCLAIM
- I *proclaim* to you my undying love and devotion.
- Do not *proclaim* your love to me unless you really mean it.

## R-S

### RELY
- I *rely* on your love to give my life purpose.
- You can *rely* on me for love and emotional support.

### RESPECT
- I *respect* you for your strength of character.
- I hope you *respect* me as much as I *respect* you.

### SACRIFICE
- Why would you *sacrifice* everlasting love for a fleeting moment of pleasure?
- Would you *sacrifice* your freedom for my love?

### SATISFY
- Only you can *satisfy* my burning desires.
- I want to *satisfy* your every need.

### SEPARATED
- When fate *separated* us, I had no idea how emotionally draining your absence would be.
- When we *separated*, I thought it was for the best, but now I regret my blindness.

**SURRENDER**
- I know that someday I will *surrender* myself to you.
- I *surrender* to you all the love I possess.

## T-Z

**TEMPT**
- You *tempt* me in a thousand ways.
- Each time you *tempt* me with a kiss, I fall for you a little more.

**THRIVE**
- I *thrive* on your nourishing love.
- Why do you *thrive* on suspicion and jealousy?
- My heart *thrives* on your sweet love.
- Our love will *thrive* if trust and mutual respect are present.

**TORMENT**
- Why do you *torment* me with your childish games?
- It's sad to see you *torment* yourself needlessly.

**TREASURE**
- I *treasure* our trusting relationship.
- I *treasure* your delicate loveliness.
- I *treasure* each and every moment we are together.
- I *treasure* the memories of our first encounter.

**YEARN**
- I *yearn* for your tender kiss.
- I *yearn* for your safe return.
- I *yearn* to caress your firm physique.
- Do you *yearn* for the good times?

# Adverb Key Words

## A-D

**AFFECTIONATELY**
- I always think of you *affectionately*.
- Your letters are *affectionately* written and gratefully received.

**DIVINELY**
- Your *divinely* elegant ways stimulate my senses.
- Our love is *divinely* inspired.

## E-G

**ENDLESSLY**
- A love such as ours will continue *endlessly*.
- *Endlessly*, you give to me your unselfish love and devotion.

**FAITHFULLY**
- I will love you *faithfully* forever.
- I will always remain *faithfully* by your side.

**GRACEFULLY**
- Love flows *gracefully* from your heart.
- *Gracefully*, you came into my life.

## H-S

**HAPPILY**
- *Happily*, I will fall into your waiting arms.
- My life flows *happily* from day to day thanks to your sustaining love.

**JOYFULLY**
- You make me feel *joyfully* alive.
- *Joyfully*, I await our next encounter.

**MADLY**
- I am *madly* and hopelessly in love with you.
- I have fallen *madly* head over heels for you.

## T-Z

**TENDERLY**
- I dream of you holding me *tenderly* in your arms.
- Only you can kiss me so *tenderly* yet so passionately at the same time.

**TOTALLY**
- I am *totally* at your loving command.
- I just realized how *totally* in love I am with you.

**TRULY**
- Do you love me *truly*?
- *Truly*, you are my soul's desire.
- You *truly* are my most intimate friend.
- Do you *truly* believe that our love will survive?
- I am *truly* fortunate to have you as my friend.
- I can *truly* say that I love you.

# Part II:
# THE LOVE POEM

# PART II / THE LOVE POEM

The final portion of this handbook concerns itself with the *Love Poem*, the second of the two major forms of romantic communication. A love poem is considered "lyric" in nature, which means it is composed, for the most part, to stir emotions and to give pleasure. Indeed, you will find that a love poem can express every shade of personal feeling imaginable.

This part has been divided into three sections which contain the following: 1) a discussion of the elements of poetry and a step-by-step procedure for writing a love poem, 2) twenty-five complete, original love poems which you can modify or use as is, and 3) over two hundred two-line mini-poems which you can combine with ease to create larger, more complex love poems taylor made to your own unique situation.

As you can see, this second and final part on the love poem addresses itself to several levels of involvement, so it doesn't make any difference whether you feel lazy or ambitious; either way, you've got it made.

# SECTION 1 / THE ELEMENTS OF POETRY

The Love Poem is one of the most powerful and effective ways of communicating your innermost thoughts and feelings to someone you love or admire. If properly composed, it has the ability to stir the reader's emotions to passionate heights.

But what really is a love poem? To gain an understanding, you must first familiarize yourself with the various elements of poetry: *Imagery*, *Rhythm* and *Rhyme*. This section will help you do this, for it is a basic overview of the topic and contains a very helpful step-by-step *procedure* for writing a love poem. After reading it, you should possess the basic tools with which you can compose love poems of beauty and emotional impact.

# ELEMENTS OF POETRY

## Rhythm

*Rhythm* is found all around us as well as within us. It gives to our lives the beauty of order and structure. In fact, even our speech has a natural rhythm which most of us are not conscious of. This is true for many things on Earth, organic as well as manmade. Take a poem for example. Often, its lines contain elements which establish a certain rhythmic pattern. This is pleasurable to our senses because our minds are attuned to the beauty of order and structure which surrounds us.

## The Verse

Each line of a poem is called a *verse*. At least two verses are needed to create the most basic poem:

> The feelings from within me shout,
> Proclaiming love without a doubt.

If you were to examine these two verses closely, you would find that each has a certain *length* and *meter* which when combined determine its *rhythm*.

## Verse Length

The *length* of each verse is measured in terms of a unit called the *metric foot*. The most common metric foot contains two syllables:

> | The feel | ings from | with/in | me shout |
> | Pro/claim | ing love | with/out | a doubt |

As illustrated in the two verses above, each two-syllable metric foot can consist of one of the following: a) two one-syllable words such as

| me shout |, b) one two-syllable word such as | with/in |, c) the first or second syllable of a two-syllable word combined with a one-syllable word such as | ings from |, or d) the third syllable of a three-syllable word combined with a one-syllable word such as | ing love |.

The *total length* of a verse is described by the number of metric feet present:

**Octameter** *(Eight metric feet)*
| I love | you more | than life | it/self | for you | are sweet | and true | to me |

**Septameter** *(Seven metric feet)*
| I love | you more | than life | it/self | for you | are sweet | and true |

**Hexameter** *(Six metric feet)*
| One lone | ly day | has all | but passed | since we | em/braced |

**Pentameter** *(Five metric feet)*
| I think | of you | my pret | ty coun | try love |

**Tetrameter** *(Four metric feet)*
| You are | my one | and on | ly love |

**Trimeter** *(Three metric feet)*
| I miss | you my | sweet love |

**Dimeter** *(Two metric feet)*
| You are | my love |

**Monometer** *(One metric foot)*
| I love |

Of these eight lengths, *pentameter*, *tetrameter* and *trimeter* are the most common in poetry. The others, although occasionally used, are not recommended because they are either too lengthy or too short.

## Verse Meter

Each *metric foot* in a verse has an obvious pattern of *emphasized* and *nonemphasized* syllables. Acting together, these give a verse a distinct meter. Several of these rythmic patterns exist and are used in identifying the different types of metric feet:

### The Iamb

The most common type of two-syllable metric foot is called an *Iamb*. It has a nonemphasized first syllable and an emphasized second syllable:

| Ĭ lŏ́ve | • | ă/bŏ́ve | • | ŏne lŏ́ne | • | lў̆ dắy |

## The Trochee

A two-syllable metric foot with an emphasized first syllable and a nonemphasized second syllable is known as a *Trochee*:

| lŏ́ve/lў̆ | • | śoft/lў̆ | • | kĭ́s/sĭng |

## The Spondee

A two-syllable metric foot with both syllables equally emphasized is called a *Spondee*:

| heắrt/ắche | • | swĕ́et/heắrt | • | gŏ́r/geŏ́us |

Spondees are used sparingly in a verse of a poem for emphasis.

Occassionally, a two-syllable metric foot may be replaced by a three-syllable metric foot. There are two types:

## The Dactyl

A three-syllable metric foot which has an emphasized first syllable and a nonemphasized second and third syllable is called a *Dactyl*:

| hắp/pĭ/nĕss | • | sў́m/pă/thў̆ | • | Cŏ́me tŏ mĕ |

## The Anapest

A three-syllable metric foot which has an emphasized third syllable and a nonemphasized first and second syllable is known as an *Anapest*:

| dĭs/rĕs/pĕ́ct | • | ańd oŭr lŏ́ve | • | iń/sĭn/cĕ́re |

If you were to substitute a Dactyl or Anapest for an *Iambic* foot in a verse, you would obtain something similar to the following:

*Dactyl:*    | Ĭ́ crắve | sў́m/pă/thў̆ | ănd lŏ́ve | frŏm yŏ́u | ḿy deắr |

*Anapest:*    | Dĭs/rĕs/pĕ́ct | căn/ńot | ĕx/ĭ́st | ĭf lŏ́ve | ĭs trŭ́e |

# Verse Types

A verse is partially described by the type of meter found in the majority of its metric feet:

## Pure Iambic *(All Feet Are Iambs)*

| Ĭ lŏvé | tŏ hŏ́ld | yŏu ĭ́n | m̆y ărms |

## Pure Trochaic *(All Feet Are Trochees)*

| Slŏ́w/lў | s̆oft/lў | ắnd s̆o | gĕ́nt/lў |

## Iambic with a Trochee And Spondee

| Sŏ́ft/lў | Ĭ wắlk | ĭn/tŏ́ | hĕ́r rŏ́om |

A verse is also partly described by its *length* (Tetrameter, Trimeter, etc.). But to fully identify a verse type, both its *meter* and *length* must be used:

## Iambic Pentameter

| Ĭ thĭ́nk | ŏf yŏ́u | m̆y prĕt | tў cŏ́un | trў lŏvé |

In this verse, the five metric feet present are all *Iambs* because in each case the second syllable is emphasized. The complete description of this verse type is *Iambic Pentameter*.

When a majority of a poem's verses are of this type and there is no rhyme present, a form of poetry known as *Blank Verse* is created. Such poetry is fairly easy to write:

| Ĭ thĭ́nk | ŏf yŏ́u | m̆y prĕt | tў cŏ́un | trў lŏvé |

| Ănd wŏ́n | dĕr whĕ́n | ŏur pắths | wĭll crŏ́ss | ŏn̆ce mŏ́re |

| Fŏr Wĭ́n | tĕr cŏ́mes | ănd nĭ́ghts | grŏw lŏ́ng | ănd c̆old |

| Thŭs sŏ́on | Ĭ'll nĕ́ed | thĕ wărmth | ŏf yŏ́ur | ĕm/brắce |

Although Blank Verse can be used in writing love poems, it is not recommended for reasons which will be made clear later.

## Iambic Tetrameter

| Ĭ lŏvé | tŏ kĭ́ss | yŏur sĕ́x | ў lĭ́ps |

This verse has four metric feet and each is an *Iamb* due to an emphasized second syllable. The complete description of this verse type is *Iambic Tetrameter*.

Love poems with verses of this rhythm are one of the most desirable types to compose since the *meter* is one of the most common types found in English poetry and the *length* is of the most natural duration:

> I dream of fragrant, flowered nights;
> Of passioned love and sweet delights.
> Such moments of my life do stay
> Alive within my mind each day.

As you can see, the verses flow smoothly and the rhythm seems natural - not abrupt or labored.

## Trochaic Tetrameter

| Slŏw/lў | sŏft/lў | ańd sŏ | gént/lў |

The four metric feet of this verse have emphasized first syllables and are considered *Trochees*, hence the verse rhythm is *Trochaic Tetrameter*. This verse type is not as common as Iambic Tetrameter. Often, such verses are interspersed within primarily Iambic Tetrameter poems to create a variety of rhythmic textures:

*Iambic:*    | Thĕ swéet | pĕr/fuḿe | yŏu áll | wăys uśe |

*Trochaic:*  | Kín/dlĕs | páss/siŏns | cŕa/vĭngs | ănd lúst |

*Iambic:*    | Sŭch féel | ĭngs lóng | hăd Í | sŭp/préssed |

*Iambic:*    | Bŭt nów | frŏm déep | wĭth/ín | me thrúst |

## Iambic Trimeter

| Ĭ kíss | yŏu ín | my dréams |

Each of the three metric feet in this verse has an emphasized second syllable, thus its rhythm is *Iambic Trimeter*.

This verse type is not as desirable as Iambic Tetrameter for use in love poems because such a verse, due to its shorter length, tends to be more abrupt and is less capable of being fully developed:

*Iambic Trimeter:*    | Ĭ kíss | yŏu ín | my dréams |

*Iambic Tetrameter:*  | Ĭ kíss | yŏu ín | my dréams | eách níght |

Often, Iambic Trimeter verses are combined with those of Iambic Tetrameter:

| Iambic Tetrameter: | \| You are \| the Sun \| shine of \| my life \| |
| Iambic Trimeter: | \| You lift \| my spi \| rits high \| |
| Iambic Tetrameter: | \| With joy \| un/bound \| you give \| to me \| |
| Iambic Trimeter: | \| A love \| to fill \| the sky \| |

Such verse combinations are called *Ballad Stanzas* and are used in the composition of *Ballads* (poems which tell a story). These will be discussed further under *Rhyme*.

## Variations

Verses may be composed with the second syllable of the last foot omitted:

> | Love/ly | wo/man | how are | you — |
> | Are you | hap/py | are you | blue — |
> | If you | feel the | way I | do — |
> | Then, my | love, you | will pur | sue — |

As you can see, the verses above are basically four metric feet *(tetrameter)* in length. In each case, however, the final syllable has been dropped. This can be done for any verse length to permit variations of rhythm.

## Free Verse

Most poems are made up of verses which have a pronounced rhythm *(meter and length)*. There is, however, a form of poetry known as *Free Verse* which is an exception to this. In addition to the absence of any regular rhythm in its verses, there is an obvious absence of the element of *rhyme* which will be discussed later in this section.

A Free Verse love poem may look something like the following example:

> I love you!
> And you believe me not.
> What must I do or say
> To make you see how wrong you are?
> For, in my heart, there is
> No doubt
> That truly
> I love you.

The power and effectiveness of a love poem depends greatly upon the presence of aesthetic elements such as *Rhythm* and *Rhyme* to stir emotions. A Free Verse poem, in effect, has neither. For comparison sake, let us now rewrite the above poem giving to it a distinct rhythm and rhyme:

> My heart is full of love for you;
>    Why do you not believe this true?
> How must I act - what must I say
>    To make you fling your doubts away?
>
> For, in my heart there is no doubt,
>    That love exists and needs to shout-
> "I love you dear!, now more and more;"
> "'Tis you I love and do adore."

It is obvious that the elements of *Rhythm* and *Rhyme*, especially Rhyme, add a third dimension to a love poem giving to it an enticing quality which is pleasing to our senses. Since Free Verse poems lack these two aesthetic elements, they are not recommended at this time as a form for use in the writing of love poems.

# Rhyme

The ability of sound to create within us a wide range of moods is an accepted reality. The poems of Edgar Allan Poe attest to this. Through the wise choice of words and their proper placement within his poems, Poe effectively uses sound repetition (*Rhyme*) to influence the emotions of the reader by creating a certain mood:

> Hear the sledges with the bells-
>    Silver bells!
> What a world of merriment their melody foretells!
>    How they tinkle, tinkle, tinkle,
>       In the icy air of night!
>    While the stars, that oversprinkle
>    All the heavens, seem to twinkle
>       With a crystalline delight;
>       Keeping time, time, time,
>       In a sort of Runic rhyme,
> To the tintinnabulation that so musically wells
>    From the bells, bells, bells, bells,
>       Bells, bells, bells-
> From the jingling and the tinkling of the bells.

**—Edgar Allan Poe** from *"THE BELLS"*

Just what makes a word rhyme? Where in a poem is rhyme used? How is rhyme used? These questions will now be discussed.

# Sound

Each word in the English language is made up of a combination of two types of letters known either as *Vowels* or *Consonants. A, E, I, O* and *U* are considered vowels. When pronounced, a vowel does not require you to use your tongue, teeth, lips or mouth to stop or restrict, for any length of time, the movement of air through your throat. *B, C, D, F, G, H, J, K, L, M, N, P, Q, R, S, T, V, W, X, Y,* and *Z* are consonants. When pronounced, they do require the stopping or restriction of air movement for a certain length of time. In certain cases, the consonants, *W* and *Y* produce vowel sounds, thus they are called *Semi-vowels*.

## Types Of Rhyme

To achieve Rhyme, you need at least two words which possess similar sounds when read or spoken. There are two basic catagories of rhyming words: *Exact Rhymes* and *Near Rhymes*.

### Exact Rhymes

Words which have identically sounding endings are called *Exact Rhymes*:

seed / bead • said / fed • flower / hour

All of the above words end with a *pronounced consonant*. To be considered exact rhymes, the last pronounced vowel and consonant sounds must be the same in both words even though their spelling is not identical.

knee / flea • weigh / today • beau / snow

All of these words end in a *pronounced vowel* or *silent consonant*. To be considered exact rhymes, the final vowel sound must be the same in both words even though their spelling is not identical.

### Near Rhymes

When writing a poem, if you are not able to find a word that is an exact rhyme for a previously used word, you may want to utilize a *Near Rhyme*. Such a word sounds similar to the word it is supposed to rhyme with:

seed / beads • flower / hours • devine / designed

Even though a Near Rhyme is not the perfect solution, it can help you finish your poem with very satisfactory results. If, however, you are unwilling to compromise, you may have to rewrite the verse or verses so that you will be able to use an Exact Rhyme.

## Sound Effects

Sounds may be used over and over again, that is, repeated to create sound effects within a verse of a poem. Words which promote this type of sound repetition cannot be considered Near Rhymes although, in some cases, they come close. There are four different types of sound effects: *Alliteration, Consonance, Assonance* and *Bracket Rhyme*:

### Alliteration

stroke / strafe • poke / pinch • talk / tell

*Alliteration* is a type of sound effect in which the only similarity between two words is that they share the same *beginning consonant sound*. This method of sound repetition is not as popular today as it was in the past.

### Consonance

late / night • read / bed • lock / take

*Consonance* is a type of sound effect in which two words share only the same *ending consonant sound*.

### Assonance

sleeve / leaf • wise / side • home / loan

*Assonance* is created when two words have in common only the *internal vowel sound*.

### Bracket Rhyme

roll / rail • seem / same • dare / door

When two words have identical *beginning and ending consonant sounds*, they are said to exhibit *Bracket Rhyme*.

## Rhyme Placement

The concept of Rhyme can be described not only in terms of sound similarities but also in terms of placement within a poem. There are two basic types of Rhyme placement: *Internal Rhyme* and *End Rhyme*.

### Internal Rhyme

If rhymed words are placed within a verse, the technique is called *Internal Rhyme*. The words should be exact rhymes. Often, the end result can be quite exciting:

> My heart is *racing* as I am *facing*
> Another day without your kiss.
> My mind is *tracing*; my thoughts are *embracing*
> The memories of the one I miss.

### End Rhyme

If rhymed words are placed at the end of selected verses, the technique is called *End Rhyme*. Such words should preferably be exact rhymes although near rhymes are acceptable. End Rhyme is pleasing to the ear, but most important, it can be used to set off a thought or idea by creating a distinct unit *(verse grouping)* within a poem.

## Verse Groupings

### The Couplet

If the last words of two consecutive verses are made to rhyme, a pair grouping is formed known as a *Couplet*. The couplet is the *basic poetic unit*. It is the smallest grouping of end-rhymed verses which can, in effect, form a poetic paragraph *(Stanza)*. In practice, however, single couplets are usually added on to other couplets to create more complex groupings which develop and express thoughts and sentiments more completely.

### *The Closed Couplet*

If two consecutive end-rhymed verses complete a thought or statement, the couplet is considered *closed*:

> My love for you will always *be,*
> As vibrant as the surging *Sea.*

The *Closed Couplet* is by far the easiest type of end-rhymed grouping to create since you have to end-rhyme only two consecutive verses.

## The Open Couplet

If the two end-rhymed verses of a couplet do not complete a thought or statement and there is need for additional verses, the couplet is considered *open*. In this case, the couplet's second verse is called a *Run-On-Line*:

|  |  |  |
|---|---|---|
| | Cycles, cycles every *place;* | *Open Couplet* |
| *Run-on-line:* | Even in my life I *face* | |
| | The fact that cycles often flow, | *Completing Couplet* |
| | To places full of pain and woe. | |

## The Heroic Couplet

A couplet may be made of any verse type. If, however, it is composed of two *Iambic Pentameter* verses, it is considered a *Heroic Couplet*:

> You cannot know how much I crave your *kiss,*
> For never have you known love's deep *abyss.*

## The Triplet *(Tercet)*

Three-verse groupings are occassionally used in poetry. This type of unit is called a *Triplet* or *Tercet*. Two or more of the three verses must be end-rhymed with the possible rhyming patterns *(a b a)* and *(a a a)*:

> Your love for me is strong and *pure,*     (a)
> It does not waiver at every bend,     (b)
> But walks with grace and will *endure.*     (a)

## The Quatrain

The most popular stanza in English poetry is the four-verse grouping known as the *Quatrain*. This unit of poetry has at least two end-rhymed verses patterned *(a b c b)* and can have up to four patterned *(a a a a)*. A quatrain may be composed of any verse type or combination of verse types:

## Iambic Pentameter (The Heroic Quatrain)

| | |
|---|---|
| You cannot know how much I crave your *kiss*, | (a) |
| For spirit free and innocent are thee. | (b) |
| You do not know the pain of Love's *abyss*, | (a) |
| Nor can you see my eyes' empassioned plea. | (b) |

This stanza is made up of four *Iambic Pentameter* verses with the rhyming pattern *(a b a b)*. Any stanza which has this combination of rhythm and rhyme is known as a *Heroic Quatrain*.

## Iambic Tetrameter

| | |
|---|---|
| I love to kiss your sexy *lips*, | (a) |
| And lightly touch your *fingertips*; | (a) |
| I love to hold you in my arms, | (b) |
| Experience your many charms. | (b) |

This Quatrain is made up of four *Iambic Tetrameter* verses with the rhyming pattern *(a a b b)*. Note that the Quatrain is, in essence, composed of two closed couplets.

## Iambic Trimeter

| | |
|---|---|
| I kiss you in my *dreams*, | (a) |
| Include you in my *schemes*. | (a) |
| For life without you dear, | (b) |
| Would leave me much to fear. | (b) |

Four *Iambic Trimeter* verses grouped into a pair of closed couplets make up this quatrain.

## The Ballad Stanza

| | |
|---|---|
| So far apart are we again; | (a) |
| It is not fair I *say*. | (b) |
| For I was dealt a rotten hand, | (c) |
| And now I have to *pay*. | (b) |

This stanza is composed of alternating verses of *Iambic Tetrameter* and *Iambic Trimeter* rhythm and has a rhyming pattern *(a b c b)*. This rhythm and rhyme format is called the *Ballad Standza*.

As you can see from these few examples, the quatrain may have many variations of rhythm and rhyme. It can create many different moods and is, therefore, a very versatile poetic grouping - one which you can effectively use to express your true inner feelings.

## The Sonnet

If you become adept at writing *Heroic Couplets* and *Heroic Quatrains*, you may want to try writing a *Love Sonnet*. The *English Sonnet* has fourteen end-rhymed Iambic Pentameter verses, which are broken down into *three Heroic Quatrains* and *one Heroic Couplet*. Usually each quatrain develops and communicates a certain idea while the final couplet brings these ideas together in a conclusion:

*——-Heroic Quatrain #1*
Shall I compare thee to a Summer's day?
Thou art more lovely and more temperate.
Rough winds do shake the darling buds of May,
And Summer's lease hath all too short a date.

*——-Heroic Quatrain #2*
Sometime too hot the eye of heaven shines,
And often is his gold complexion dimm'd.
And every fair from fair sometime declines,
By chance or Nature's changing course untrimm'd

*——-Heroic Quatrain #3*
But thy eternal Summer shall not fade,
Nor lose possession of that fair thou owest;
Nor shall death brag thou wander'st in his shade,
When in eternal lines to time thou grow'st,

*——-Heroic Couplet*
So long as men can breathe, or eyes can see,
So long lives this, and this gives life to thee.

**—William Shakespeare**

# Words And Imagery

By now, you should be quite familiar with *Rhythm* and *Rhyme* which can be considered a love poem's *Technical Ingredients*. To complete your understanding, you will need to familiarize yourself with *Words* and *Imagery*, a love poem's *Creative Ingredients*.

## Words

A poet is an artist who uses words instead of paint to create an artistic statement. In effect, the entire English vocabulary is his or her color pallette.

When you assume the poet's role, your task will be to select those words which best express your true feelings, emotions and intentions within the context of the poem. The words you choose should, therefore, be packed with as much meaning as possible because a poem, unlike a letter, requires that you say just as much but in a smaller amount of space. In order to accomplish this, you will have to turn to the final creative ingredient: *Imagery*.

## Imagery

*Words* give a love poem *taste* but *images* give it *flavor*. Images play an important role in love poetry, for they give to the reader *visual, physical*, and/or *emotional impressions* which can possess the potency of a thousand words yet take up only a small amount of space within a verse. The creation and use of images within a poem is called *Imagery*. The remaining portion of this section will identify and discuss its various forms.

### Allusion

An *Allusion* is a one or two word reference to a person, object, place or event from literature, history or legend which brings forth in the mind of the reader a preconceived image. When using Allusion, you must make sure that the person, object, place or event being alluded to is known to the reader or else your effort will be wasted:

> Your *arms* are my *Eden,* I cannot leave,

In this verse, the allusion is to the biblical *Garden Of Eden*. Taken at face value, however, the idea of *Your arms* being a *Garden* is ridiculous. We must, therefore, look to our preconceived image of *Eden* to find the correlation.

To most of us, the word, *Eden* brings forth a number of visual and emotional impressions which describe the type of place the Garden Of Eden was. For instance, it was a *beautiful place*. It provided Adam and Eve a *secure home, comfort, warmth* and *contentment*. In light of this, we can now understand the imagery being created here. In effect, by alluding to the Garden Of Eden, the poet is saying:

> *Your arms are my...*(secure home—They are a beautiful
> place to be. They comfort me and give me warmth and
> contentment. Because of this)...*I cannot leave,*

## Personification

*Personification* is the creation of an image in which the visual impression suggests that something not human has human qualities:

Breezes gently *caress* your silken hair,

This verse brings forth the visual impression that the breezes have somehow acquired *hands* and are gently *caressing* the subject's silken hair. Even though this is impossible, you will accept the overall image which is of the subject's silken hair being *disturbed* by the gentle winds. The personification merely gives the description more eloquence and poetic charm.

## Simile

A *Simile* is the creation of an image in which the visual impressions cause a comparison between two different types of objects. Words such as *like* and *as* are usually signs of a Simile:

Our *love* is **like** *Gibraltar,*

In this Simile, *love* is being compared to the *Rock Of Gibraltar*. Once again, taken at face value, such a comparison is ridiculous. However, if you consider the visual impressions which make up your preconceived image of Gibraltar, then the comparison becomes more acceptable. To most people, the word Gibraltar should stir up impressions of *solidity, stability, indestructability,* etc. Thus, the poet, by using Simile, is saying:

Our *love* is...(solid, stable and indestructable).

## Metaphor

A *Metaphor* is the creation of an image in which the visual impressions cause a certain object to be described by, and not just compared to, a completely dissimilar object. To accomplish this, the poet makes a direct statement without the use of comparative words such as *like* and *as*:

Our *love* **is** an *island,*

This Metaphor describes *love* as being *an island* and not merely *like an island*. Again, you might ask how such a strong statement can be made. Actually, it does sound a bit extreme. In order to understand this relationship, you will have to compare your preconceived image of *love* with the visual and emotional impressions which make up your image of an *island*. To many, an island is a *haven* surrounded by a threatening sea. It provides *nourishment* to sustain life as well as *beautiful surroundings* to make life more pleasurable. Consequently, through this Metaphor, the poet is saying:

> *Our love is...*(a haven which protects us from all that is negative around us—It provides us with physical and emotional nourishment and a beautiful existence).

## Symbolism

A *Symbol* is an image which is perceived at face value, although it may also suggest other visual impressions:

> My *broken heart* will never heal,

Taken literally, a heart breaking in half is certainly a life-threatening experience. To many, however, a *broken heart* symbolizes the trauma of being rejected which can be considered just as serious. Thus, through the use of symbolism, the poet is saying:

> My...(traumatic illness, caused by your rejection of me and whose symptoms are sadness, despair, melancholy and loneliness)...*will never heal.*

## Hyperbole

A *Hyperbole* is a far-fetched written expression which creates a very powerful visual, physical and/or emotional impression:

> I am **dying** of a *broken heart,*

This is obviously an overstatement. Very few people, if any, die of a *broken heart*. Yet, you will probably accept this expression, not at face value, but through the visual and emotional impressions which surround the process of dying due to a broken heart. Through Symbolism, you will realize that the words *broken heart* refer to the *hurt of rejection* and, as a consequence, that *dying* refers to a *spiritual or emotional death*. By exaggerating or overstating events, the poet is expressing to the reader how deep his or her love actually is.

## Understatement

An *Understatement* is the opposite of a Hyperbole. It is a subdued written expression which creates a very restrained visual, physical and/or emotional impression:

> Your picture which I have in hand,
> By itself can never stand.

Taken again at face value, this written expression creates the visual impressions of a person setting a picture on end and letting go. Having only two dimensions, it will most likely fall. For some reason, this seems too simple. There must be some underlying meaning. In truth, there is, for the poet is implying that:

> *Your picture...*(is only two-dimensional
> with no substance; therefore, it is a poor
> substitute for the real you.)

## Paradox

A *Paradox* is a written expression which creates an image in which the impressions cause an apparent contradiction. However, this contradiction is short-lived and easily resolved by the reader:

> The *silence* of a day without you
> Is *deafening* and hard to live through.

This seems impossible. How can *Silence* (the absence of sound) be *deafening*? Yet, in the context of these two verses, such an expression is accepted. Why? Perhaps, because your mind reasons that the absence of sound, especially desirable sound, can be psychologically and emotionally devastating - in effect, *deafening* to the person being deprived of it. With this realization, the paradox is resolved. Thus, in the above verses, the poet is saying:

> *The...*(absence of your loving, reassuring
> voice for even a day creates a silence which is
> psychologically and emotionally)...*deafening*
> *and hard to live through.*

## Oxymoron

An *Oxymoron* is a very short expression which creates an image in which the visual, physical and/or emotional impressions cause an apparent contradiction through the use of two opposites. In the reader's mind, this type of contradiction tends to be resolved more quickly than a Paradox:

> Your *guilty innocence* is hard to bear.

*Guilt* and *innocence* are the two opposites used in this Oxymoron. Taken at face value, they could never exist side by side - a person is either guilty or innocent but never both. Yet, what if someone was guilty but pretended to be innocent. Furthermore, what if the other person knew of this person's guilt. By accepting the fact that such a scenario is possible, you will have resolved the apparent contradiction and the Oxymoron will become more acceptable.

## Verbal Irony

*Verbal Irony* is the creation of a written expression whose actual meaning is the opposite of its meaning at face value:

> I hate you for being so beautiful,
> So cheerful and so faithful.

Taken at face value, these two verses proclaim the poet's intense dislike of a "beautiful" woman. However, such a statement does not seem logical. Why would the poet hate a beautiful girl, especially one who is also "cheerful" and "faithful"? Perhaps, because the poet has become a prisoner of love and cannot accept the fact that he has lost control of his emotions and, as a direct result, his freedom and independence. Thus, the poet, through the use of Verbal Irony is really saying:

> I am a prisoner of your beauty,
> Thus I am hopelessly in love with you.

As you can see, *Imagery* in all its forms, can spice up and add flavor to a love poem. As a creative ingredient, however, it should be used sparingly in order to achieve maximum impact.

# Love Poem Writing Procedure

The following step-by-step procedure has been developed to aid you in the writing of your own original love poem. It identifies the most important considerations which should be dealt with prior to, as well as during the actual writing process.

1. Select the type of Rhythm you are going to utilize (*Iambic Pentameter, Iambic Tetrameter,* etc.).

2. Determine the Verse Grouping (*stanza*) you are going to use (*Couplet, Tercet, Quatrain,* etc.).

3. Select the primary Rhyming Pattern you will be using (*abcb, abab, aabb,* etc.). Keep in mind that several different rhyming patterns may be used in the same poem, especially if the poem is made up of quatrains.

4. Identify the poem's Main Theme (*You mean so much to me, I love you, I miss you, I can't live without you, You're beautiful, You're handsome,* etc.).

5. Set down the Primary Words which you wish to use in the poem (*passion, yearning, desire, honesty, sincerity, loneliness, beauty, charm, divine, embrace,* etc.).

6. Write down any images which might be appropriate. Remember, you have many forms of imagery from which to choose, such as **Allusion:** *Your arms are my Eden.*, **Simile:** *Our love is like Gibraltar.*, **Symbolism:** *My broken heart will never heal.*, etc. You will also find many helpful *Imagery Terms* in Appendix D.

7. Determine if there is any progression or logical order of thought which can be followed from stanza to stanza (See the complete love poem, *I Can't Imagine* which may be found in Section Two: *Original Love Poems*).

8. If possible, create a verse which states the poem's theme. You can then use this in one or more stanzas (*I Can't Imagine, One Lonely Day,* etc.). This Theme Verse can act as the thread which binds the poem's stanzas together.

9. Sometimes, a special word or phrase can be used to start and end a poem. Like the theme verse, this too can be an effective way to increase a poem's potency (See the complete love poem, *An Animated Woman.*).

Once you have completed these preliminaries, you may begin to write your love poem. As you proceed, however, keep in mind the following:

10. Stick to your chosen rhythm as much as possible. Some deviation is good but it should not be overdone.

11. Use the Rhyming Dictionary in Appendix E to help you to achieve end-rhyme.

12. If a verse isn't working out, don't hesitate to change it.

13. If you cannot find an appropriate rhyme for an end word, modify the verse and obtain an end word which lends itself better to rhyming or use a Near Rhyme.

14. Use internal rhyme whenever possible to create special moods.

15. Use Sound Effects such as *Alliteration, Assonance,* and *Consonance* to give a verse greater vitality.

A love poem is your own personal "work of art" which can inspire, delight and motivate. You should never feel self-conscious or inhibited in any way in regards to expressing yourself using this form of romantic communication.

# SECTION 2 / ORIGINAL LOVE POEMS

The following twenty-five original love poems are presented in this section for you to use in any way you desire. You may modify them to suit your needs or use them as they are written.

You will find poems composed in several rhythmic patterns including *Iambic Pentameter*, *Iambic Tetrameter*, *Iambic Trimeter* and various combinations thereof. You will also discover a fourteen verse *English love sonnet*.

Remember, these love poems were especially written for you to use. Take good advantage of them if they apply to your situation.

# ORIGINAL LOVE POEMS

### I LOVE YOU

You're kissable and cuddly;
   You're lovable and sweet;
You thrill me every minute,
   And sweep me off my feet.

You're charming and disarming,
   Desirable and true.
You inspire and impress me,
   And that's why I love you.

### LOVE

Love is bliss
   And a tender kiss.

Love is sharing
   And always caring.

Love is giving
   And healthy living.

Love is laughter
   Forever after.

## TRIUMPH

I stretch my mind across the space,
   Which keeps us both apart.
I try to kiss your lovely face,
   With all the strength within my heart.

And when, at last, I do succeed,
   I feel contentment deep.
I bask in the triumph of my deed,
   Then gently fall asleep.

## YEARNING

I yearn to see you once again;
   It's been too long a time.
I crave your soft caress and then
   Your passioned love sublime.

I will not let myself despair,
   For soon we will unite.
And then, again, I will ensnare
   You in my arms at night.

## A PLAIN OLD KISS

Some people need a peck or two;
   For others a simple smooch will do;
To many, a graze will stimulate;
   A few may want to osculate.

And then there are those who need a smack;
   For flowery words, they have a knack.
But all I want from you is bliss,
   Which you can give me with a plain old kiss.

## YOU ARE

You are my brave Centurion;
   You are my learned historian;
You are my Knight in shining armor;
   You are my handsome, courtly charmer.

You are my personal troubadour;
   You are a man I can't ignore.
You are my loyal Samurai;
   You are one dynamic, hell of a guy!

## CYCLES

Wildflowers bloom on a mountainside,
   As icy waters on their tumbling ride,
Flow in haste to meet the Sea,
   On a cycle that will always be.

Cycles, cycles everyplace,
   Even in my life I face,
The fact that cycles often race
   With no regard to proper pace.

So I was born and grew up fast,
   And now I'm free to love at last,
And need you to complete the chain
   Of the cycle that is in my name.

## HEALING

My heart is racing as I am facing
   Another day without your kiss.
My mind is tracing; my thoughts are embracing
   The memories of the one I miss.

I have the feeling that you'll be stealing
   My heart from me, again, come night.
And I'll be dealing with the need for healing
   When the darkness finally turns to light.

## NEEDS

You don't need fancy jewelry
     To make me fall for you.
You don't need a lot of makeup,
     To cause me to pursue.

You don't need clothes from Gucci
     To make me like you more.
You do not need to put on airs
     To make my passions soar.

All you need is honesty,
     And a smiling face;
Sincerity and loyalty,
     And a warm embrace.

## FLOWERING LOVE

My love for you will always be
     As vibrant as the surging Sea.
Since I was made for you to love,
     And you were made by the Lord above,
To share with me in every way,
     A love that flowers day by day.

## MY LEADING MAN

You are my handsome leading man,
   And, dear, I am your staunchest fan;
For you are skilled beyond compare
   In the art of loving with a flair.

Of all the parts you've played to date,
   Your greatest one is as my mate.
For in this very challenging role,
   You make my life complete and whole.

## LUCK

How lucky can a woman be
   To find in life a man like thee?
A man who knows what makes her smile;
   A man with charm, quick wit and style.

How lucky can a woman be
   To find in life a man like thee?
A man who knows when to be strong,
   And when to sing a tearful song.

How lucky can a woman be
   To find in life a man like thee?
A man who knows the Art of Love,
   And lives by the light of God above.

## JASMINE, ROSE AND DAISY

You are the Jasmine of all my senses;
  Your stunning beauty drops my defenses,
And I am stripped of all pretences,
  As I accept all consequences.

You are the wild Rose of my heart;
  I yearn for you when we're apart,
For then my passions on fire start,
  Desperately desiring your lover's art.

You are the Daisy of my being;
  You give my soul a love enduring,
Which makes each day a day worth living,
  And makes you ever more alluring.

## I CAN

I can idolize a man who is handsome and strong;
  I can treasure a man who has in his heart a song;
    I can admire a man who is quick and decisive;
      I can revere a man who knows well how to live;
I can adore a man who is kindhearted and warm;
  I can respect a man who can weather the harshest storm;
    I can cherish a man who can shed a loving tear;
      I can love a man who is honest and sincere.

## TWO BIRDS

Two birds begin a journey long,
  From different points in a far off land;
With a luring urge - in heart a song,
  Two novices heed life's command.

As they make their great migration,
  Their feeble feet turn to taloned hands;
And the two reach their destination
  As seasoned travelers in the northern lands.

Still unaware that the other lives,
  Each alights upon the very same tree;
And there the two, as if guided by God,
  Fall madly in love and marry.

Thus so it is with you and me;
  Two birds which Heaven's winds did blow
To this blessed rendezvous of life,
  Like the two Swallows at Capistrano.

## LOVE'S REVELATION

How wondrous a transformation!
How glorious a stimulation!
How divine an inspiration,
  Is Love's great revelation.

## AN ANIMATED WOMAN

An animated woman
    Should never be confined.
And one so energetic,
    Like you is hard to find.

Your charming personality,
    And wholesome, winning ways,
Bring me happiness constantly,
    And add zest to my days.

Your lively conversations
    And spirited debate,
Are welcome confrontations,
    Which always stimulate.

Your healthy, vibrant body
    Is divine to say the least;
It is expressive poetry
    And a sensorial feast.

An animated woman
    Like you who's so refined,
Is a blessing to any man,
    And truly hard to find.

## ONE WAY LOVE

A one way love can never thrive;
    It needs reciprocation.
And so, in order to survive
    My love needs affirmation.

So throw your caution to the sky,
    And let your heart command.
You'll find that it will not deny
    A love which must expand.

Come now, to me, with open arms
    And sweep me off my feet;
And then display for me your charms,
    To make my love complete.

My one way love will terminate
    Without your inspiration.
So, therefore, please reciprocate
    With no more hesitation.

## ON GOSSAMER WINGS

When first we touched, my heart flew high,
   On gossamer wings through a cloudless sky.
People told me this love would die,
   They said it was built upon a lie.

They told me my feelings would surely fade;
   Passions would cease and foes would be made.
To this I said, "Why are you so blind?"
   "Can you not put the past behind?"

True love can change a river's course,
   Or pierce the strongest vault with ease.
True love can turn coal into gold,
   Or tame the Tempest to a balmy breeze.

Quite some time has passed since then;
   People no longer criticize;
For now they see that truth exists,
   Where once there might've been only lies.

Thus my feelings are the same today,
   As they were on that very first day;
For when we touch, my heart still flies,
   On gossamer wings through cloudless skies.

## I CAN'T IMAGINE

I can't imagine a day
    Without your charming smile;
Nor can I justly convey
    How much I love your style.

I can't imagine a week
    Without your warm embrace;
Nor the absence of your pleasing form
    And lovely, flawless face.

I can't imagine a year,
    Without you near to share
The times that do endear,
    Or the moments of despair.

I can't imagine a lifetime
    Without you at my side;
For if I want a love divine,
    I need you as my guide.

I can't imagine eternity
    Without the love I've known.
My spirit would wander hopelessly
    In agony - alone.

## FEELINGS

Endlessly, you inspire me
  By what you say and do.
Thus, with great sincerity,
  I'll tell my feelings true.

You always use your eloquence
  To raise my self-esteem.
You help me boost my confidence
  To realize a dream.

You comfort me in times of stress;
  You hold me tenderly.
Your soothing words do then suppress
  All my anxiety.

You love me with a passioned grace,
  Which gives me ecstacy.
And there within your warm embrace,
  My spirit wanders free.

In mind and body, I do thrive
  Within your loving sphere.
And easily I do survive
  Each and every passing year.

So now you know in words sincere,
  My feelings pure and true.
They reaffirm what should be clear,
  That I'm in love with you.

## THE PICTURE

Your picture which I have in hand,
   By itself could never stand;
For in dimensions, it does lack
   The third and foremost of the pack.

It will not kiss me on command;
   It cannot love me on demand;
And warmth it never can imbue
   To this poor soul who yearns for you.

Torture me no more, my sweet;
   Pictures can't such passions treat;
And if they burn as mine do now,
   They need to be relieved somehow.

Thus to this truth, I do adhere,
   That only you, my Doctor dear,
In three dimensions can you clear
   This burning which is so severe.

So fly to me - do not delay;
   I cannot wait another day;
And free me from the torments of
   This raging three-dimensioned love.

## MY BROKEN HEART

You possess the fury of a Spring storm,
The gentleness of a tropical shower.
You have a charm which is quick to warm
The coldest men's hearts and make love flower.
Michelangelo must have sculpted you;
Truly perfect is your figure and face;
Your soft silken hair with its golden hue;
An image to adorn a Roman vase.
You do not know how much I crave your kiss,
For spirit free and innocent are thee.
You cannot know the pain of love's abyss,
Nor can you see my eyes' empassioned plea.
With great charm and beauty you lure my heart,
Then, with abandon, you break it apart.

## ONE LONELY DAY

One lonely day has all but passed
  Since last I held you in my arms.
And truly did I think I'd last
  At least a day without your charms.

Hard work, I thought will keep me sane;
  Blot you out and dull the pain;
And easily I will contain,
  A love from which I must abstain.

But all day long my thoughts do shout
  Your name without a moment's rest.
In truth, I cannot blot you out,
  For I am hopelessly possessed.

Alas, its done, from where they dwell,
  My passions rise and then they swell;
To frenzied heights they heave and thrust,
  And fill me with desire and lust.

One lonely day has all but passed;
  I really thought that I would last.
But since I'm so in love with thee,
  A day - alone - is agony.

## WELL-TEMPERED LOVE

The fires of my loneliness,
  Once filled my life with much distress;
And constantly they did suppress
  My every chance at happiness.

In truth, I lost all zest for life,
  And every day was filled with strife;
Until, that is, the day you came
  Into my life and called my name.

With tenderness you gave to me,
  The strength to set my spirit free,
And then you showed me lovingly,
  How wonderful my life could be.

As our new friendship grew and grew,
  A joyous feeling did ensue.
I know that I was born anew,
  When I realized my love for you.

This love has bounds I cannot see,
  It is universal poetry;
And with its durability,
  It shall continue endlessly.

So future trials will not repress;
  Life's tribulations will not suppress
This well-tempered love which I possess;
  Forged in the fires of my loneliness.

# SECTION 3 / PICK-A-POEM

The following section contains over two hundred end-rhymed couplets. Many different thoughts and sentiments are stated and a variety of emotions are addressed. These couplets are, in effect, mini-poems which you can use to create larger love poems tailor made to your needs.

You will discover twenty-five *Primary Couplets* which begin a thought or sentiment. Each primary couplet has listed below it six *Secondary Couplets* which resolve or complete the idea. All together, there are over one hundred and fifty of these. Any combination of primary and secondary couplet is acceptable:

1. My friends all tell me you're a saint,  *Primary Couplet*
   So, therefore, I will use restraint;
   +
   e) And slowly to my saint acquaint,  *Secondary Couplet*
   A love which will not cause complaint.

Or

1. My friends all tell me you're a saint,  *Primary Couplet*
   So, therefore, I will use restraint;
   +
   f) Unless, that is, my friends are wrong,  *Secondary Couplet*
   And in your heart a love burns strong.

You may also combine any two Secondary Couplets if, together, they make sense:

b) You did not see me watching you,
   Yet this I did the whole night through.
   +
a) And as I gazed at you that night,
   My senses felt supreme delight.

165

You will also find sixty miscellaneous rhymed couplets listed under various topics:

### Valentine's Day

> 1) Throughout the year, dear Valentine,
>    You gave my soul a love divine.
>
> 2) To me, you are the rarest wine;
>    My sweetly scented Valentine.
>
> 3) You look so good - you feel so fine;
>    You are my lovely Valentine.

You may join any of these Miscellaneous Couplets with any other Primary or Secondary Couplet listed in this section or with an Original Couplet of your own creation. Make sure that the two couplets you are combining are compatible. Thoughts or ideas must flow logically from one couplet to the other, or else, you may have to change some of the words. Often, you can add *And, For* or *Thus* to the beginning of the second couplet to help make the tie:

> 1) Throughout the year, dear Valentine,      *Miscellaneous Couplet*
>    You gave my soul a love divine.
>
>                     +
>
> e) It carries me to heights unknown,        *Secondary Couplet*
>    To where I've never been alone.

When modified and combined, these two couplets become the following quatrain:

> Throughout the year, dear Valentine,
> You gave my soul a love divine.
> And carried me to heights unknown,
> To where I've never been alone.

Finally, you may join individual verses from any two existing couplets to create new and different couplets. This can be done only if the two existing couplets have the same end-rhyme, and the thoughts stated are compatible:

> You gave my soul a love divine;
> You are my lovely Valentine.

Remember, two couplets make a quatrain. A love poem may be composed of any number of quatrains. You are limited only by your imagination.

# PICK-A-POEM

1. My friends all tell me you're a saint,
   So, therefore, I will use restraint.

   a) For love needs time to germinate,
      To fascinate and captivate.

   b) A perfect gentleman, I'll be;
      This I promise and decree.

   c) And in degrees I will convey,
      The true love which I must display.

   d) A proper lady I shall be;
      This I promise and decree.

   e) And slowly to my saint acquaint,
      A love which will not cause complaint.

   f) Unless, that is, my friends are wrong,
      And in your heart a love burns strong.

2. I saw you enter from afar;
   To me you were the northern star.

    a) And as I gazed at you that night,
        My senses felt supreme delight.

    b) You did not see me watching you,
        Yet, this I did the whole night through.

    c) And everything around you there,
        Could not compete; could not compare.

    d) And in that instant of first sight,
        I felt the sting of Love's first bite.

    e) And I was a voyager in Space,
        My guiding light was your lovely face.

    f) In all your radiant glory bright,
        I watched you move throughout the night.

3. My heart is full of love for you,
   Why do you not believe this true?

    a) Why do you not yourself allow,
        To fall in love and pledge a vow?

    b) Have you been hurt at love before,
        And thus committment you ignore?

    c) What makes you doubt that this can be?
        What will it take for you to see?

    d) Is it because you cannot trust
        A person full of life and lust?

    e) What can I say - what can I do,
        To make you change your point of view?

    f) How must I act - what must I say,
        To make you fling your doubts away?

4. My love for you will always stay,
   As vibrant as it is today.

      a) Time's swift torrent will not decay
        The freshness of its Spring bouquet.

      b) And even when we're split apart,
        It will not fade within my heart.

      c) And all the miles 'tween you and I,
        Will never cause this love to die.

      d) For it is truly Heaven made,
        And will not falter; will not fade.

      e) For in its nature strong and pure,
        Are qualities that will endure.

      f) For nothing earthly can destroy,
        This Heavenly bond which gives great joy.

5. My dearest love, be not so glum,
   Our day of joy will surely come.

      a) The torments which we felt before,
        Will fade away and hurt no more.

      b) But patience, you must now display,
        Until we reach that joyous day.

      c) And those who are so blind will see
        How powerful true love can be.

      d) And all those who spoke ill of us,
        Will ne'er again make such a fuss.

      e) And give to us the promise of,
        A long, uninterrupted love.

      f) And I will leave this lonely place,
        And fly back to your warm embrace.

6. Each day you are away from me,
   Seems longer than eternity.

    a) Your safe return is my only plea,
       So I'll be rid of this agony.

    b) If I am to survive at all,
       I need your letter or your call.

    c) How will I ever make it through
       Such desperate times without you?

    d) And makes life empty and lonely;
       To this, do you likewise agree?

    e) Each night you cannot be with me,
       Seems longer than infinity.

    f) Thus every letter which you write,
       I read and reread through the night.

7. I dream of fragrant flowered nights,
   Of passioned love and sweet delights;

    a) Such moments of my life do stay
       Alive within my mind each day.

    b) I dream of you my handsome lad,
       My wandering Sir Galahad.

    c) These times which you and I did share,
       Gave pleasures which are truly rare.

    d) I dream of you fairest woman,
       My faraway Maid Marion.

    e) These moments which I hope to live;
       These pleasures which to you, I'll give.

    f) Such times which make life worth it all,
       Are times which gladly I recall.

8. You touched me just the other day,
   Quite gently, in a special way.

> a) And by that gesture so divine,
>    You sent a quiver up my spine.

> b) And suddenly the Sun shone bright,
>    And filled my senses with delight.

> c) So thrilled was I, by your caress,
>    My passions, I could not suppress.

> d) And by that gesture so discreet,
>    You caused my heart to skip a beat.

> e) My body quivered - my senses swirled,
>    My heart flew half-way round the World.

> f) Your love for me, you did convey,
>    And now my fears have gone away.

9. Dear love, for you, my heart does yearn,
   My senses stir - my passions burn.

> a) Thus difficult, it is to keep
>    From dreaming of you in my sleep.

> b) Your safety is my great concern;
>    My prayers are for your swift return.

> c) And yet, I know I'll have to wait
>    Until that long-awaited date.

> d) They cry out in lonely agony,
>    For you mean everything to me.

> e) Each night alone in bed, I lay,
>    For ages, you have been away.

> f) From deep within, my feelings churn,
>    From left to right to left, they turn.

10. Dear love, I promise to devote
    My all to keep our love afloat.

    a) With perseverance and restraint,
       A brighter future, I will paint.

    b) For up until this very time,
       Our problems have been mostly mine.

    c) With self-control and no more lies,
       Our love, I will revitalize.

    d) My jealous ways, I will contain.
       From hurtful talk, I will refrain.

    e) For without you, my life would be,
       So very lonely and empty.

    f) First I'll change my attitude,
       Then try hard not to be so crude.

11. Fly to me - do not delay,
    I cannot wait another day;

    a) For only you can cure my pain,
       And in so doing, keep me sane.

    b) My self-control has gone astray;
       My patience has melted away.

    c) Dear love, I hope you will obey;
       For this, I yearn and truly pray.

    d) For I must hold you in my arms,
       And quench my passions with your charms.

    e) So give me reason to rejoice,
       And let me hear your loving voice.

    f) If, in your arms, I do not lay,
       Quite likely I will pine away.

12. Great passions lie in the prison keep
    Of my yearning heart, so dark and deep;

     a) They wait for me to set them free,
         But only you possess the key.

     b) And will remain in silence there,
         Unless, somehow, you start to care.

     c) And only when my term is through,
         Can they display themselves to you.

     d) They wait for the precious light of day,
         Which only you can bring my way.

     e) They can't be properly conveyed
         To you, my love, through poems made.

     f) They need to be expressed to you,
         In hopes that love will then ensue.

13. You left me and my heart does ache,
    As if you pierced it with a stake.

     a) What made you leave without regret?
         Was it boredom or was it debt?

     b) Now listlessly, I meet each day,
         With spirit dulled, in hues of grey.

     c) My future, now, is so unclear,
         For loneliness is what I fear.

     d) Please torture me no more, I plead;
         Come back to me, your love, I need.

     e) And now I know the torments of
         A passionate, forsaken love.

     f) And now you will not answer me,
         Whene're I call to make my plea.

14. The vision of your lovely face,
    Occupies a most special space;

    a) For only it, can I embrace,
       In this foreboding, lonely place.

    b) From where it gives my life a lift;
       It really is a precious gift.

    c) Where, always ready to delight;
       It shows itself each lonely night.

    d) And beckons me to soon retrace,
       The steps which lead back to your place.

    e) From where it helps me to subdue,
       The loneliness which does ensue.

    f) And on its charm, I do rely
       To keep my spirits always high.

15. You give to me a tender love,
    Which surely comes from God above;

    a) Thus words can never quite convey,
       The happiness I feel each day.

    b) For it is pure in thought and deed,
       And will in years to come succeed.

    c) You give to me your loving hand,
       Which helps me confidently stand.

    d) You are considerate and kind,
       You are forever on my mind.

    e) To this great truth, I am not blind;
       A love like you is hard to find.

    f) Neither anger nor jealousy,
       In your eyes, do I ever see.

16. I want to hold you in my arms,
 And partake of all your charms.

  a) I want to love you openly,
   So all my passions can be free.

  b) I want to hear your loving sighs,
   And gaze into your dreamy eyes.

  c) I want to taste your honeyed kiss;
   This, I crave and really miss.

  d) This, I yearn for in my dreams,
   And include within my schemes.

  e) But, alas, you do not express,
   The same desires which I possess.

  f) This course of treatment, I must start
   To quench the fires within my heart.

17. True understanding must prevail,
 So that our love will never fail;

  a) Thus we should settle any fight,
   Before we go to sleep at night.

  b) And selfish feelings must be fought,
   Or else they'll dictate every thought.

  c) And always we should both discuss,
   All problems which are serious.

  d) And if our thoughts don't harmonize,
   We both should try to compromise.

  e) Thus if we don't mean what we say,
   Someday our passions will decay.

  f) Thus honesty must be the rule,
   Or else our bond will surely cool.

18. I love to kiss your sexy lips,
    And lightly touch your fingertips.

    a) I love to nip your pretty nose,
       And fondle both your little toes.

    b) I love to stroke your flowing hair,
       For you are my own Maiden fair.

    c) I love to feel your strong physique,
       For it is really quite unique.

    d) I love to hold you in my arms,
       Experience your many charms.

    e) I love the feel of lace on you,
       But better yet, I love the view.

    f) I love to nibble on your ears,
       And lick away your happy tears.

19. When I, at last, do hear your voice,
    Dear love, my heart will then rejoice.

    a) For you'll be in the flesh once more,
       When you pass through my open door.

    b) For I have craved its golden tone,
       Ever since you began to roam.

    c) For, once again, with you so near,
       My days will not be filled with fear.

    d) For it will mean that you've come home,
       And no more will I be alone.

    e) It, in that instant, will regain,
       Its freedom from torment and pain.

    f) For we have been apart too long;
       It's time you're back where you belong.

20. You are my Angel of the night,
    From the darkness deep, you bring me light;

    a) You fill my life with love and bliss,
       When we're apart, it's you I miss.

    b) And with your charms, you do excite
       My deepest passions which then burn bright.

    c) You lead me to a world divine,
       Where both our spirits do entwine.

    d) You soothe the pains of living well;
       Without you, life would sure be Hell.

    e) And in my dreams, you do delight;
       My inner passions, you ignite.

    f) And so you help me find my way,
       Through the labyrinth of life each day.

21. Forsake me for another, why?
    How could you, thus, our love deny?

    a) How could you break my heart this way?
       How could you throw our love away?

    b) What do you see in your new beau
       Which I could not give or bestow?

    c) How could you lead me on so long,
       Proclaiming that your love was strong?

    d) How could you turn your back on me,
       How could your love so shallow be?

    e) And make my heart, in anguish cry,
       For having fallen for a lie.

    f) Or are you punishing me for
       Some thoughtless act you can't ignore?

22. For many days, I have not heard
    From you, my sweet, a single word.

    a) Distressing thoughts go through my head
        And fill my yearning heart with dread.

    b) Did all the miles at last subdue
        The precious love 'tween me and you?

    c) So with a note or call convey,
        If I've displeased you in some way.

    d) Your silence is too hard to bear;
        It raises doubts and brings despair.

    e) Have you forgotten I exist,
        Or did you break your writing wrist?

    f) Can't you find the time to write,
        Or are you busy every night?

23. Whenever my thoughts turn to you,
    Strange feelings once again ensue.

    a) I am not sure why this takes place,
        I only know my heart does race.

    b) This has happened for quite some time,
        Ever since that night sublime.

    c) They reaffirm to me each time,
        The presence of a love divine.

    d) And in their strength, they do reveal,
        How much to me you do appeal.

    e) And make me wish I could renew,
        A love which now I know is true.

    f) And torment me for being blind
        To the truest love I'll ever find.

24. I met you only days ago,
    And yet so quickly love does grow.

> a) For my heart tells me you're a girl,
>    Who is as precious as a Pearl.

> b) So all my doubts, I'll cast away,
>    And then to you my love display.

> c) For my heart tells me you're a boy,
>    Who'll give to me love, warmth and joy.

> d) That, suddenly, I've come to know,
>    The sweet joys that it can bestow.

> e) It carries me to heights unknown,
>    To where I've never been alone.

> f) That I can easily express,
>    The passioned love which I possess.

25. We've been best friends for many years,
    We've shared each other's joys and fears;

> a) And through these times we've grown so near
>    That now I think I love you, dear.

> b) And built a bond which will endure
>    The trials of marriage, I am sure.

> c) Thus, now your absence makes me fear
>    Another day without you near.

> d) These sure have been the best of times;
>    A change would be the worst of crimes.

> e) But now I can't believe my ears;
>    You're leaving me to drown in tears.

> f) Don't you see what is plain to me,
>    That true love has now come to be?

# Miscellaneous

## A. Mother

1) Mother dear, it's you I miss,
   So with this verse, I send a kiss.

2) Mom, I miss your smiling face,
   Your loving voice and warm embrace.

3) Mother, to you, I must convey
   How much I miss you every day.

4) Please, Mom, will you prepare for me
   A package full of ecstacy?

5) Mother, to you, I must express
   My wish for health and happiness.

## B. Father

1) Father, I send my best to you,
   And wish you health and happiness too.

2) Father dear, you taught me well,
   For all my fears I now can quell.

3) Dearest Dad, I finally see,
   How much you really mean to me.

4) Dad, times between us have been hard,
   Yet still I hold you in high regard.

5) Dearest Dad, I want to convey,
   The love I feel for you this day.

## C. Christmas, New Years and Hanukkah

1) My greatest Christmas gift would be,
   To spend all Christmas Eve with thee.

2) I send to you my Christmas love,
   Blessed by God and Christ above.

3) A Christmas spent without you , dear,
   Is lonely and devoid of cheer.

4) This Christmas season I must face,
   The absence of your warm embrace.

5) This Christmas, dear, I do express
   My wish for health and happiness.

6) During Hanukkah, I send to you
   My deepest love and kisses too.

7) A Hanukkah without you here,
   Is empty of all warmth and cheer.

8) I resolve this coming New Year,
   To spend more time with you, my dear.

9) This New Year holds the promise of
   The fulfillment of our tortured love.

10) My wish for you this coming year
    Is health and wealth and lots of cheer.

11) May the new year bring you happiness,
    A healthy body and much success.

12) May the new year give you strength to last
    Until these trying times have passed.

13) This New Year's Eve I send to you,
    My warmest love, sincere and true.

14) This New Year's Eve we'll be apart;
    But never so within my heart.

15) I hope this coming year will bring,
    An end to our great suffering.

## D. Valentine's Day

1) Throughout the year, dear Valentine,
   You gave my soul a love divine.

2) To me, you are the rarest wine;
   My sweetly scented Valentine.

3) You look so good - you feel so fine;
   You are my handsome Valentine.

4) Dear Valentine, I love you so,
   My passions burn; my heart's aglow.

5) My yearnings, I cannot confine;
   Will you be my Valentine?

6) All I need is one small sign
   Which shows you love me, Valentine.

7) Cupid's arrow has pierced my heart,
   So I feel sad when we're apart.

8) This Valentine's Day I do convey,
   The love I feel for you each day.

9) You send a quiver up my spine
   Each time you kiss me, Valentine.

10) I hope that Cupid will impart
    Into your heart his potent dart.

11) I do not want to stand in line;
    I want to be your Valentine.

12) A Valentine as sweet as you,
    Will always cause me to pursue.

13) You are my sexy Valentine,
    You make this life of mine divine.

14) My heart is once again aflame;
    Could Cupid be the one to blame?

15) It's hard to keep this heart of mine
    From skipping beats, sweet Valentine.

## E. Potpourri

1) I love to hug you, Teddy Bear,
   For you are my Koala rare.

2) I'd love to make a potion
   To stir within you great devotion.

3) I love to dream of what might be;
   I love the thought of you and me.

4) True love burns bright deep in my heart,
   Kindled by Cupid's potent dart.

5) The love we share flows straight and sure;
   You should not feel so insecure.

6) I reaffirm my love for you,
   And once again proclaim it true.

7) Lovely daydreams do allay,
   The torments of each lonely day.

8) How many love's have you enjoyed?
   How many hearts have you destroyed?

9) The feelings from within me shout,
   Proclaiming love without a doubt.

10) I'm not quite sure but could it be
    That you are now in love with me?

11) Do share with me in every way
    A love that flowers day by day.

12) Each letter which you send to me
    I kiss, with love, quite tenderly.

13) Never will the miles subdue
    This precious love I have for you.

14) You take me to a land divine,
    Where love prevails and hearts entwine.

15) At last, I heard your silken voice,
    And in its tones, I did rejoice.

16) Once again, the charms you loose
    Will break my will and then seduce.

17) Yesterday, I saw a girl,
    Who made me dream of you, my Pearl.

18) The other day, your knee touched mine;
    My passions swelled to heights divine.

19) You are the answer to my prayer;
    You are the man for whom I care.

20) Your large and sparkling azure eyes
    Reflect the beauty of the skies.

21) I'm not quite sure but could it be,
    What I feel for you, you feel for me?

22) Your striking beauty can disarm
    This strong-willed soldier with its charm.

23) With charm and grace, you do inspire;
    With silk and lace, you spark desire.

24) When you get mad, you look so cute;
    This, even I cannot dispute.

25) My heart weakens as time goes by,
    So please return before I die.

26) Quite anxiously, I wait each day,
    For your letter to come my way.

27) Your silken skin is so sublime;
    It doesn't seem to age with time.

28) You know I like to flirt a lot;
    Why do you always get so hot?

29) Jealousy will never let
    A selfish person to forget.

30) I will tolerate your extremes,
    For I do understand your dreams.

# APPENDICES

# /PARTS OF SPEECH

In English, every word must be used in a certain way as dictated by its *function*. A word's function is directly related to what *part of speech* it is. There are several parts of speech in English, but only six are of major importance. The following discussion will deal with these six: *Nouns, Pronouns, Adjectives, Verbs, Adverbs* and *Prepositions*:

## Nouns

A *Noun* is a word which acts as the name of something such as a *person, animal, plant, place, thing, substance, quality, idea, action* or *state of being*. There are two major types:

1. **Proper Nouns** *(Specific Names Of People And Places)*

   God • Heaven • Cynthia • Paradise

2. **Common Nouns** *(Four Sub-catagories)*

   a) Concrete Nouns *(Names Of Objects)*

   heart • legs • face • lips • man • woman

   b) Mass Nouns *(Names Of Materials Of A General Nature)*

   water • fire • wine • wind

   c) Collective Nouns *(Names Of Groups Of Objects)*

duet • family • sorority • kingdom

   d) Abstract Nouns *(Names Of Qualities, Ideas And Actions)*

gentleness • love • faith • desire • passion

# Pronouns

A *Pronoun* is a word which can be substituted in place of a noun. It is often used within a love paragraph to prevent a noun from having to be repeated too many times:

| | |
|---|---|
| *Wrong:* | **Ann** is a beautiful girl and **Ann's** gown is exquisite. **Ann** is the answer to all my dreams. |
| *Correct:* | **Ann** is a beautiful girl and **her** gown is exquisite. **She** is the answer to all my dreams. |

There are several different types of pronouns:

  1. **Personal Pronouns** *(Three Sub-catagories)*

    a) Subjective *(Acting As A Subject Of A Sentence)*

I • We • You • He • She • It • One • They

**She** is beautiful.

    b) Possessive *(Showing Possession)*

my/mine • our/ours • your/yours • his • her/hers • its • one's • their/theirs

**Her** beauty is eternal.

    c) Objective *(Acting As The Object Of The Sentence)*

me • us • you • him • her • it • one • them

I love **you**.

  2. **Relative Pronouns**

who/whom • which/whose • that • what • whoever/whomever • whatever

I need a girl **who** is sincere and honest.

## 3. Indefinite Pronouns *(No Definite Quantity)*

all • anybody • anything • each • everyone • somebody • many

**Many** people have told me how charming you are.

## 4. Demonstrating Pronouns *(Which Person, Object, Etc.?)*

this • these • that • those • first • second

The **first** moment was Heaven.

## 5. Reflexive Pronouns *(Reflect Action Back To Subject)*

myself • ourselves • yourself • himself • themselves • herself • itself

*You* should see **yourself** as I see you.

## 6. Questioning Pronouns *(Begin A Question)*

who • which • what • whom • whose

**What** do you want from me?

## 7. Numeral Pronouns *(State The Number Or Quantity)*

one • two • three • first • second • third

**Two** people become one under God.

These numeral pronouns may also be considered adjectives.

# Functions

A Noun or Pronoun may be placed in various locations within a love sentence. Its placement often determines its specific function:

## 1. Subject Of A Love Sentence *(Begins A Sentence)*

*Pronoun:*   **I** love you.

*Noun:*   Your **beauty** is inspiring.

## 2. Object Of A Verb *(Follows The Action Word/Verb)*

The *Object* receives the action of the verb:

*Pronoun:*   I love **you**.

*Noun:*   I can love a **man** like you.

### 3. Object Of A Preposition *(Follows A Preposition)*

Some common prepositions are:

at • by • for • from • in • of • on • it • with

The Preposition and its Noun or Pronoun Object create what is known as a *Prepositional Phrase*:

*Pronoun As Object:*     with **me**

*Noun As Object:*        with my **heart**

The Prepositional Phrase can then be used to describe either a *noun* or *verb* which comes before it:

*Verb Describer:*        Always, you *walk* **with me.**

*Noun Describer:*        You are the *love* **of my heart.**

### 4. Predicate Noun *(Follows A Linking Verb)*

*Are* and *Is* are linking verbs. The *Predicate Noun* follows one or the other and renames the subject of the love sentence:

*John* is the most handsome **man** I've ever known.

### 5. Showing Possession *(Placed Before Another Noun)*

A Possessive Pronoun or a Noun in its possessive form may be used to describe another noun:

**Our** • Heaven/**Heaven's** • flowers/**flowers'**

*Possessive Pronoun:*          *Our* love is boundless.

*Possessive Singular Noun:*    When we kiss, I pass through *Heaven's* gate.

*Possessive Plural Noun:*      The *flowers'* aroma was overwhelming.

### 6. Appositive *(Placed After Another Noun)*

A Noun or Noun Phrase set off by commas may be used to rename another noun. Usually, one of the two is a Proper Noun while the other is a Common Noun:

**Mary,** *my love,* when will I see you again?

Both nouns can also be Proper Nouns. In this case, commas are not used:

You are my **Princess** *Mary.*

7. **Noun Modifier** *(Placed Before Another Noun)*

A Noun may describe or modify another noun:

Your *beauty* **mark** looks very sexy.

8. **Verb Modifier** *(Follows A Verb)*

A Noun or Noun Phrase may modify or describe a verb in order to complete its action:

We danced **every** *night.*

# Adjectives

An *Adjective* is a word which describes or modifies a Noun. It usually relates to a *quality, quantity* or *distinction.* There are three basic types of adjectives:

1. **Descriptive Adjectives** *(Describe A Quality Or Condition)*

**luminous** beauty    •    **Heavenly** caress    •    **azure** eyes

**silent** desperation    •    **fluttering** eyelashes    •    **broken** heart

2. **Limiting Adjectives** *(Describe The Quantity And Number)*

**seven** days    •    **all** night    •    **first** encounter

**our** love    •    **a** kiss    •    **the** night

Some limiting adjectives such as *our* are also Pronouns.

3. **Proper Adjectives** *(Describe Origins, Location, Etc.)*

*Proper Adjectives* are derived from Proper Nouns and are usually Limiting Adjectives:

**Roman** Conquests    •    **Arctic** Circle    •    **Greek** Islands

# Functions

An Adjective may be placed in various locations within a love sentence. Its placement determines its function:

1. **Attributive Adjective** *(Placed Before Or After A Noun)*

   Describes the Noun's attribute or quality:

   > Your *sweet kiss* is divine.

   > Your *kiss*, **sweet and tender**, is an earthly delight.

2. **Predicate Adjective** *(Placed After The Verb)*

   The *Predicate Adjective* usually modifies or describes the Subject of the love sentence and follows some form of the verb *be* or some other verb such as *look, smell* or *feel*:

   > *You* are **gorgeous.**

   > *Your body* feels **warm.**

3. **Preposition Object Modifier** *(Placed Before The Object)*

   An Adjective may modify the Noun which serves as the Object of the Preposition:

   > I feel safe *in your* **loving arms.**

# Verbs

A *Verb* is a word which expresses an *action* or *state of being*. It usually follows the Subject of the love sentence and is the most important element of the sentence Predicate which is discussed in Part I, Section 2: *The Basics Of Love Letter Writing.*

# Conjugation

A Verb must be made to agree with its Subject. This is accomplished through a change of form known as *Conjugation*:

| The Verb: *Be* | The Verb: *Kiss* | The Verb: *Dream* |
|---|---|---|
| I *am* in love. | I *kiss.* | I *dream.* |
| You *are* in love. | You *kiss.* | You *dream.* |
| He *is* in love. | He *kisses.* | He *dreams.* |
| We *are* in love. | We *kiss.* | We *dream.* |
| They *are* in love. | They *kiss.* | They *dream.* |

In addition to making the verb relate to its Subject, you may also relate it to a certain time period by changing its form or creating a short phrase. This simply means that a Verb can be written in a *Tense* which relates its action or state of being to the *Past, Present* or *Future*:

|                | The Verb: *Be*            | The Verb: *Kiss* |
|----------------|---------------------------|------------------|
| *Past Tense:*    | I *was* in love with you.   | I *kissed.*        |
| *Present Tense:* | I *am* in love with you.    | I *kiss.*          |
| *Future Tense:*  | I *will be* in love with you. | I *will kiss.*     |

## Verb Types

There are several different types of Verbs. A few of the most important ones are:

### 1. Infinitives

An *Infinitive* is a verb in its general, non-conjugated form. That is, it has not been modified to agree with any subject. In English, an Infinitive is usually made by putting *to* in front of the base form of the verb:

**to** love • **to** kiss • **to** embrace • **to** caress

You can not use an Infinitive by itself as the verb of a love sentence. It must always follow another conjugated verb which agrees with the love sentence subject:

I *want* **to** *love* you.

She *likes* **to** *kiss* me.

*To* is dropped especially when the infinitive is placed after verbs such as *Can* and *Must*:

I *can love* you.

You *must kiss* me.

### Function

An Infinitive, in addition to its verbal uses, may function as the Subject of a love sentence:

**To love** is my greatest need.

## 2. Linking Verbs

A *Linking Verb* suggests a state of being and connects the subject of the love sentence directly with a Noun or Adjective Modifier:

*Subject To Adjective Modifier:*        You **look** *beautiful.*

*Subject To Noun Modifier:*             You **are** *my love.*

Some linking verbs may also be action verbs:

I **look** for you each day.

## 3. Helping Verbs

A *Helping Verb* is used to modify another verb which follows it. It creates a small verbal phrase:

I *was kissing* you in my dreams.

You *can hold* me if you want.

*Be, Can, Do, Have, Must, Ought, Should* and *Will* are examples of Helping Verbs.

## 4. Gerunds

A *Gerund* is a verb which ends in *-ing*.

kissing • touching • embracing • loving

### Functions

Although A Gerund is a verb form, it functions primarily as a Noun and can be used in the following ways:

### 1. Subject Of A Love Sentence *(Begins The Sentence)*

**Kissing** is my favorite passtime.

### 2. Object Of A Verb *(Placed Directly After The Verb)*

I enjoy **kissing**.

### 3. Predicate Noun *(Placed Directly After The Verb)*

The *Predicate Noun* renames the Subject:

My favorite *passtime* is **kissing**.

4. **Noun Modifier/Adjective** *(Placed Before A Noun)*

The *Kissing Bug* has bitten you.

# Adverbs

An *Adverb* is a word which describes or modifies a *verb, an adjective* or, on occassion, another *adverb*. Each adverb belongs to one of several groups of adverbs each of which is identified by a question:

## 1. How?

Adverbs which answer the question, *How?*, describe the *manner* in which something is done or the *quality* of the doing:

*Manner:*     He kissed me *passionately.*

*Quality:*     We *look alike* in many ways.

## 2. When?

If an adverb answers the question, *When?*, it is describing the *time* of the doing or in what *order* the doing will take place:

*Time:*     We *will soon be together* again.

*Order:*     I *will marry* you *after* I return.

## 3. Where?

Adverbs which answer the question, *Where?*, describe the *location* of the doing or the *direction* in which it occurs:

*Location:*     I *want to return here* to your loving arms.

*Direction:*     My heart *flies up* into the clouds each time you kiss me.

## 4. How Much?

If an adverb answers the question, *How Much?*, it is describing the *degree* of the doing or the *measure* of its intensity:

*Degree:*     I *am totally devastated* by this news.

*Measure:*     When you left, I *cried a lot.*

# Functions

Adverbs have four primary functions within a sentence:

1. **Single Word Modifier** *(Three Catagories)*

    a) Verb Modifier *(Placed Before, After Or Separated From Verb)*

    > You *kiss* **passionately.**
    >
    > You **certainly** *look* beautiful.
    >
    > *Do* you *love* me **truly?**

    b) Adjective Modifier *(Placed Before The Adjective)*

    > You are **too** *beautiful* for words.

    c) Adverb Modifier *(Placed Before The Adverb)*

    > You kiss **incredibly** *well.*

2. **Sentence Modifier** *(Begins A Love Sentence)*

    > **Joyfully,** I await our next encounter.

3. **Clause Connector** *(Placed Between Clauses)*

    > Our love is strong; **consequently,** my overseas tour of duty is but an inconvenience.

4. **Question Introducer** *(Begins A Love Sentence)*

    > **When** will I see you again?

APPENDIX B / **PUNCTUATION**

*Punctuation* is a major tool for indicating within a sentence changes of ideas, areas of emphasis, special phrases and complex thoughts. All punctuation can be broken down into three catagories: *Sentence Punctuation, Internal Punctuation* and *Quotation Punctuation.*

## Sentence Punctuation *(Mainly Used To Mark The Sentence End)*

### 1. The Period [.]

a) Identifies the end of a statement:

I love you[.]

b) Ends abbreviations:

L[.] A[.] and San Diego are in Southern Calif[.]

c) Acts as a Decimal Point in numbers:

Pi = 3[.]1417

### 2. The Question Mark [?]

a) Ends a direct question:

Do you love me[?]

b) Ends a direct question within a sentence:

"How much do you love me[?]" you ask.

3. **The Exclamation Point [!]**

a) Ends a highly emphasized sentence:

You are gorgeous[!]

b) Identifies a highly emphasized word:

Wow[!]

Wow[!] You look beautiful.


# Internal Punctuation *(Mainly To Separate Sentence Elements)*

*Words, Phrases* and *Clauses* are the love sentence elements which may be separated or affected by Internal Punctuation. Before our discussion continues, however, we should briefly identify the differences between Phrases and Clauses.

A *Phrase* is a grouping of words which does not contain a conjugated verb *(action word)*, thus the phrase cannot stand on its own:

| | |
|---|---|
| *Participial Phrase:* | **Embracing you every day** |
| *Gerund Phrase:* | **My needing you** |
| *Infinitive Phrase:* | **To kiss you passionately** |

A Clause is a grouping of words which usually contains a Subject and Verb:

Since *I met* you

Because *I care* for you

*You are* in love

Two Clauses of equal importance create a *compound sentence.* The two clauses are often connected by words such as *And, But, Or* and *For*:

**Dearest, write to me often if you can, for your letters help me overcome my loneliness.**

If one clause is of lesser importance than the other, the love sentence is said to be *complex*. In this case, the less important clause begins with a word such as *Because, Since, When, As, That, Who* or *Which*:

> My outlook on life is better **since I met you.**

## 1. The Comma [,]

The *Comma* creates a pause between words, phrases or clauses and is used:

a) Before the word *But* or *For* if it is serving as a connector between clauses of equal importance:

> You can't imagine how I feel[,] **for** I am hopelessly
> in love with you.

b) Before the word *And, Or, Nor* or *Yet* if it is serving as a connector between two clauses of equal importance but with *different* Subjects:

| | |
|---|---|
| *Different Subjects:* | My love for you is apparent[,] **yet** you choose to ignore it. |
| *Same Subject:* | **My love for you** is apparent *yet* **it** is ignored. |

c) After a short clause or long phrase which comes before the main love sentence clause:

| | |
|---|---|
| *Long Phrase:* | **In the shelter of your arms**[,] I can find refuge from the demands of society. |
| *Short Clause:* | **Since compassion means weakness**[,] there is no place here for a man with your sensitivity. |

d) After short modifying words or phrases which come before the main love sentence clause. Such commas are for emphasis and clarity:

| | |
|---|---|
| *Word:* | **Truthfully**[,] I can't live without you. |
| *Phrase:* | **Many times**[,] I've kissed you in my dreams. |

e) Before and after a describing word or phrase which renames or modifies a preceeding noun:

*Word:*    Dearest[,] **John**[,] when will I see you again?

*Phrase:*    My heart[,] **now broken in two**[,] will never heal without your love.

f) Before and after an expressive or modifying phrase or clause which hinders the flow of a love sentence:

*Phrase:*    Our love[,] **now more powerful than ever before**[,] will sustain us through these trying times.

*Clause:*    My passions[,] **which are locked deep within my heart**[,] yearn for expression.

g) Before and after adverbs such as *However, Therefore, Hence* and *Moreover* which come immediately after the first phrase of the love sentence:

*Your loyalty and devotion*[,] **moreover**[,] serve as the foundation of our loving relationship.

h) After a connective adverb which begins a love sentence:

**Consequently**[,] you are the most important person in my life.

i) To separate three or more items in a series:

**Trust**[,] **devotion**[,] **forgiveness** and **love** are the cornerstones of a lasting relationship.

j) After the salutation at the beginning of a love letter:

*Dear John*[,] • *My dear Judy*[,] • *Dearest Wayne*[,]

k) After words of exclamation which are not emphasized:

Well[,] • Oh[,] • Gee[,] • Why[,]

l) In addresses:

Fresno[,] California[,] 93703[,] U.S.A.

m) In dates:

June 16[,] 1949

## 2. The Semicolon [;]

The *Semicolon* signifys a greater pause or separation between elements than the comma. The semicolon is used:

a) Between two clauses if there is no connecting word:

> If you love me, show me[;] if you don't, tell me.

b) Before a *connecting adverb* located between two clauses of equal importance:

> Our separation is the loneliest time of my life[;] **consequently,** I am very depressed.

## 3. The Colon [:]

The *Colon* is a mark which indicates that something is to follow. The Colon is placed:

a) Between two clauses of equal importance, if the second clause *restates* the first in some way:

> There are things in life which are inevitable[:] only God has the power to control them.

b) After a phrase or clause which introduces a short series of items:

> A good marriage requires four sturdy cornerstones[:] **Love, Devotion, Forgiveness** and **Tolerance.**

c) After a formal letter salutation:

> *Gentlemen*[:] • *Dear Mr. Johnson*[:] • *Dear Ms. Turner*[:]

## 4. The Dash [-]

The *Dash* signals a break in the love sentence. It is more powerful than the comma and is usually placed before a change of thought or an expression of strong emotion:

a) At the end of a love sentence:

> You ask me how many times I've dreamt of you [-] *I cannot count.*

b) Within a love sentence:

> Our rendezvous [-] *such a sweet interlude* [-] was one of the happiest times of my life.

# Quotation Punctuation *(To Identify Quotations)*

1. **Double Quotation Marks["]**

   *Double Quotation Marks* are used:

   a) To identify direct quotations.

   Quotation marks are placed at the beginning and end of conversations, speeches and excerpts from books, articles, etc.:

   > The man said, ["]Wow! She sure is beautiful.["]
   >
   > Did that man say, ["]Wow, she sure is beautiful["]?
   >
   > I asked, ["]How are you?["] and you didn't answer.

   b) To set off Titles.

   Quotation marks are placed before and after the Titles of poems, songs, book chapters and magazine articles:

   > "On Gossamer Wings" is one of the poems
   > found in this book.
   >
   > *Pearls Of Love* contains a section
   > entitled "Pick-A-Poem".

   c) To set off special words.

   Quotation marks are placed before and after Slang words or expressions:

   > He sure is one "hunk" of a guy!

2. **Single Quotation Marks [']**

   *Single Quotation Marks* are used to identify quotations within quotations:

   > He asked her, "Didn't you say, [']*I love you*['] just the other day?"

# APPENDIX C/LOVE TERMS

Over 650 *Key Love Terms* have been selected and listed in this appendix. They represent some of the most colorful and expressive words in use today. Each Key Love Term is followed by several *Synonyms* which can be used as substitutes. These will help you say the same thing in a slightly different way so that you can avoid repetition and add language variety to your love letters.

## Love Term Catagories

The Key Love Terms have been catagorized according to what part of speech they are. This has been done to help you increase your word knowledge and to make it easier for you to use the love terms in your writing. In some cases, a love term which has more than one possible function may be listed in two or more of the four catagories: *Nouns, Adjectives, Verbs* and *Adverbs*.

## Structure And Content

Each Key Love Term is alphabetically listed in boldface type and has a corresponding listing of synonyms:

### Adjectives cont.

**GLORIOUS**
    gorgeous, grand, magnificent, superb; see DIVINE
**GORGEOUS**
    splendid, sublime; see GLORIOUS
**GRACEFUL**
    agile, nimble ‖ elegant, eloquent ‖ polished, refined
**GRACIOUS**
    affable, congenial, cordial, sociable ‖ courtly, stately

**H**

**HANDSOME**
see CUTE
**HAPPY**
cheerful, glad, joyful, joyous, merry, pleased
**HEAVENLY**
see DELICIOUS ‖ see DIVINE
**HOPEFUL** [also noun]
hoping, optimistic ‖ promising

Key love terms which are listed in two or more of the four catagories are referenced as follows:

**HOPEFUL** [also noun]
hoping, optimistic ‖ promising

Key love terms which have basically one meaning have their synonyms listed alphabetically in the following manner:

**HAPPY**
cheerful, glad, joyful, joyous, merry, pleased

Key love terms which have two or more subtle meanings may require their synonyms to be listed in groups which correspond to the different meanings. Double slash marks separate such synonym groupings:

**GRACEFUL**
agile, nimble ‖ elegant, eloquent ‖ polished, refined

Key love terms may be referenced to other key love terms in the following three ways:

1. Direct reference to one key love term:

**HANDSOME**
see CUTE

2. Direct reference to two or more key love terms:

**HEAVENLY**
see DELICIOUS ‖ see DIVINE

As you can see, HEAVENLY has been referenced to the two key love terms: DELICIOUS and DIVINE. Both are separated by a double slash mark which signifies that the synonyms under each referenced key love term are not interchangeable with one another due to the fact that HEAVENLY has two subtle meanings. One meaning is expressed by DELICIOUS and its synonyms and the other by DIVINE and its synonyms. Note that if the two referenced key love terms were separated by a semi-colon [;] instead of a double slash mark [‖], they and their synonyms would be interchangeable.

    3. Reference to a key love term for additional synonyms:

> **GLORIOUS**
> gorgeous, grand, magnificent, superb; see DIVINE

In this example, the listed synonyms for the key love term, GLORIOUS, agree in concept or meaning with the referenced key love term, DIVINE and its synonyms, thus a semi-colon [;] and not a double slash mark [‖] is used between the final synonym, *superb*, and the referenced key love term, DIVINE.   If you were to look up DIVINE, you would find the following:

> **DIVINE**
> godlike, godly, heavenly ‖ *glorious*, wonderful, wondrous

Note that DIVINE has two groupings of synonyms. However, the only grouping which is usable contains the original key love term, GLORIOUS, as a cross-reference.

You will find over 3,000 synonyms listed throughout the following pages. Use these substitute words whenever the need arises, for they will give your love letters great vitality. If you have any doubts as to the appropriateness of any synonym, do not hesitate to consult a dictionary or thesaurus. After all, it's better to be "safe than sorry" especially when it comes to love.

# LOVE TERMS

## Nouns

### A-B

**ATTRACTION**
allurement, appeal, charisma, charm, magnetism, pull
**BABE**
baby, darling, dear, honey, love, sweetie, sugar
**BEAUTY**
attractiveness, charm, elegance, grace, loveliness
**BOY**
lad, laddie, pup, son, sonny, young buck

### C

**CARESS** [also verb]
brush, graze, kiss, love pat, nudge, touch
**CARESSING**
cuddling, feeling, fondling, stroking, touching
**CATCH**
conquest, find, godsend ‖ plum, prize, trophy
**CHARM** [also verb]
fascination, glamour; see ATTRACTION
**CHEER** [also verb]
delight, exhilaration, gaiety, glee, merriment, revelry
**CONSORT**
companion, comrade, mate, partner, spouse
**CRAVING**
addiction, appetite, desire, lust, passion, urge

### D

**DELIGHT** [also verb]
enjoyment, gladness, happiness, joy, pleasure
**DELIRIUM**
fever, frenzy, furor, hysteria, incoherence, madness

**DESIRE** [also verb]
see CRAVING
**DESPAIR** [also verb]
agony, anguish, desperation, hopelessness, torment, woe
**DEVOTION**
affection, attachment ‖ fidelity, loyalty ‖ dedication
**DIGNITY**
elegance, grace ‖ proud bearing, stateliness

## E-G

**ECSTACY**
bliss, exaltation, rapture, ravishment
**ELEGANCE**
dignity, eloquence, grace; see BEAUTY
**FLAME**
beau, beloved, honey, ladylove, sweetheart, truelove
**FOCUS**
center, core, focal point, heart, hub, nucleus, seat
**FOREVER** [also adverb]
always, eternity, perpetuity
**FRENZY**
bewilderment, chaos, rage; see DELIRIUM
**GIRL**
babe, chick, damsel, doll, filly, maid, maiden, nymphet
**GLOW** [also verb]
bloom, gleam, incandescence, rosiness ‖ warmth
**GRACE**
see ELEGANCE

## H

**HAPPINESS**
bliss, cheerfulness, contentment, delight, joyfulness
**HEART**
soul ‖ guts, spirit, spunk ‖ see FOCUS
**HEARTACHE**
affliction, anguish, grief, sadness, sorrow, woe
**HEAVEN**
bliss, Nirvana ‖ Paradise, promised land, wonderland
**HONEY**
see BABE; see FLAME
**HOPE** [also verb]
faith, optimism, reliance ‖ belief, desire, wish
**HOPEFUL** [also adjective]
applicant, aspirant, aspirer, candidate
**HUG** [also verb]
bear hug, clasp, clinch, embrace, enfoldment, hold
**HURT** [also verb]
distress, loss, misery, outrage ‖ injury, pain, wound

HUSBAND
see MAN

# I

IMAGE
likeness, picture ‖ idea, memory, vision, visualization
INDIFFERENCE
apathy, carelessness, coldness, inattention, unconcern
INFATUATION
craze, crush, fascination, fondness, mania, passion
INFIDELITY
disloyalty, faithlessness, falsity, unfaithfulness
INFINITY
boundlessness, endlessness, vastness; see FOREVER
INFLUENCE [also verb]
authority, control, clout, power, prestige, pull
INHIBITION
hinderance, repression, restraint, suppression
INNOCENCE
guiltlessness, harmlessness ‖ purity, virtue ‖ ignorance
INSPIRATION
brainstorm, insight ‖ encouragement, infusion
INSTANT [also adjective]
crack, flash, jiffy, minute, moment, second, wink
INTEREST [also verb]
commitment, concern, regard ‖ attraction, appeal, charm

# J-K

JOY
bliss, delight, elation, gladness, happiness, rapture
KING
czar, emperor, prince, ruler, sovereign ‖ top dog, tycoon
KISS [also verb]
buss, graze, nudge, osculation, peck, smack, smooch

# L

LIFT [also verb]
aid, assistance, support ‖ charge, kick ‖ rise, uplift
LIGHT [also adjective/verb]
brightness, Dawn, sight ‖ enlightenment, truth
LONGING
aching, craving, hankering, pining, yearning
LOVE [also verb]
romance ‖ darling, honey ‖ see DEVOTION
LOVE LETTER
billet-doux [Fr.], mash note

**LOVELINESS**
    prettiness, handsomeness, exquisiteness; see BEAUTY
**LOVER**
    adorer, admirer, paramour; see FLAME
**LOYALTY**
    allegiance, constancy, devotion, faithfulness, fidelity
**LUST** [also verb]
    carnality, lechery ‖ see CRAVING

# M

**MAN**
    gentleman, guy, male ‖ husband, lord, lover, master
**MARRIAGE**
    matrimony, nuptials, wedding, wedlock ‖ bond, union
**MEMORY**
    musing, recollection, remembrance, reminiscence
**MIRACLE**
    marvel, phenomenon, sensation, wonder ‖ wonderment
**MOLD** [also verb]
    brand, cast, form, frame, impression, model, pattern
**MOONLIGHT**
    moonbeam, moonglow, moonshine

# N-O

**NEED** [also verb]
    deficiency, lack ‖ desire, want, wish ‖ necessity
**NIGHT**
    blackness, dark, darkness, nighttide, nighttime

# P-Q

**PASSION**
    agony, misery, suffering ‖ ardor, ferver ‖ see LUST
**PERFECTION**
    completeness, faultlessness, flawlessness, wholeness
**PHYSIQUE**
    anatomy, build, figure, form, frame, hulk, shape
**PINNACLE**
    apex, crest, crown, zenith ‖ ultimate ‖ see CLIMAX
**PLAYBOY**
    pleasurist, pleasure-seeker, man-about-town
**PLAYGIRL**
    woman-about-town; see PLAYBOY
**PLAYMATE**
    bedmate, concubine, lover, lovemate, paramour
**PLEASURE**
    pleasantness, pleasantry; see DELIGHT

**POEM**
rhyme, rune, song, verse ‖ picture, vision
**POET**
bard, minstrel, troubadour ‖ scribe, writer ‖ artisan
**POETRY**
rhyme, song, verse ‖ grace, gracefulness
**POISE**
bearing, behavior, conduct, demeanor, manner, presence
**PRIDE**
arrogance, conceit, egotism, hauteur, pomposity, vanity
**PRINCE**
see KING
**PRINCESS**
see QUEEN
**PRIZE** [also verb]
award, reward, trophy ‖ catch, champion
**PROMISE** [also verb]
pledge, vow ‖ forecast ‖ word ‖ prospect
**QUALITY**
attribute, characteristic, trait ‖ caliber, value, worth
**QUEEN**
czarina, duchess, empress, princess
**QUIVER** [also verb]
flicker, flutter, rush, tremor, shake, shiver, shudder

**R**

**RENDEZVOUS** [also verb]
appointment, date ‖ gathering, meeting
**RENEWAL**
enlivenment, invigoration, regeneration, revival
**RESISTANCE**
immunity, nonsusceptibility ‖ toughness, withstanding
**RESPECT** [also verb]
admiration, appreciation, esteem, favor, honor, regard
**RETURN** [also verb]
comeback, reappearance, reentry ‖ homecoming ‖ recurrance
**ROMANCE**
affair, entanglement, intrigue, liason, love affair
**ROMANTIC** [also adjective]
romancer, romanticist ‖ dreamer, idealist, visionary

**S**

**SACRIFICE** [also verb]
dedication, devotion ‖ forfeiture, denial ‖ offering
**SAINT**
angel, angel of love
**SATISFACTION**
fulfillment, gratification ‖ atonement, retribution

**SECLUSION**
alienation, detachment, isolation, withdrawal
**SELF-CONTROL**
discipline, restraint, self-command, willpower, poise
**SELF-ESTEEM**
dignity, self-respect ‖ self-confidence, self-reliance
**SELF-INTEREST**
egotism, individualism, self-concern, selfishness
**SENSATION**
feeling, sense ‖ thrill, titillation ‖ see MIRACLE
**SEPARATION**
detachment, division ‖ dissolution, disunion, partition
**SEX**
coupling, intercourse, lovemaking, mating ‖ gender
**SIGH** [also verb]
breathy voice, moaning, murmuring, sighing, whining
**SINCERITY**
candidness, candor, frankness, genuineness, honesty
**SIREN**
enchantress, seductress, temptress ‖ mermaid, sea nymph
**SMOOCH** [also verb]
see KISS
**SOFTNESS**
daintiness, delicacy, gentleness, mildness, tenderness
**SOLITUDE**
aloneness, isolation, loneness, solitariness ‖ privacy
**SORROW**
see HEARTACHE
**SPELL** [also verb]
charm, curse, enchantment, hex, incantation
**SPIRIT**
being, heart, mind, psyche, soul ‖ energy, life, verve
**STYLE**
craze, fad, fashion, mode, rage, trend ‖ manner, way
**SUFFERING**
agony, distress, grief, hurt, misery, pain, passion
**SUPPORT** [also verb]
aid, assistance, backing, sustenance ‖ encouragement
**SUSTENANCE**
nutriment, nourishment ‖ maintenance; see SUPPORT
**SWEETHEART**
see BABE; see FLAME
**SYMPATHY**
condolence, consolation ‖ concern, empathy ‖ accord

**T**

**TECHNIQUE**
approach, manner, method, procedure ‖ expertise, knowhow

TEMPER [also verb]
dander, hot-headedness ‖ disposition, nature, temperament
TENDERNESS
youthfulness ‖ softheartedness; see SOFTNESS
THOUGHT
conception, idea, image, notion, perception ‖ reflection
THRESHOLD
brink, edge ‖ entrance, portal ‖ ceiling, upper limit
THRILL [also verb]
sensation, titillation ‖ tingle, tingling ‖ kick, wallop
TINGLING [also adjective]
pricking, prickling, ringing, stinging ‖ see THRILL
TORMENT [also verb]
desolation, misery, passion, torture; see DESPAIR
TORRENT
flood, deluge, inundation, river ‖ rush, gush
TORTURE [also verb]
persecution ‖ see TORMENT
TOTALITY
all, completeness, Creation, entirety, unity, wholeness
TOUCH [also verb]
contact, feel, stroke, tap; see CARESS
TRANQUILITY
calmness, peacefulness, quietude, restfulness, serenity
TRIUMPH [also verb]
hit, success ‖ conquest, victory ‖ exultation, jubilation
TRUTH
actuality, fact, reality, truthfulness, trueness
TURMOIL
commotion, confusion, disorder, ferment, tumult, unrest

# U-V

ULTIMATE [also adjective]
perfection ‖ absolute ‖ see PINNACLE
UNDERSTANDING [also adjective]
conception, intelligence mentality ‖ agreement, bargain
UNSELFISHNESS
altruism, generosity, largess, magnanimity
VALUE [also verb]
dearness, merit, preciousness, worth ‖ benefit, service
VERSATILITY
adaptability, adjustability, flexibility, variability
VIGOR
energy, force, might, power ‖ potency, virility, vitality
VIRGIN
damsel, maiden, vestal, vestal virgin
VIRGINITY
freshness, newness, pristineness ‖ maidenhood

**VIRILITY**
manly vigor, masculinity ‖ see VIGOR

**VIRTUE**
goodness, morality, righteousness ‖ attribute, quality

**VISION**
revelation ‖ apparition, conception; see IMAGE

**VISIONARY** [also adjective]
escapist, seer, utopian; see ROMANTIC

**VITALITY**
exuberance, hardiness, spirit, vivacity; see VIGOR

**VIVACITY**
animation, liveliness, robustness, zest; see VITALITY

## W-Z

**WANT** [also verb]
passion ‖ shortcoming; see NEED

**WARMTH**
cordiality, friendliness, geniality, graciousness

**WEAKNESS**
faintness, feebleness ‖ failing, infirmity, vice ‖ fondness

**WEALTH**
assets, fortune, means, property, resources, riches

**WEDDING**
alliance, association, merger ‖ fusion ‖ see MARRIAGE

**WIFE**
see WOMAN

**WILLINGNESS**
eagerness, readiness ‖ aptness, propensity ‖ motivation

**WISDOM**
wiseness ‖ intelligence ‖ insight ‖ judgement ‖ knowledge

**WISH** [also verb]
see CRAVING; see LONGING

**WOE**
see HEARTACHE; see TORMENT

# Adjectives

## A

**ADAPTABLE**
conformable, flexible, plastic ‖ versatile
**AFFECTIONATE**
adoring, caring, considerate, devoted, loving
**AGREEABLE**
congenial, pleasant, pleasing, pleasurable
**ATTRACTIVE**
alluring, appealing, captivating, charming, magnetic

## B

**BALANCED**
harmonious, poised, proportioned, symmetrical
**BALMY**
aromatic, fragrant, perfumed ‖ gentle, mild, soft
**BEAUTIFUL**
attractive, comely, fair, lovely, pretty, stunning
**BRILLIANT**
beaming, bright, radiant, vivid ‖ intelligent, knowledgeable

## C

**CHARMING**
bewitching, glamorous, seductive; see ATTRACTIVE
**CHEERFUL**
bright, cheery, happy, joyful, radiant, sunny
**COMELY**
see BEAUTIFUL
**CURVACEOUS**
curvy, rounded, rotund ‖ built, buxom, shapely, stacked
**CUTE**
attractive, charming, pretty, handsome

## D

**DAINTY**
choice, delicate, elegant, exquisite, rare, select
**DELICIOUS**
delightful, delectable, heavenly, luscious, scrumptious
**DELIGHTFUL**
see DELICIOUS

**DELIRIOUS**
   frantic, frenzied, raving, wandering, wild
**DESIRABLE**
   advisable, expedient ‖ appealing, likable, pleasing
**DIVINE**
   godlike, godly, heavenly ‖ glorious, wonderful, wondrous

# E

**ELEGANT**
   see DAINTY
**ENCHANTING**
   bewitching, captivating, charming, fascinating
**ENDLESS**
   continual, eternal, perpetual, unceasing, unending, unremitting
**ETERNAL**
   infinite ‖ ceaseless, perpetual, timeless; see ENDLESS
**EXCITING**
   exhilarating, inspiring, stimulating, stirring, rousing
**EXQUISITE**
   see DAINTY

## F-G

**FAITHFUL**
   constant, loyal, staunch, steady, steadfast, true
**FOND**
   affectionate, dear, devoted, doting, loving
**FRIENDLY**
   amicable, neighborly ‖ harmonious ‖ receptive
**GALLANT**
   courageous, fearless ‖ courtly, gracious
**GENTLE**
   amiable, genial ‖ faint; see BALMY
**GLORIOUS**
   gorgeous, grand, magnificent, superb; see DIVINE
**GORGEOUS**
   splendid, sublime; see GLORIOUS
**GRACEFUL**
   agile, nimble ‖ elegant, eloquent ‖ polished, refined
**GRACIOUS**
   affable, congenial, cordial, sociable ‖ courtly, stately

# H

**HANDSOME**
   see CUTE
**HAPPY**
   cheerful, glad, joyful, joyous, merry, pleased

HEAVENLY
see DELICIOUS ‖ see DIVINE
HOPEFUL [also noun]
hoping, optimistic ‖ promising
HYPNOTIC
mesmeric, mesmerizing ‖ narcotic, opiate ‖ sleepy

# I

IMMEASURABLE
incalculable, measureless, uncountable ‖ endless
IMMENSE
colossal, enormous, huge, mammoth, massive, mighty
IMPETUOUS
abrupt, hasty, hurried, rushing, sudden
IMPISH
elvish ‖ mischievous, playful, prankish
IMPULSIVE
automatic, instinctive, involuntary, spontaneous
INCOMPATIBLE
conflicting, discordant, dissonant, inconsistent
INCOMPLETE
fractional, fragmentary, partial, unfinished
INCONSISTENT
changeable, fickle, unstable, variable ‖ conflicting
INCREDIBLE
inconceivable, unbelievable, unimaginable, unthinkable
INDESCRIBABLE
inexpressible, undescribable, unspeakable, unutterable
INDISCREET
ill-advised, imprudent, injudicious, unseemly, unwise
INEVITABLE
certain, inescapable, predestined, unavoidable
INFINITE
endless, eternal ‖ limitless, unbounded ‖ immeasurable
INFLAMED
ablaze, afire, aflame, blazing, burning, flaming, fiery
INFLATED
bloated, distended, overblown, swelled, swollen ‖ windy
INHIBITED
passionless, restrained, suppressed, unresponsive
INNOCENT
blameless, guiltless ‖ good, righteous ‖ naive, pure
INSATIABLE
quenchless, unappeasable, unsatisfiable, unquenchable
INSECURE
unassured, unconfident, unsure ‖ unstable, wavering
INSENSITIVE
insensible, numb, senseless, unfeeling ‖ insusceptible

**INSEPARABLE**
    inalienable, indivisable, inseverable ‖ intimate
**INSIGNIFICANT**
    little, minor, petty, trivial ‖ meaningless ‖ unimportant
**INSINCERE**
    artificial ‖ double-dealing, hypocritical, false hearted
**INSTANT**
    immediate ‖ imperative, pressing, urgent ‖ current, present
**INTIMATE**
    close, confidential, familiar ‖ innermost, private
**IRRESISTIBLE**
    captivating, compelling ‖ forceful, potent, powerful

## J-L

**JOYFUL**
    blissful, cheerful, glad, happy, joyous, lighthearted
**LIGHT** [also noun/verb]
    agile, graceful ‖ blond, fair ‖ lightweight, unheavy
**LIVELY**
    animated, energetic, robust, spirited, vivacious, zesty
**LOFTY**
    elevated, high, soaring, towering ‖ exalted, sublime
**LONELY**
    lone, lonesome
**LOVABLE**
    adorable, desirable, likable, lovely, sweet, winning
**LOVELY**
    see BEAUTIFUL
**LOVING**
    affectionate, dear, devoted, doting, fond
**LOYAL**
    see FAITHFUL
**LUSCIOUS**
    see DELICIOUS
**LUSTFUL**
    hot, licentious, lascivious, passionate, rutty, satyric
**LUSTY**
    bouncing, dynamic ‖ energetic, hearty, strong, vigorous

## M

**MAGNIFICENT**
    august, majestic; see GORGEOUS
**MARRIED**
    marital, matrimonial, nuptial, spousal, wedded
**MARVELOUS**
    amazing, miraculous, spectacular, wonderful, wondrous
**MIRACULOUS**
    fantastic, remarkable, sensational; see MARVELOUS

# N

**NAIVE**
innocent, simple ‖ unschooled ‖ unaffected ‖ gullible
**NATURAL**
inborn, innate, inherited ‖ native, wild
**NAUGHTY**
bad, misbehaving, mischievous ‖ disobedient, unruly
**NOBLE**
august, royal ‖ ethical, moral, virtuous ‖ honorable
**NONCHALANT**
blasé, cool, collected, composed, unruffled
**NUDE**
bare, naked, raw, stark, unclad, unclothed, undressed

# O

**OBSESSED**
fixated, held, infatuated, preoccupied; see POSSESSED
**OFFENSIVE**
disgusting, repulsive, sickening ‖ obscene ‖ ungrateful
**OLD-FASHIONED**
antiquated, archaic, dated, outdated, passé ‖ vintage
**ONLY** [also adverb]
alone, lone, sole, solitary, unique
**OPEN**
unobstructed ‖ exposed ‖ accessible ‖ usable ‖ frank, candid
**OPTIMISTIC**
bright, sunny, upbeat; see HOPEFUL
**OPULENT**
affluent, moneyed, rich, wealthy ‖ luxurious, sumptuous
**OUTRAGEOUS**
atrocious, monstrous, scandalous, shocking ‖ uncivilized
**OUTSTANDING**
noticeable, prominent, striking ‖ magnificent, superb

# P

**PASSIONATE**
impassioned, fervent; see LUSTFUL
**PEACEFUL**
placid, quiet, serene, still, undisturbed ‖ nonviolent
**PERFECT**
flawless, ideal, impeccable, pure, unflawed, whole
**PERPETUAL**
see ENDLESS
**PLACID**
calm, hushed, restful, tranquil; see PEACEFUL

**PLEASANT**
　agreeable, genial ‖ gratifying, pleasing, pleasurable
**PLEASING**
　see PLEASANT
**PLIABLE**
　flexible, plastic, pliant, supple, willowy ‖ adaptable
**POETIC**
　lyric, romantic, visionary
**POIGNANT**
　pungent, racy, spicy ‖ moving, impressive, touching
**POSSESSED**
　bewitched, controlled, obsessed, owned
**POWERFUL**
　forceful, mighty, potent, strong
**POWERLESS**
　helpless, impotent, ineffectual
**PRICELESS**
　precious, inestimable, invaluable, valuable
**PRIVATE**
　personal, intimate ‖ concealed, hidden ‖ secret
**PUNGENT**
　bitter, harsh, sharp, strong; see POIGNANT

## R

**RADIANT**
　brilliant, dazzling, luminous, lustrous, scintillating
**RARE**
　choice, exquisite, select, superior, uncommon, unique
**RAVEN**
　ebony, black, jet-black, inky
**RAVISHING**
　captivating, entrancing, enthralling, stunning
**REELING**
　spinning, staggering, swimming, swirling, turning, whirling
**REFRESHING**
　invigorating, rejuvenating, renewing, restoring
**REMARKABLE**
　extraordinary, outstanding, phenomenal, sensational
**RESILIENT**
　elastic, flexible, springy, stretchy, supple
**REVEALING**
　betraying, disclosing, exposing, telling
**RISING**
　ascending, climbing, mounting, soaring
**ROMANTIC** [also noun]
　dreamy, idealistic ‖ loving, mushy, sentimental

## S

**SAINTLY**
angelic, divine, godly, holy ‖ virtuous
**SCINTILLATING**
sparkling; see RADIANT
**SECLUDED**
cloistered, isolated, sequestered, withdrawn
**SECURE** [also verb]
assured ‖ safe ‖ firm, solid, sound, stable
**SEDUCTIVE**
engaging, mesmeric; see CHARMING
**SEETHING**
boiling, burning, fuming, simmering, stewing
**SELFISH**
egocentric, egotistic, self-centered, self-seeking
**SELF-RELIANT**
independent, self-dependent, self-supporting
**SENSATIONAL**
arresting, remarkable, striking, wonderful
**SENSITIVE**
impressionable, susceptible ‖ perceptive ‖ touchy
**SENSUAL**
carnal, voluptuous ‖ sensory, sensuous
**SENSUOUS**
luscious, lush, luxurious, sensory
**SENTIMENTAL**
maudlin, mawkish, moist, mushy, romantic
**SERENE**
see PEACEFUL
**SEXY**
erotic ‖ racy, risque, spicy, suggestive
**SHAPELY**
statuesque, trim ‖ well-built, well-proportioned
**SHOWY**
flamboyant, ostentatious, pretentious, splashy
**SILKEN**
cottony, satiny, silky, velvety
**SINCERE**
genuine, honest, real, unfeigned ‖ heartfelt
**SLEEK**
smooth, slinky ‖ glassy, glossy, polished
**SLENDER**
narrow, slight, slim, slinky, svelte, thin
**SLIM**
see SLENDER
**SLINKY**
see SLEEK
**SMILING**
beaming, grinning ‖ cheerful, happy

**SMOOTH**
even, flat ‖ effortless, flowing, fluent ‖ tactful

**SOARING**
ascending, rising, spiring, towering

**SOFT**
cottony, velvety ‖ mushy, yielding ‖ gentle ‖ smooth

**SOOTHING**
calming, quieting ‖ easing, subduing

**SOPHISTICATED**
complex, complicated, elaborate ‖ cosmopolitan, worldly

**SPECIAL**
distinguished, unique ‖ individual, particular, specific

**SPECTACULAR**
see MARVELOUS

**SPIRITUAL**
immaterial, metaphysical ‖ sacred

**SPLENDID**
august, luxurious, sumptuous; see GORGEOUS

**SPONTANEOUS**
automatic, impulsive, instinctive, involuntary

**STARVED**
famished, hungry, ravenous, starving

**STARVING**
see STARVED

**STATUESQUE**
see SHAPELY

**STEADFAST**
fixed, immovable, rigid ‖ firm, steady, unyielding

**STIMULATING**
exciting, exhilarating, inspiring, stirring

**STIRRING**
see STIMULATING

**STRIKING**
conspicuous; see OUTSTANDING

**STUNNING**
astounding, bewildering, dazzling, devastating

**SUAVE**
civilized, disarming, smooth, urbane

**SUBDUED**
low-key, restrained, unobtrusive ‖ quiet ‖ soft

**SUBLIME**
see GORGEOUS

**SUBMISSIVE**
docile, domesticated, tame ‖ subdued

**SUBTLE**
delicate, refined ‖ artful, crafty, cunning

**SUGGESTIVE**
evocative; see SEXY

**SUNNY**
fair, sunshiny ‖ cheery, pleasant; see OPTIMISTIC

**SUPERB**
outstanding, splendid; see GLORIOUS
**SUPPLE**
limber, lithe; see RESILIENT
**SUPPORTING**
backing, sustaining ‖ encouraging ‖ bearing
**SUPREME**
greatest, highest, ultimate ‖ incomparable, unmatchable
**SUSCEPTIBLE**
exposed, open ‖ prone, subject; see SENSITIVE
**SVELTE**
see SLENDER
**SWEET**
aromatic, balmy, fragrant ‖ engaging, winsome ‖ melodic
**SWELLING**
ballooning, bulging, expanding, growing, increasing
**SWIRLING**
rotating, twirling; see REELING

# T

**TACTFUL**
delicate, mindful, thoughtful ‖ diplomatic, statesmanlike
**TASTEFUL**
appetizing, flavorsome, savory, tasty ‖ unobtrusive
**TAUNTING**
insulting, offending, ridiculing, scorning, teasing
**TEARFUL**
crying, sobbing, teary, weeping, weepy
**TEASING**
harassing, needling, pestering; see TAUNTING
**TEMPTING**
enticing, inviting, luring, titillating
**TENACIOUS**
stout, sturdy, tough ‖ firm, secure, set
**TENDER**
compassionate, sympathetic, warm, warmhearted
**THOUGHTFUL**
pensive, thinking ‖ attentive, considerate; see TACTFUL
**THRILLING**
breathtaking, electrifying, exhilarating, intoxicating
**THRIVING**
flourishing, prospering, successful ‖ robust
**TIMELESS**
ageless, dateless ‖ everlasting, perpetual; see ETERNAL
**TINGLING** [also noun]
prickling, ringing, stinging, tinkling
**TITILLATING**
tantalizing, teasing, tickling; see TEMPTING

**TOLERANT**
broad-minded, liberal || indulgent || lenient
**TORRID**
blistering, boiling, burning, fiery, hot, sizzling
**TOTAL**
complete, entire, whole || absolute, pure, sheer, utter
**TOUCHING**
affecting, mournful, saddening; see POIGNANT
**TRANQUIL**
composed, serene; see PLACID
**TREMBLING**
quaking, quivering, shaking, shivering, shuddering
**TREMENDOUS**
awesome, terrific || immense, monumental, stupendous
**TRIUMPHANT**
elated, exultant, jubilant, triumphal
**TROUBLED**
distraught, distressed, tormented, worried
**TRUE**
faithful, loyal, steadfast || genuine, honest, sincere
**TRYING**
arduous, difficult, oppressive, rough, taxing
**TURBULENT**
chaotic, disorderly, rowdy, stormy, unruly, wild

# U

**ULTIMATE** [also noun]
absolute || final, last || see SUPREME
**UNBEARABLE**
unendurable, insufferable, intolerable
**UNBEATABLE**
indomitable, invincible, invulnerable, unconquerable
**UNBOUNDED**
boundless, limitless, unlimited
**UNBRIDLED**
uncontrolled, uninhibited, unrestrained, unsuppressed
**UNBROKEN**
intact, perfect, unblemished, undamaged, whole
**UNCEASING**
ceaseless, continuous, everlasting; see ENDLESS
**UNCERTAIN**
chancy, erratic, unpredictable || doubtful, dubious
**UNCHANGING**
constant, even, stable, steady, uniform, unvarying
**UNCOMMON**
extraordinary, scarce, unusual; see RARE
**UNCONTROLLED**
unconfined, ungoverned, rampant; see UNBRIDLED

UNCONVENTIONAL
   deviant, different, irregular, unorthodox
UNCORRUPTED
   ethical, principled, uncorrupt, untarnished
UNDENIABLE
   certain, incontestable, sure, undisputable
UNDERSTANDING [also noun]
   indulgent, tolerant ‖ sympathetic ‖ patient ‖ agreeable
UNDIMINISHED
   unabated, unfaded, unreduced, unwithered, unworn
UNDISTORTED
   faithful, true, undeviating ‖ unaffected
UNDISTURBED
   unagitated, unbothered, unperturbed, untroubled
UNDIVIDED
   concentrated, whole ‖ coupled, joined, united
UNDYING
   deathless, immortal ‖ eternal, everlasting
UNEASY
   edgy, tense, unsettled, unsure, uptight
UNENDING
   see ENDLESS
UNEVENTFUL
   common, commonplace, ordinary, unexceptional
UNEXPRESSED
   silent, unspoken, unuttered, unvoiced, wordless
UNFADED
   untouched, unweakened; see UNDIMINISHED
UNFADING
   enduring, lasting, undying, unfailing
UNFAILING
   certain, sure ‖ constant, invariable, unchanging
UNFAITHFUL
   disloyal, treacherous, unloyal, untrue
UNFALTERING
   steadfast, steady, unhesitating, unwavering
UNFAVORABLE
   adverse, bad, detrimental, negative
UNFINISHED
   crude, rough, unpolished ‖ deficient
UNFLINCHING
   relentless, ruthless, unrelenting, unyielding
UNFORGETTABLE
   memorable, notable ‖ persistent, recurrent
UNFORTUNATE
   mournful, ominous, regrettable, unlucky, woeful
UNFOUNDED
   baseless, groundless, ungrounded, unwarranted
UNFULFILLED
   unattained, unrealized ‖ ungratified, unsatisfied

**UNGROUNDED**
see UNFOUNDED
**UNIMAGINED**
unconceived, unconsidered, undreamt, unimaged
**UNINHIBITED**
uncurbed, ungoverned; see UNBRIDLED
**UNINTENTIONAL**
inadvertent, undesigned, undevised, unplanned
**UNIQUE**
see RARE
**UNITING**
combining, fusing, merging, unifying
**UNIVERSAL**
omnipresent ‖ cosmic, global, worldwide
**UNKNOWN**
obscure, uncelebrated, unrenowned ‖ nameless
**UNLIMITED**
see UNBOUNDED
**UNMARRIED**
spouseless, unwed ‖ single, sole
**UNMISTAKABLE**
clear, distinct, evident, obvious, plain
**UNNECESSARY**
unessential, unneeded, unrequired
**UNOBSTRUCTED**
clear, open, unhampered, unrestricted
**UNPARALLELED**
peerless, unequaled, unmatched, unrivaled, unsurpassed
**UNPLANNED**
aimless, indiscriminate ‖ unintended; see UNINTENTIONAL
**UNPREDICTABLE**
see UNCERTAIN
**UNPROTECTED**
defenseless, helpless, undefended, unguarded
**UNQUENCHABLE**
see INSATIABLE
**UNQUESTIONABLE**
absolute, genuine, indisputable, incontestable
**UNQUESTIONING**
abiding, steady, unfaltering, unshaken, unwavering
**UNREALISTIC**
impractical, storybook, unpractical
**UNREALIZED**
uncompleted, unexecuted; see UNFULFILLED
**UNREASONABLE**
illogical, irrational, unreasoned ‖ unjustifiable
**UNRELIABLE**
dubious, questionable, undependable, untrustworthy
**UNRELIEVED**
unabated, undiminished, unreduced ‖ uninterrupted

**UNREMITTING**
see ENDLESS
**UNRESERVED**
candid, direct, frank ‖ casual, easygoing, relaxed
**UNRESPONSIVE**
impassive, insensitive, insusceptible, unimpressionable
**UNRESTRAINED**
excessive, immoderate; see UNBRIDLED
**UNRESTRICTED**
accessible, open; see UNOBSTRUCTED
**UNSELFISH**
selfless, self-forgetting, self-sacrificing
**UNSHAKEN**
firm, staunch, steadfast; see UNQUESTIONING
**UNSOCIABLE**
aloof, distant, reserved, solitary, withdrawn
**UNSPOKEN**
see UNEXPRESSED
**UNSTABLE**
uncertain, unsettled, unsure ‖ fickle, variable ‖ unsteady
**UNSURE**
skeptical ‖ insecure, unassured; see UNSTABLE
**UNSURPASSED**
see UNPARALLELED
**UNTAINTED**
unspoiled, unspotted, untarnished ‖ immaculate, pure
**UNTARNISHED**
unsoiled, unstained; see UNTAINTED
**UNTHINKABLE**
inconceivable, incredible, unbelievable, unimaginable
**UNTIRING**
inexhaustible, tireless, unflagging, unwearying
**UNTRUE**
false, erroneous, truthless ‖ faithless; see UNFAITHFUL
**UNUSUAL**
bizarre, erratic, strange; see UNCOMMON
**UNUTTERED**
see UNEXPRESSED
**UNVOICED**
see UNEXPRESSED
**UNWANTED**
undesirable, undesired, unsought, unwelcome
**UNWISE**
ill-advised, imprudent, indiscreet ‖ inadvisable
**UNYIELDING**
inflexible, rigid ‖ steadfast, stubborn, unflinching

# V

**VALIANT**
bold, brave, courageous, gallant, heroic, valorous
**VALUABLE**
costly, invaluable, precious, priceless
**VERSATILE**
adaptable, all-around, many-sided ‖ changeable, flexible
**VIBRANT**
intense, strong, vivid ‖ dynamic, energetic, vigorous
**VIGOROUS**
hardy, potent, tough, vital ‖ forceful; see VIBRANT
**VIRILE**
macho, male, manly, masculine ‖ potent
**VIRTUOUS**
ethical, moral, noble, principled, pure, righteous
**VISIONARY** [also noun]
dreamy, idealistic, lofty, utopian
**VITAL**
alive, animated, essential; see VIGOROUS
**VIVACIOUS**
effervescent, exuberant, sprightly; see LIVELY
**VIVID**
expressive, graphic; see BRILLIANT
**VOLUPTUOUS**
carnal, luscious, luxurious, sensual, sensuous
**VORACIOUS**
gluttonous, rapacious, ravening, ravenous
**VULNERABLE**
conquerable, pregnable ‖ defenseless, helpless

# W

**WANTING**
deficient, incomplete, insufficient, lacking, missing
**WARM** [also verb]
compassionate, sympathetic, tender ‖ enthusiastic
**WARMHEARTED**
see TENDER
**WASTING**
deteriorating, fading, failing, shriveling, withering
**WAVERING**
faltering, hesitating, timid, uncertain ‖ unstable, weak
**WEAK**
feeble, frail ‖ inadequate, impotent ‖ see WAVERING
**WEAKENING**
debilitating, draining, exhausting, fatiguing, grueling
**WEALTHY**
affluent, loaded, moneyed, rich

**WHIRLING**
see REELING

**WHOLE**
complete, entire, flawless, intact, perfect, total

**WHOLESOME**
curative, curing, healing ‖ good, healthful, healthy

**WILD**
barbaric, savage, vicious ‖ frantic, frenzied, unruly

**WILLING**
agreeable, eager, game, inclined, ready ‖ voluntary

**WILLOWY**
see PLIABLE

**WINNING**
appealing, charming, engaging, sweet, winsome

**WOEFUL**
afflicted, miserable, sorrowful, wretched

**WONDERFUL**
see MARVELOUS

**WONDROUS**
see MARVELOUS

**WOOING**
chasing, courting, pursuing, sparking

**WORLDLY**
cosmopolitan, sophisticated ‖ materialistic, temporal

**WORTHY**
capable, deserving, desirable, suited ‖ honorable, noble

## X-Z

**YEARNING** [also noun]
longing, wishful, wistful

**YIELDING**
passive, resigned, submissive, unresisting

**YOUNG**
juvenile, youthful ‖ green, immature, inexperienced

**YOUTHFUL**
see YOUNG

**ZEALOUS**
anxious, eager, enthusiastic, fervent, warm, zestful

**ZESTFUL**
dynamic, energetic, lively, vigorous; see ZEALOUS

# Verbs

## A

**ADMIRE**
appreciate, cherish, favor, respect, revere
**ADORE**
honor, idolize, love, revere, venerate, worship
**AROUSE**
awaken, enliven, excite, impassion, inflame, kindle
**ATTRACT**
appeal, captivate, charm, excite, fascinate, interest

## B-C

**BEWITCH**
captivate, charm, enchant, entrance
**CALM**
allay, lull, quiet, settle, soothe, still, tranquilize
**CAPTIVATE**
allure, bewitch, draw, magnetize; see ATTRACT
**CARESS** [also noun]
brush, cuddle, fondle, graze, kiss, love, pet, rub, stroke
**CHARM** [also noun]
see ATTRACT; see BEWITCH
**CHEER** [also noun]
cry, shout, yell ‖ brighten, comfort, gladden, hearten
**CHERISH**
esteem, prize, treasure ‖ cultivate, foster, nurture
**CODDLE**
humor, indulge, oblige, pamper, spoil ‖ dandle, fondle
**CRAVE**
hanker, hunger, thirst, yearn ‖ desire, need ‖ require
**CUDDLE**
burrow, nestle, nuzzle, snuggle ‖ see CARESS

## D

**DELIGHT** [also noun]
gladden, gratify, please ‖ exult, jubilate, triumph
**DESIRE** [also noun]
request, solicit ‖ want, wish; see CRAVE
**DESPAIR** [also noun]
abandon hope, despond, falter, give up, lose heart
**DWELL**
abide, exist, hang out, lie, live, reside

## E-F

**ENCHANT**
see BEWITCH
**ENTHRALL**
entrance, fascinate, grip, hold, mesmerize, spellbind ‖ enslave
**ENTRANCE**
enrapture, enravish, ravish, trance; see ENTHRALL
**EXCITE**
delight, elate, stimulate ‖ move, motivate, provoke
**FONDLE**
see CARESS
**FULFILL**
accomplish, complete, realize ‖ fill, meet, satisfy

## G-H

**GLOW** [also noun]
beam, gleam, sparkle ‖ blush, redden ‖ blare, flame, flare
**HOPE** [also noun]
anticipate, await, count on, expect
**HUG** [also noun]
bosom, clasp, clinch, embrace, enfold, holl, squeeze
**HUNGER**
see CRAVE
**HURT** [also noun]
damage, harm, injure, irritate, pain, sting, wound

## I

**IDOLIZE**
see ADORE
**IMAGINE**
conceive, envision, fancy, visualize
**IMBUE**
impress, infuse, ingrain, instill, invest
**IMPEL**
drive, mobilize, move, propel, push, shove, thrust
**IMPRESS**
etch, imprint, inscribe ‖ influence, inspire, move, sway
**INFLAME**
aggravate, irritate, provoke, rile ‖ see AROUSE
**INFLUENCE** [also noun]
affect, induce, touch; see IMPRESS
**INHABIT**
dwell in, live in, occupy, people, populate, reside
**INHIBIT**
ban, forbid, prohibit ‖ bridle, curb, restrain, temper

**INSCRIBE**
engrave, mark, record, write; see IMPRESS
**INSPIRE**
excite, exhilarate, motivate, stimulate; see IMPRESS
**INTEREST**
see ATTRACT

## J-L

**JUSTIFY**
substantiate, validate, verify ‖ vindicate
**KINDLE**
fire, ignite, light; see AROUSE
**KISS** [also noun]
brush, buss, graze, peck, osculate, smack, smooch
**LIFT** [also noun]
arise, mount, soar ‖ boost, elevate, raise, uplift
**LIGHT** [also noun/adjective]
illuminate, lighten ‖ see KINDLE
**LIKE**
adore, love ‖ enjoy, savor ‖ choose, desire, fancy, wish
**LONG**
ache, crave, dream, hunger, lust, pine, yearn
**LOVE** [also noun]
see ADORE; see CARESS
**LUST** [also noun]
see LONG

## M-O

**MARRY**
espouse, wed ‖ combine, couple, hitch, mate, link, unite
**MESMERIZE**
see ENTHRALL
**MOLD** [also noun]
cast, fashion, forge, form, frame, model, shape, sculpt
**NEED** [also noun]
require, want
**OVERWHELM**
overpower, overrun, trounce ‖ engulf, flood, inundate

## P

**PERMEATE**
impregnate, penetrate, pervade, saturate
**PINE**
see LONG
**PLEASE**
satisfy, suit; see DELIGHT

POSSESS
control, have, hold, occupy, own, retain ‖ obsess
PRIZE [also noun]
appreciate, value; see CHERISH
PROMISE [also noun]
pledge, vow ‖ hint, imply, suggest
PROPEL
goad, prod, spur ‖ see IMPEL
PURSUE
chase, follow, tail, trail ‖ court, spark, woo

## Q-R

QUENCH
quash, quell, suppress ‖ satisfy, slake ‖ douse, extinguish
QUIVER [also noun]
quake, quaver, shake, shiver, shudder, tremble, twitter
RAVISH
defile, outrage, spoil, violate
RECONCILE
reunite ‖ adapt, fit ‖ conform, harmonize, integrate
REEL
lurch, spin, stagger, sway, totter, twirl, whirl
REFRESH
freshen, rejuvenate, renew, renovate, restore, revive
REKINDLE
relight ‖ renew, resurrect, resuscitate, revitalize
RENDEZVOUS [also noun]
assemble, congregate, gather, meet, muster
RENEW
regenerate, restart; see REFRESH; see REKINDLE
REPLENISH
refill, replace, restore, return
RESIST
buck, combat, fight, oppose, repel, withstand
RESOLVE
clear up, settle, solve, unravel, unriddle, work out
RESPECT [also noun]
honor, regard, value; see ADMIRE
RESTORE
re-establish, reinstate; see REFRESH
RESTRAIN
control, moderate, subdue, suppress ‖ see INHIBIT
RETURN [also noun]
come back ‖ regress, revert, turn back ‖ replace, restore
REUNITE
bring together, come together again, reconcile
REVEAL
bare, disclose, divulge, tell ‖ uncover, unmask, unveil

**REVERE**
see ADORE
**REVIVE**
see REFRESH

# S

**SACRIFICE** [also noun]
drop, forfeit, lose, relinquish, surrender ‖ victimize
**SATIATE**
gratify, satisfy ‖ glut, gorge, saturate ‖ quench, slake
**SATISFY**
appease, gratify ‖ fulfill, meet ‖ convince, persuade
**SATURATE**
drench, soak, sop, souse, waterlog ‖ see PERMEATE
**SECURE** [also adjective]
obtain, procure ‖ capture, catch ‖ assure, insure ‖ protect
**SEDUCE**
ensnare, entice, entrap, lure, tempt ‖ deceive, betray
**SEETHE**
churn, rage, stir ‖ boil, burn, simmer, smolder, stew
**SIGH** [also noun]
grieve, lament, moan, mourn, sob, sorrow, wail, whine
**SMOOCH** [also noun]
see KISS
**SOAR**
ascend, aspire, arise, climb, fly, lift, mount, rise
**SOFTEN**
dampen, diminish, moderate, reduce, subdue, temper
**SOOTHE**
diminish, soften; see CALM
**SPELL** [also noun]
becharm, mesmerize; see BEWITCH
**STIMULATE**
exhilarate, inspire; see EXCITE
**STIR**
arouse, awaken, rouse; see SEETHE
**STRENGTHEN**
energize, fortify, harden, invigorate, toughen, temper
**SUBDUE**
conquer, defeat, master, quell, tame; see SOFTEN
**SUBMIT**
bow, buckle under, defer, succumb, surrender
**SUCCUMB**
fall, go down, yield ‖ relent, resign; see SUBMIT
**SUFFER**
bear, endure, sustain, tolerate ‖ ache, anguish, hurt
**SUPPORT** [also noun]
brace, carry, prop ‖ maintain, provide ‖ back, champion

**SUPPRESS**
crush, quell, quench ‖ squelch, stifle ‖ muffle, repress
**SURRENDER**
give up, hand over, relinquish, resign, submit, yield
**SUSTAIN**
maintain, preserve ‖ brace, bolster ‖ endure, tolerate
**SWELL**
bloat, distend, expand, inflate ‖ grow, mount, rise
**SWOON**
black out, drop, faint, pass out ‖ succumb

# T

**TEMPER** [also noun]
harden, toughen ‖ tame ‖ control, restrain; see SOFTEN
**TEMPT**
allure, tantalize, titillate, tease; see SEDUCE
**THRILL** [also noun]
glow, tingle ‖ delight, electrify, enthuse, titillate
**THRIVE**
boom, flourish, grow, prosper, succeed
**TINGLE**
jingle, tinkle ‖ see THRILL
**TITILLATE**
see TEMPT ‖ see THRILL
**TOLERATE**
bear, endure, stand, stomach, sustain, take, withstand
**TORMENT** [also noun]
persecute, punish, rack, torture ‖ harass, haunt, plague
**TORTURE** [also noun]
agonize, distress, hound; see TORMENT
**TOUCH** [also noun]
contact, feel, finger, handle, paw ‖ see INFLUENCE
**TRANQUILIZE**
see CALM
**TREMBLE**
see QUIVER
**TRIUMPH** [also noun]
conquer, master, overcome, prevail ‖ delight, exult
**TRY**
attempt, endeavor, offer, strive, undertake ‖ prove, test
**TUMBLE**
fall, drop, plunge, skid, topple

# U-V

**UNCHAIN**
free, liberate, release ‖ unbind, unlock, unstrap, untie
**UNITE**
connect, converge, join, meet, merge, unify ‖ see MARRY

UNLOCK
expose, reveal, uncover ‖ solve, resolve ‖ see UNCHAIN
VALUE [also noun]
assess, evaluate, rate ‖ appreciate; see PRIZE
VENERATE
prize, value; see ADORE
VITALIZE
animate, arouse, enliven, invigorate, stimulate

# W-Z

WANT [also noun]
desire, fancy, like, love, lust for, need, require, wish
WARM [also adjective]
arouse, awaken, excite, stir ‖ heat, kindle
WASTE
blow, squander ‖ decimate, destroy, devastate, ruin
WAVER
falter, hesitate ‖ flounder, stagger, vacillate, wobble
WHIRL
see REEL
WISH [also noun]
see DESIRE
WITHOLD
inhibit, restrain ‖ keep, retain ‖ deny, refuse ‖ refrain
WITHSTAND
see RESIST
WOO
chase, court, pursue, spark
WORSHIP
see ADORE
YIELD
give, break, collapse ‖ relinquish; see SUCCUMB

# Adverbs

## A-D

**ABRUPTLY**
bluntly, brusquely, curtly, gruffly, suddenly

**ADEQUATELY**
amply, enough, sufficiently ‖ properly, suitably, well

**AFFECTIONATELY**
dearly, devotedly, dotingly, fondly, lovingly

**BEAUTIFULLY**
attractively, handsomely, stunningly

**BRILLIANTLY**
beamingly, luminously, lustrously, radiantly, vividly

**CHEERFULLY**
blithely, cheerily, gladly, happily

**DELIGHTFULLY**
delectably, deliciously, exquisitely, pleasingly

**DIVINELY**
blissfully, gloriously, splendidly, sublimely

## E-F

**ELEGANTLY**
becomingly, delicately, exquisitely, gracefully

**ENDLESSLY**
ceaselessly, constantly, forever, incessantly, interminably

**EVENTUALLY**
finally, someday, sometime, ultimately

**FAITHFULLY**
realistically ‖ rigorously, strictly ‖ devotedly, loyally

**FINALLY**
see EVENTUALLY

**FONDLY**
see AFFECTIONATELY

**FOREVER** [also noun]
eternally, everlastingly, permanently; see ENDLESSLY

## G-H

**GALLANTLY**
boldly, bravely, chivalrously, courageously, valiantly

**GENTLY**
delicately, slowly ‖ faintly, softly ‖ meekly, quietly

**GLORIOUSLY**
magnificently, marvelously, wonderfully; see DIVINELY

**GRACEFULLY**
graciously; see ELEGANTLY
**GRACIOUSLY**
agreeably, genially ‖ hospitably ‖ see GRACEFULLY
**HAPPILY**
blissfully, joyfully, joyously; see CHEERFULLY
**HARD**
forcefully, vigorously, violently ‖ closely, intently

# I

**IMMENSELY**
immeasurably ‖ superbly, tremendously
**IMPULSIVELY**
hastily, impetuously, quickly, rashly, suddenly
**INCREDIBLY**
amazingly, astonishingly, awesomely, surprisingly
**INDISCREETLY**
imprudently, incautiously, injudiciously, unwisely
**INFINITELY**
boundlessly, limitlessly ‖ incalculably, immeasurably
**INNOCENTLY**
blamelessly, faultlessly ‖ naively, naturally ‖ harmlessly
**INTIMATELY**
confidentially ‖ deeply, profoundly
**IRRESISTIBLY**
forcefully, mightily, potently ‖ ravishingly, temptingly

# J-L

**JOYFULLY**
see HAPPILY
**LIGHTLY**
barely, hardly, slightly ‖ fancifully ‖ frivolously
**LOVINGLY**
tenderly, thoughtfully; see AFFECTIONATELY

# M-O

**MADLY**
fiercely, frantically, furiously, turbulently, wildly
**MAGNIFICENTLY**
grandly, superbly; see GLORIOUSLY
**MIRACULOUSLY**
fabulously, fantastically, remarkably
**ONLY** [also adjective]
alone, entirely, exclusively, solely ‖ merely, purely

## P-R

**PASSIONATELY**
amorously, ardently, fervently, intensely, warmly
**PEACEFULLY**
calmly, reposefully, restfully, tranquilly
**PERFECTLY**
absolutely, faultlessly, flawlessly, impeccably ‖ ideally
**PLEASANTLY**
agreeably, congenially, genially ‖ enjoyably
**PLEASINGLY**
aesthetically, artistically ‖ pleasurably
**POSITIVELY**
absolutely, assuredly, certainly, decidedly, definitely
**PRESENTLY**
directly, shortly, soon
**PRIVATELY**
individually, personally ‖ covertly, secretly, stealthily
**RAVENOUSLY**
greedily, insatiably, rapaciously, voraciously
**ROMANTICALLY**
sentimentally, softly, tenderly

## S

**SECURELY**
fast, firmly, tight ‖ dependably, reliably, safely
**SINCERELY**
genuinely, honestly, really ‖ heartily, wholeheartedly
**SMOOTHLY**
artfully, craftily ‖ evenly, uniformly ‖ fluently ‖ placidly
**SOFTLY**
see GENTLY
**SPECIALLY**
distinctively, expressly, particularly, specifically
**SPIRITUALLY**
metaphysically, immaterially ‖ morally
**SPONTANEOUSLY**
automatically, instinctively ‖ freely, voluntarily
**SWEETLY**
aromatically, fragrantly ‖ engagingly

## T

**TACTFULLY**
delicately, thoughtfully, sensitively ‖ diplomatically
**TENACIOUSLY**
doggedly, persistently, relentlessly ‖ cohesively

**TENDERLY**
compassionately, sympathetically, warmly
**THOUGHTFULLY**
considerately, heedfully, mindfully; see TACTFULLY
**TOTALLY**
absolutely, completely, entirely, fully, purely, wholly
**TRULY**
genuinely, really, truthfully, undeniably, verily

# U

**ULTIMATELY**
see EVENTUALLY
**UNDENIABLY**
indubitably, irrefutably, undoubtedly ‖ see TRULY
**UNFORTUNATELY**
sadly, unfavorably, unhappily, unluckily
**UNINTENTIONALLY**
inadvertently, unconsciously, unwillingly, unwittingly
**UNIQUELY**
singularly, solely ‖ exceptionally ‖ incomparably
**UNREASONABLY**
exorbitantly, illogically, irrationally, outrageously
**UNSELFISHLY**
selflessly ‖ ungrudgingly
**UNUSUALLY**
extremely, uncommonly, unnaturally, unordinarily ‖ rarely

# V-Z

**VALIANTLY**
see GALLANTLY
**VIGOROUSLY**
energetically, exuberantly, forcefully, intensely
**VIVIDLY**
expressively, graphically ‖ intensely; see BRILLIANTLY
**WARMLY**
cordially, genially; see PASSIONATELY ‖ see TENDERLY
**WELL**
correctly, properly ‖ entirely, fully ‖ see ADEQUATELY
**WHOLLY**
see TOTALLY
**WILDLY**
desperately, fanatically; see MADLY
**WILLINGLY**
contently, dutifully, readily, receptively, voluntarily

# APPENDIX D / IMAGERY TERMS

This appendix contains a listing of various *Names*, *Places*, *Objects*, and *Events* of worldly importance which you can utilize in creating Imagery. The Items listed have been selected from the areas of *Mythology*, *The Bible*, *History*, *Folklore*, *Legend*, *Literature*, *Geology*, *Geography* and *Biology*. If used effectively and in moderation, they have the ability to make your Love Poem or Love Letter more vibrant and expressive.

# IMAGERY TERMS

## Greek And Roman Gods And Goddesses

| | |
|---|---|
| ZEUS<br>JUPITER | *God Of Weather, Of Destiny, Of Lightning,<br>Of Thunder, Of Heaven; Ruler Of Gods And Men* |
| JUNO<br>HERA | *Goddess Of Beginings, Of Heaven, Of Light,<br>Of Womanhood, Of Marriage; Queen Of The Gods* |
| MARS<br>ARES | *God Of War* |
| ATHENA<br>MINERVA | *Goddess Of War, Of The Arts, Of Lightning,<br>Of Science, Of Navigation, Of Wisdom* |
| VENUS<br>APHRODITE | *Goddess Of Beauty, Of Love* |
| APOLLO<br>PHOEBUS | *God Of The Sun, Of Light, Of Poetry, Of<br>Music And Song* |
| PERSEPHONE<br>PROSERPINA | *Goddess Of Spring, Of Flowers* |
| DIANA<br>ARTEMIS | *Goddess Of The Moon, Of Hunting, Of Rivers,<br>Springs And Fountains* |
| MERCURY<br>HERMES | *God Of Commerce, Of Thieves, Of Gambling;<br>Messenger Of The Gods* |
| CUPID<br>EROS | *God Of Love* |
| FORTUNA<br>TYCHE | *Goddess Of Chance, Of Luck* |
| AURORA<br>EOS | *Goddess Of The Dawn* |
| SATURN<br>KRONOS | *God Of Time* |

## Greek And Roman Gods
## And Goddesses cont.

| | |
|---|---|
| PSYCHE | *Goddess Of The Soul* |
| POLLUX<br>HERCULES | *God Of Sports* |
| VULCAN<br>HEPHAESTUS | *God Of Fire, Of Blacksmithing* |
| PLUTO<br>PLUTUS | *God Of Wealth* |
| BACCHUS<br>DIONYSUS | *God Of Wine* |
| NEPTUNE<br>POSEIDON | *God Of The Ocean And Sea* |
| EREBUS<br>LETO | *God Of Darkness* |
| PLUTO<br>HADES | *God Of The Underworld; Ruler Of The Dead* |

## Greek And Roman Mythology

### Mythological Characters

| | | |
|---|---|---|
| Achilles | Circe | Minos |
| Adonis | Daphne | Narcissus |
| Agamemnon | Echo | Orion |
| Ajax | Electra | Orpheus |
| Amazons, The | Europa | Pandora |
| Andromeda | Hector | Paris |
| Antigone | Helen Of Troy | Penelope |
| Arachne | Hero And Leander | Perseus |
| Argonauts, The | Io | Phaedra |
| Ariadne | Jason | Ulysses |
| Cassandra | Midas | |

### Mythological Creatures

| | | |
|---|---|---|
| Centaur | Gorgon, The | Medusa, The |
| Cyclops, The | Griffin | Minotaur, The |
| Dryad, The | Hydra | Pegasus |
| Faun | | |

## Mythological Places

| | | |
|---|---|---|
| Atlantis | Hades | Parnassus, Mount. |
| Delphi, Oracle Of | Hercules, Pillars Of | Styx, The River |
| Elysian Fields | Labyrinth, The | Thebes, City Of |
| Etna, Mount. | Olympus, Mount. | Troy, City Of |

## Mythological Objects And Symbols

| | | |
|---|---|---|
| Ambrosia | Golden Fleece | Wooden Horse |
| Apple Of Discord | Gordian Knot | Of Troy |

# Astronomy And Astrology

## Constellations

ANDROMEDA: *The Chained Lady*
APUS: *The Bird Of Paradise*
AQUARIUS: *The Water Bearer*
AQUILA: *The Eagle*
ARIES: *The Ram*
AURIGA: *The Charioteer*
BOOTHES: *The Herdsman*
CAPRICORN: *The Horned Goat*
CASSIOPIA: *The Lady In The Chair*
CEPHEUS: *The Monarch*
CYGNUS: *The Swan*
DRACO: *The Dragon*
GEMINI: *The Twins*
HERCULES
HYDRA: *The Sea Serpent*

HYDRUS: *The Water Snake*
LEO: *The Lion*
LEPUS: *The Hare*
LIBRA: *The Balance*
LUPUS: *The Wolf*
MONOCEROS: *The Unicorn*
ORION: *The Giant Hunter*
PEGASUS: *The Winged Horse*
PERSEUS
PHOENIX: *The Phoenix*
PISCES: *The Fishes*
SAGITTARIUS: *The Archer*
SCORPIO: *The Scorpion*
TAURUS: *The Bull*
VIRGO: *The Virgin*

## Important Stars

| | | |
|---|---|---|
| Alpha Centauri | Mira | Rigel |
| Antares | North Star, The | Sirus |
| Betelgeuse | | |

## Planets And Planetary Bodies

| | | |
|---|---|---|
| Asteroids | Mercury | Pluto |
| Comets | Meteors | Saturn |
| Halley's Comet | Moon | Uranus |
| Jupiter | Neptune | Venus |

**Signs Of The Zodiac**

| | | |
|---|---|---|
| Aquarius | Gemini | Sagittarius |
| Aries | Leo | Scorpio |
| Cancer | Libra | Taurus |
| Capricornus | Pisces | Virgo |

# Biblical Characters, Places And Terms

| | |
|---|---|
| Abraham | Joseph |
| Adam And Eve | Joshua |
| Ararat, Mount. | Judah |
| Armageddon | Messiah |
| Bethlehem | Moses |
| Cedars Of Lebanon | Nazareth, City Of |
| David, King | Noah |
| Eden, Garden Of | Noah's Ark |
| Galilee, Sea Of | Olives, Mount Of |
| Gethsemane, Garden Of | Pontius Pilate |
| Golden Rule | Prophet |
| David And Goliath | River Jordan, The |
| Herod, King | Samson And Delilah |
| Immaculate Conception | Solomon, King |
| Jerusalem | Ten Commandments, The |
| Jesus Christ | Tower Of Babel |
| Jonah | Virgin Mary |

# World Folklore And Legend: Stories Characters And Objects

| | |
|---|---|
| Androcles | Joan Of Arc |
| Billy The Kid | Johnny Appleseed |
| Blarney Stone, The | Kit Carson |
| Buffalo Bill | Lady Godiva |
| Damon And Pythias | Leprechaun |
| Daniel Boone | Miles Standish |
| Davy Crockett | Paul Bunyan |
| Don Juan | Pocahontus |
| El Cid | Romulus And Remus |
| Excaliber | Rubicon |
| Fountain Of Youth | Werewolf |
| Holy Grail | William Tell |

# World Literature:
# Characters And Stories

| | |
|---|---|
| Aesop's Fables | Jack The Giant Killer |
| Alice In Wonderland | King Arthur |
| Arabian Nights | Lochinvar |
| Alladin | Maid Marion |
| Ali Baba | Midsummer Night's Dream |
| Scheherazade | Mother Goose |
| Sinbad | Peter Pan |
| Canterbury Tales | Peter Rabbit |
| Cinderella | Rip Van Winkle |
| Don Quixote | Romeo And Juliet |
| Evangeline | Robin Hood |
| Gulliver's Travels | Sir Galahad |
| Hiawatha | Sir Lancelot |
| Iliad And Odessey | Snow White |

## Famous Painters Of The World

| | | |
|---|---|---|
| Cezanne | Michelangelo | Rockwell |
| Dali | Mondrian | Rubens |
| da Vinci | Monet | Toulouse-Lautrec |
| Degas | Picasso | VanDyke |
| El Greco | Raphael | van Gogh |
| Gauguin | Rembrant | Whistler |
| Matisse | Renoir | Wyeth |

## Famous Sculptors Of The World

| | | |
|---|---|---|
| Bernini | Giacometti | Picasso |
| Calder | Michelangelo | Rodin |
| da Vinci | | |

## Famous Writers And Poets Of The World

| | | |
|---|---|---|
| Aesop | Dostoevski, Fedor | Plato |
| Anderson, Hans C. | Eliot, T.S. | Poe, Edgar Allan |
| Aquinas, St. Thomas | Emerson, Ralph W. | Pope, Alexander |
| Aristotle | Faulkner, William | Sandburg, Carl |
| Balzac, Honore de | Frost, Robert | Shaw, George B. |
| Browning, E. B. | Hawthorne, Nathaniel | Shelly, Percy B. |
| Browning, Robert B. | Hemingway, Ernest | Socrates |
| Burns, Robert | Holmes, Oliver W. | Steinbeck, John |
| Byron, George, Lord | Homer | Tennyson, Alfred |
| Cervantes | Hugo, Victor | Thoreau, Henry D. |

## Famous Writers And Poets Of The World cont.

| | | |
|---|---|---|
| Chekhov, Anton | Joyce, James | Tolstoi, Leo |
| Cicero | Keats, John | Twain, Mark |
| Coleridge, Samuel T. | Kipling, Rudyard | Voltaire |
| Confucious | London, Jack | Whitman, Walt |
| Dante | Longfellow, Henry W. | Whittier, John G. |
| Dickens, Charles | Melville, Herman | Wolfe, Thomas |
| Dickenson, Emily | Milton, John | Wordsworth, William |
| Donne, John | Omar Khayyam | Yeats, William B. |

## Rulers Of The World

| | |
|---|---|
| Alexander The Great | Herod The Great |
| Antoinette, Marie | Isabella I, Queen |
| Antony, Mark | Ivan The Great |
| Attila The Hun | Kublai Khan |
| Augustus | Louis XIV, King |
| Caesar, Gaius Julius | Marcus Aurelius |
| Caligula | Mary Queen Of Scots |
| Charlemagne | Mohammed |
| Claudius | Montezuma |
| Cleopatra | Napoleon I |
| Constantine The Great | Nero |
| Cyrus The Great | Peter The Great |
| David, King | Solomon, King |
| Elizabeth I, Queen | Tamerlane |
| Elizabeth II, Queen | Tutankhamon |
| Ferdinand V, King | Victoria, Queen |
| Genghis Khan | William The Conqueror |
| Henry VIII, King | |

## Flowers Of The Earth

| | | |
|---|---|---|
| Acacia | Honeysuckle | Morning-Glory |
| African Violet | Hyacinth | Orchid |
| Aster | Hydrangea | Passion Flower |
| Azalea | Jasmine | Periwinkle |
| Baby's Breath | Larkspur | Petunia |
| Bachelor Button | Lilac | Poinsetta |
| Begonia | Lily | Poppy |
| Bluebell | Lily Of The Valley | Primrose |
| Buttercup | Lotus | Rhododendron |
| Camellia | Magnolia | Rose |
| Candytuft | Marigold | Shooting Star |
| Carnation | Mayflower | Snapdragon |
| Christmas Rose | Forget-Me-Not | Snowberry |

## Flowers Of The Earth cont.

| | | |
|---|---|---|
| Chrysanthemum | Forsythia | Strawflower |
| Crocus | Foxtail | Sunflower |
| Daffodil | Fushsia | Sweet Pea |
| Dahlia | Gardenia | Tulip |
| Daisy | Geranium | Viola |
| Dandelion | Gladiolus | Violet |
| Delphinium | Goldenrod | Water lily |
| Edelweiss | Heather | Wisteria |
| Fleur-De-Lis [Fr.] | Hibiscus | Zinnia |

## Fruits Of The Earth

| | | |
|---|---|---|
| Apple | Guava | Pear |
| Apricot | Honeydew | Persimmon |
| Avocado | Huckleberry | Pineapple |
| Banana | Kiwi | Plum |
| Blackberry | Kumquat | Pomegranate |
| Blueberry | Lemon | Prune |
| Cherry | Lime | Quince |
| Cranberry | Nectarine | Raspberry |
| Fig | Orange | Strawberry |
| Grape | Papaya | Tangerine |
| Grapefruit | Peach | Watermelon |

## Trees Of The Earth

| | | |
|---|---|---|
| Acacia | Elm | Orange |
| Alder | Eucalyptus | Palm |
| Almond | Fig | Papaya |
| Apple | Fir | Peach |
| Ash | Ginkgo | Pear |
| Aspen | Grapefruit | Pecan |
| Banyan | Juniper | Pine |
| Baobab | Kumquat | Pistachio |
| Bayberry | Laurel | Plum |
| Beech | Lemon | Poplar |
| Birch | Lime | Redwood |
| Camphor | Linden | Rosewood |
| Cedar | Locust | Sandalwood |
| Cherry | Magnolia | Sequoia |
| Chestnut | Mahogany | Spruce |
| Coconut | Maple | Sycamore |
| Cottonwood | Mountain Ash | Tangerine |
| Cypress | Mulberry | Teak |
| Dogwood | Oak | Walnut |
| Ebony | Olive | Willow |

# Gems Of The Earth

| | | |
|---|---|---|
| Agate | Emerald | Opal |
| Alexandrite | Fire Opal | Ruby |
| Amethyst | Garnet | Sapphire |
| Aquamarine | Jade | Star Sapphire |
| Black Opal | Lapis Lazuli | Topaz |
| Diamond | Onyx | Turquoise |

# Mammals Of The Earth

| | | |
|---|---|---|
| Antelope | Elk | Otter |
| Arctic Fox | Fox | Ox |
| Arctic Hare | Gazelle | Pack Rat |
| Badger | Giraffe | Panda |
| Bat | Goat | Panther |
| Bear | Gray Fox | Polar Bear |
| Beaver | Gray Wolf | Polecat |
| Bighorn Sheep | Grizzly Bear | Possum |
| Bison | Groundhog | Prairie Dog |
| Black Bear | Guinea Pig | Rabbit |
| Blue Fox | Hamster | Raccoon |
| Boar | Hare | Red Fox |
| Bobcat | Hippopotamus | Reindeer |
| Brown Bear | Horse | Rhinoceros |
| Buffalo | Jackrabbit | Sheep |
| Burro | Jaguar | Shrew |
| Camel | Kangaroo | Silver Fox |
| Cat | Koala | Squirrel |
| Cheetah | Leopard | Swamp Rabbit |
| Chinchilla | Lion | Tiger |
| Chipmunk | Llama | Tiger Cat |
| Cinnamon Bear | Lynx | Timber Wolf |
| Cottontail Rabbit | Meadow Mouse | Water Buffalo |
| Cougar | Mink | Weasel |
| Cow | Moose | Wild Boar |
| Coyote | Mountain Lion | Wildcat |
| Deer | Mouse | Wolf |
| Duckbill Platypus | Mule | Wolverine |
| Elephant | Muskrat | Zebra |

# Fishes Of The Sea

| | | |
|---|---|---|
| Albacore | Marlin | Sea Horse |
| Angel Fish | Minnow | Shark |
| Barracuda | Perch | Silver Salmon |
| Bass | Pike | Steelhead |
| Black Bass | Piranha | Sting Ray |

## Fishes Of The Sea cont.

| | | |
|---|---|---|
| Devil Fish | Rabbitfish | Striped Bass |
| Dragon Fish | Rainbow Trout | Sunfish |
| Eel | Roosterfish | Swordfish |
| Goldfish | Sailfish | Toadfish |
| Halibut | Salmon | Trout |
| Kingfish | Sea Bass | Tuna |

## Birds Of The Earth

| | | |
|---|---|---|
| American Eagle | Goldfinch | Pelican |
| Barn Swallow | Goose | Penguin |
| Bird Of Paradise | Hawk | Pheasant |
| Bluebird | Hermit Thrush | Pigeon |
| Blue Jay | Heron | Raven |
| Bobolink | Honker | Roadrunner |
| Bobwhite | Hoot Owl | Robin |
| Cardinal | Hummingbird | Sandpiper |
| Chickadee | Ibis | Sapsucker |
| Clif Swallow | Kingfisher | Seagull |
| Cockatoo | Lark | Snowbird |
| Condor | Loon | Sparrow |
| Coot | Lovebird | Stork |
| Crane | Meadow Lark | Swallow |
| Crow | Mockingbird | Swan |
| Cuckoo | Mourning Dove | Swift |
| Dodo | Mud Hen | Thrush |
| Dove | Myna Bird | Toucan |
| Duck | Nighthawk | Turkey |
| Eagle | Nightingale | Turtle Dove |
| Egret | Ostrich | Vulture |
| Falcon | Owl | Whippoorwill |
| Finch | Parakeet | Wood Duck |
| Flamingo | Parrot | Woodpecker |
| Golden Eagle | Partridge | Wren |

## Winds Of The Earth

| | | |
|---|---|---|
| Chinook | Simoom | Tradewind |
| Gale | Sirocco | Whirlwind |
| Monsoon | Tempest | Zephyr |

## Storms Of The Earth

| | | |
|---|---|---|
| Blizzard | Hurricane | Tornado |
| Cloudburst | Lightning Storm | Tropical Storm |
| Cyclone | Sandstorm | Typhoon |
| Dust Storm | Thunderstorm | Waterspout |

## Surface Features Of The Earth

| | | |
|---|---|---|
| Atoll | Desert | Mountain |
| Basin | Divide | Oasis |
| Butte | Dune | Plain |
| Canyon | Hill | Plateau |
| Cave | Mesa | Prairie |
| Crevasse | Moor | Swamp |
| Delta | Moraine | Valley |

## Mountains Of The Earth

| | |
|---|---|
| Allegheny Mountains | McKinley, Mount. |
| Alps, The | Olympic Mountains |
| Andes, The | Ozark Mountains |
| Appalachian Mountains | Parnassus, Mount. |
| Ararat, Mount. | Pike's Peak |
| Catskill Mountains | Pyrenees, The |
| Caucasus, The | Rainier, Mount. |
| Everest, Mount. | Rocky Mountains |
| Fujiyama, Mount. | Shasta, Mount. |
| Great Smokey Mountains | Sierra Madre Mountains |
| Himalayas, The | Sierra Nevadas, The |
| Hood, Mount. | Tetons, The |
| Kilimanjaro, Mount. | Whitney, Mount. |
| Matterhorn, The | Vesuvius, Mount. |

## Plains And Deserts Of The Earth

| | | |
|---|---|---|
| Gobi Desert | Moor, The | Sahara Desert |
| Kalahari Desert | Painted Desert | Serengeti, The |
| Mojave Desert | Prairie, The | Tundra, The |

## Lakes Of The Earth

| | | |
|---|---|---|
| Albert, Lake | Great Lakes, The | Ness, Loch |
| Caspian Sea | Great Salt Lake | Okeechobee, Lake |
| Champlain, Lake | Great Slave Lake | Oneida, Lake |

## Lakes Of The Earth cont.

Crater Lake
Dead Sea
Erie, Lake
Galilee, Sea Of
Geneva, Lake
George, Lake
Great Bear Lake

Huron, Lake
Lake Of The Woods
Lomond, Loch
Louise, Lake
Lucerne, Lake
Mead, Lake
Michigan, Lake

Ontario, Lake
Pontchartrain, Lake
Saint Clair, Lake
Salton Sea
Superior, Lake
Tahoe, Lake
Victoria, Lake

## Rivers Of The Earth

Alabama, The
Allegheny, The
Amazon, The
Arkansas, The
Avon, The
Colorado, The
Columbia, The
Congo, The
Danube, The
Delaware, The
Euphrates, The
Ganges, The
Hudson, The
Jordan, The River

Loire, The
Mississippi, The
Missouri, The
Monongahela, The
Niagra, The
Nile, The
Ohio, The
Pecos, The
Platte, The
Potomic, The
Red, The
Rhine, The
Rio Grande, The
Sacramento, The

Saint Lawrence, The
San Joaquin, The
Snake, The
Susquehanna, The
Tennessee, The
Thames, The
Tiber, The
Tigris, The
Ubangi, The
Volga, The
Wabash, The
Yangtze, The
Yukon, The
Zambezi, The

## Islands Of The Earth

Antilles, The
Azores, The
Bahamas, The
Barbados
Bermuda
Borneo
British Isles, The
Canary Islands, The
Capri
Catalina, Santa
Corsica
Crete
Cuba
Cyprus

Easter Island
Falkland Islands
Florida Keys, The
Galapagos Islands
Guam
Hawaiian Islands, The
Iceland
Indonesia
Jamaica
Java
Kodiak Island
Martinique
Midway
New Zealand

Philippines, The
Puerto Rico
Rhodes
Sardinia
Sicily
Singapore
Solomons, The
Sri Lanka
Sumatra
Tasmania
Tierra Del Fuego
Trinidad
Virgin Islands, The
Zanzibar

# Cities Of The World

Abadan, Iran
Abilene
Acapulco, Mexico
Adelaide, Australia
Agadir, Morocco
Akron
Alamogordo
Albany
Albuquerque
Amsterdam, Netherlands
Annapolis
Arlington
Athens, Greece
Atlanta
Austin
Baghdad, Iraq
Bakersfield
Bangor
Battle Creek
Beirut, Lebanon
Belfast, N. Ireland
Belgrade, Yugoslavia
Berkeley
Berlin, E/W Germany
Berne, Switzerland
Biloxi
Bismarck
Boise
Bologna, Italy
Bombay, India
Bonn, W. Germany
Bordeaux, France
Boston
Bowling Green
Brasilia, Brazil
Brussels, Belgium
Bucharest, Romania
Budapest, Hungary
Buenos Aires, Argentina
Buffalo
Butte
Cairo, Egypt
Calais, France
Calcutta, India
Calgary, Canada
Cambridge
Camden
Canberra, Australia

Duluth
Edmonton, Canada
Eugene
Evanston
Fargo
Fort Worth
Frankfurt, W. Germany
Freeport, Bahamas
Fresno
Galveston
Gdansk, Poland
Geneva, Switzerland
Genoa, Italy
Glasgow, Scotland
Glendale
Gloucester
Halifax, Canada
Hamburg, W. Germany
Hanoi, Viet Nam
Harrisburg
Hartford
Havana, Cuba
Helena
Helsinki, Finland
Honolulu
Houston
Indianapolis
Isfahan, Iran
Jackson
Jerusalem
Juneau
Kansas City
Knoxville
Kochi, Japan
Lahore, Pakistan
Lansing
La Paz, Bolivia
Laredo
Las Vegas
Leipzig, E. Germany
Leningrad, U.S.S.R.
Lima, Peru
Lisbon, Portugal
Little Rock
Liverpool, England
London, England
Los Angeles
Lucerne, Switzerland

Nassau, Bahamas
Newark
New Delhi, India
New Orleans
New York
Nuremburg, W. Germany
Oakland
Oklahoma City
Omaha
Orlando
Ottawa, Canada
Palermo, Sicily
Paris, France
Pasadena
Peking, China
Phoenix
Pittsburgh
Portland
Providence
Raleigh
Rangoon, Burma
Reno
Reykjavik, Iceland
Richmond
Rio De Janeiro, Brazil
Rome, Italy
Sacramento
Saint Louis
Salt Lake City
San Salvador, El Salvador
San Diego
San Francisco
San Jose
Santiago, Chile
Santo Domingo, Dom. Rep.
Sao Paulo, Brazil
Sapporo, Japan
Saskatoon, Canada
Seattle
Singapore, Malaysia
Sioux Falls
Sofia, Bulgaria
Sydney, Australia
Taipei, Taiwan
Tallahassee
Tampa
Tashkent, U.S.S.R.
Tehran, Iran

# Cities Of The World cont.

| | | |
|---|---|---|
| Canton, China | Lyon, France | Tel Aviv, Israel |
| Capetown, S. Africa | Madison | Tijuana, Mexico |
| Caracas, Venezuela | Madrid, Spain | Tokyo, Japan |
| Carmel | Malaga, Spain | Toledo |
| Carson City | Manilla, Philippines | Topeka |
| Casablanca, Morocco | Marseilles, France | Toronto, Canada |
| Casper | Mazatlan, Mexico | Trieste, Italy |
| Charleston | Melbourne, Australia | Tripoli, Libya |
| Charlotte | Memphis | Troy |
| Cheyenne | Mexico City, Mexico | Tunis, Tunisia |
| Chicago | Miami | Vancouver, Canada |
| ChristChurch, N. Zealand | Milan, Italy | Venice, Italy |
| Cleveland | Milwaukee | Versailles, France |
| Columbia | Minneapolis | Vienna, Austria |
| Columbus | Monterrey | Vladivostok, U.S.S.R. |
| Concord | Montevideo, Uruguay | Warsaw, Poland |
| Copenhagen, Denmark | Montgomery | Washington |
| Dallas | Montpelier | Wichita |
| Dayton | Montreal, Canada | Winnipeg, Canada |
| Denver | Moscow, U.S.S.R. | Wilmington |
| Des Moines | Nagasaki, Japan | Yerevan, Armenia |
| Dresden, E. Germany | Nanking, China | Zagreb, Yugoslavia |
| Dublin, Ireland | Naples, Italy | Zurich, Switzerland |

APPENDIX E / **RHYMING WORDS**

The following *Rhyming Dictionary* contains over 3,500 words which have been compiled to assist you in the writing of rhymed poetic verse. More than 150 *Key Words* are listed alphabetically and identified as to their part(s) of speech. These words head the various rhyming lists:

**MIND** [noun]

| | | | | |
|---|---|---|---|---|
| bind | kind | behind | unbind | confined |
| blind | rind | mankind | unkind | refined |
| find | wind | remind | | |
| grind | | | | |

## Rhyming Dictionary Procedure

1. Take the word which is to be rhymed and look it up in the Rhyming Dictionary.

2. If it is listed as a Key Word, it will be followed by a rhyming list which you can then use.

3. If your word cannot be found alphabetically, use the *Index Of Vowel Sounds* to determine if it has been included in the Rhyming Dictionary.

## Index Procedure

1. Determine the word's final vowel sound and any consonant sound(s) which may follow:

DOCK————————OCK

2. Check the Index Of Vowel Sounds to see if this ending is present.

3. If you find the ending, you will be referred to the *Key Word* which corresponds to it:

OCK.......(Talk)

4. When you locate the Key Word in the dictionary, you will find its rhyming list which you can then use:

**TALK** [noun/verb]

| | | | | |
|---|---|---|---|---|
| block | hock | rock | stalk | unlock |
| clock | knock | shock | stock | |
| **dock** | lock | sock | walk | |
| flock | mock | | | |

A Rhyming Dictionary such as the one found in this Appendix is a valuable tool which can make the writing of love poems and even love songs less tedious and more enjoyable.

# INDEX OF VOWEL SOUNDS
## FOR
## KEY RHYMING WORDS

**A**

**ā (ate)**

āce......(Face)
āde......(Fade)
āint.....(Saint)
āke......(Ache)
āil......(Fail)
āim......(Flame)
āne......(Pain)
ānge.....(Change)
āte......(Mate)
ātion....(Nation)
āve......(Crave)
āy.......(Day)
āze......(Gaze)

**ă (cat)**

ăck......(Back)
ăct......(Attract)
ăd.......(Sad)
ăn.......(Man)
ănce......(Dance)
ănd.......(Hand)
ănk.......(Thank)
ănt.......(Enchant)
ăp........(Trap)
ăsh.......(Clash)
ăss.......(Class)
ăst.......(Past)
ătch......(Catch)

**ä (art)**

ärd......(Hard)
äre......(Star)
ärk......(Spark)
ärm......(Arm)
ärt......(Heart)

**E**

**ēē (me)**

ēē........(Me)
ēēce......(Peace)
ēēch......(Reach)
ēēd.......(Need)
ēēf.......(Thief)
ēēk.......(Cheek)
ēēl.......(Feel)
ēēld......(Yield)
ēēm.......(Dream)
ēēn.......(Queen)
ēēng......(Spring)
ēēngle....(Tingle)
ēēnk......(Drink)
ēēp.......(Deep)
ēēr.......(Ear)
ēēz.......(Please)
ēēt.......(Feet)
ēēv.......(Grieve)

**ĕ (met)**

ĕck.......(Neck)
ĕct.......(Respect)

**ĕ (met) cont.**

ĕction...(Affection)
ĕd.......(Head)
ĕll......(Dwell)
ĕlt......(Melt)
ĕlth.....(Health)
ĕmpt.....(Tempt)
ĕn.......(Yen)
ĕnch.....(Quench)
ĕnd......(Friend)
ĕnder....(Tender)
ĕnce.....(Sense)
ĕnshen...(Tension)
ĕnt......(Scent)
ĕpt......(Accept)
ĕshen....(Freshen)
ĕss......(Caress)
ĕst......(Chest)
ĕt.......(Regret)
ĕver.....(Never)

**ē (father)**

ē-ēr.....(Rare)
ēss......(Ageless)

**I**

**ä + ēē (right)**

eye......(Cry)
ice......(Nice)
ide......(Bride)
ife......(Life)

**ä + ēē (right)** cont.

ike.......(Like)
ile.......(Smile)
ime.......(Time)
ine.......(Mine)
ined......(Mind)
ipe.......(Ripe)
ire.......(Desire)
ite.......(Light)
ive.......(Thrive)
ize.......(Prize)

**ĭ (it)**

ĭch.......(Rich)
ĭck.......(Music)
ĭd........(Splendid)
ĭft.......(Lift)
ĭll.......(Thrill)
ĭm........(Slim)
ĭn........(Skin)
ĭnce......(Prince)
ĭps.......(Lips)
ĭsh.......(Wish)
ĭshen.....(Mission)
ĭss.......(Kiss)
ĭst.......(Exist)
ĭt........(Spirit)
ĭv........(Live)

**O**

**ōō (food)**

ōō........(True)
ōōd.......(Mood)
ōōl.......(Cool)
ōōm.......(Groom)
ōōn.......(Moon)
ōōp.......(Scoop)
ōōse......(Seduce)

**ōō (food)** cont.

ōōth......(Truth)
ōōv.......(Move)
ōōz.......(Lose)

**oo (good)**

ood.......(Good)
ook.........(Look)
ool.......(Graceful)
oor.......(Lure)

**ō (home)**

ōde.......(Load)
ōh........(Glow)
ōke.......(Provoke)
ōld.......(Hold)
ōle.......(Soul)
ōme.......(Home)
ōpe.......(Hope)
ōr........(Soar)
ōrd.......(Lord)
ōrm.......(Warm)
ōrn......(Torn)
ōrt......(Consort)
ōse......(Nose)
ōte......(Float)
ōtion....(Potion)
ōwn......(Alone)

**ô (law)**

ô........(Flaw)
ôck......(Talk)
ôl.......(Call)
ôlve.....(Solve)
ôn.......(Dawn)
ônd......(Bond)
ông......(Strong)
ôp.......(Stop)
ôt.......(Sought)

**ô + ēē (boy)**

oil.......(Boil)
oy........(Joy)
oyce.....(Voice)

**ä + ōō (out)**

ound......(Sound)
our.......(Flower)
out.......(Shout)
ow........(Brow)
owd.......(Proud)

**U**

**ēē + ōō (use)**

ure.......(Pure)
use.......(Abuse)
ute.......(Cute)

**ŭ (cut)**

ŭch.......(Touch)
ŭff.......(Tough)
ŭj........(Judge)
ŭm........(Glum)
ŭn........(Sun)
ŭsh.......(Blush)
ŭss.......(Us)
ŭst.......(Lust)
ŭt........(Cut)
ŭv........(Love)
ŭver......(Lover)

**û (hurt)**

ûr........(Stir)
ûrge......(Urge)
ûrl.......(Girl)
ûrn.......(Yearn)
ûrse......(Nurse)
ûrst......(Thirst)
ûrt.......(Hurt)

# RHYMING WORDS

## A

**ABUSE** [verb]

| | | | | |
|---|---|---|---|---|
| fuse | cues | accuse | effuse | debuts |
| muse | hues | amuse | excuse | imbues |
| use | news | bemuse | infuse | previews |
| | views | confuse | misuse | renews |
| | | diffuse | refuse | |
| | | disuse | transfuse | |

**ACCEPT** [verb]

| | | | | |
|---|---|---|---|---|
| crept | swept | stepped | adept | inept |
| kept | wept | | concept | unkept |
| slept | | | except | |

**ACHE** [noun/verb]

| | | | | |
|---|---|---|---|---|
| bake | lake | snake | awake | keepsake |
| brake | make | stake | foresake | mistake |
| break | quake | steak | daybreak | outbreak |
| cake | rake | take | heartache | partake |
| fake | shake | wake | heartbreak | retake |
| flake | slake | | intake | |

**AFFECTION** [noun]

| | | | | |
|---|---|---|---|---|
| flexion | collection | dejection | erection | perfection |
| lection | complexion | detection | infection | protection |
| section | confection | direction | injection | reflection |
| | connection | ejection | inspection | rejection |
| | correction | election | objection | selection |

**AGELESS** [adjective]

| | | | | |
|---|---|---|---|---|
| boundless | flawless | helpless | matchless | restless |
| ceaseless | friendless | lawless | peerless | spotless |
| endless | groundless | limitless | priceless | timeless |
| fearless | heartless | listless | quenchless | |

## ALONE [adjective/adverb]

| | | | | |
|---|---|---|---|---|
| bone | phone | blown | atone | intone |
| cone | prone | grown | condone | postpone |
| loan | stone | known | disown | unknown |
| lone | tone | shown | enthrone | |
| moan | throne | | | |
| own | zone | | | |

## ARM [noun/verb]

| | | | | |
|---|---|---|---|---|
| charm | harm | alarm | disarm | unharm |

## ATTRACT [verb]

| | | | | |
|---|---|---|---|---|
| act | backed | abstract | enact | attacked |
| fact | cracked | compact | exact | sidetracked |
| pact | lacked | contact | extract | unpacked |
| tact | packed | contract | impact | |
| | smacked | detract | intact | |
| | stacked | distract | | |

# B

## BACK [noun/verb]

| | | | | |
|---|---|---|---|---|
| black | pack | shack | snack | attack |
| crack | rack | slack | stack | setback |
| knack | sack | smack | track | unpack |
| lack | | | | |

## BLUSH [noun/verb]

| | | | | |
|---|---|---|---|---|
| brush | gush | mush | slush | underbrush |
| crush | hush | plush | thrush | |
| flush | lush | rush | | |

## BOIL [verb]

| | | | | |
|---|---|---|---|---|
| broil | oil | spoil | despoil | turmoil |
| coil | soil | toil | embroil | uncoil |
| foil | | | recoil | |

## BOND [noun]

| | | | | |
|---|---|---|---|---|
| blond | pond | wand | donned | beyond |
| fond | | | | respond |

## BRIDE [noun]

| | | | | |
|---|---|---|---|---|
| bide | ride | abide | divide | defied |
| chide | side | aside | inside | denied |
| glide | slide | beside | outside | implied |
| guide | stride | collide | provide | untied |
| hide | tide | confide | reside | untried |
| pride | wide | decide | subside | |

**BROW** [noun]

| | | | | |
|---|---|---|---|---|
| bow | plow | vow | allow | endow |
| how | though | wow | avow | somehow |
| now | | | | |

# C

**CALL** [noun/verb]

| | | | | |
|---|---|---|---|---|
| all | hall | small | appall | forestall |
| ball | haul | sprawl | befall | install |
| brawl | mall | stall | downfall | nightfall |
| crawl | maul | tall | enthrall | recall |
| fall | pall | wall | | |
| gall | scrawl | | | |

**CARESS** [noun/verb]

| | | | | |
|---|---|---|---|---|
| bless | address | excess | princess | suppress |
| dress | assess | express | profess | transgress |
| guess | confess | finesse | process | undress |
| less | depress | impress | recess | unless |
| mess | digress | obsess | regress | happiness |
| press | distress | oppress | repress | wilderness |
| stress | duress | possess | success | |
| yes | | | | |

**CATCH** [noun/verb]

| | | | | |
|---|---|---|---|---|
| batch | match | snatch | attach | mismatch |
| hatch | patch | thatch | detach | unlatch |
| latch | scratch | | dispatch | |

**CHANGE** [noun/verb]

| | | | | |
|---|---|---|---|---|
| grange | range | arrange | exchange | interchange |
| mange | strange | estrange | | rearrange |

**CHEEK** [noun]

| | | | | |
|---|---|---|---|---|
| chic | peak | sleek | streak | physique |
| creek | reek | sneak | weak | technique |
| leak | seek | speak | week | unique |
| meek | sheik | | | |

**CHEST** [noun]

| | | | | |
|---|---|---|---|---|
| best | abreast | greatest | blessed | distressed |
| breast | arrest | highest | guessed | expressed |
| crest | attest | invest | pressed | impressed |
| guest | contest | protest | stressed | obssessed |
| jest | conquest | request | addressed | posessed |
| nest | detest | suggest | assessed | recessed |
| quest | divest | unrest | confessed | repressed |
| rest | | | depressed | suppressed |

**CHEST** [noun] cont.

| | | | | |
|---|---|---|---|---|
| test | | | digressed | undressed |
| west | | | | |
| zest | | | | |

**CLASH** [noun/verb]

| | | | | |
|---|---|---|---|---|
| ash | crash | hash | sash | stash |
| bash | dash | lash | slash | thrash |
| brash | flash | mash | smash | trash |
| cash | gash | rash | splash | |

**CLASS** [noun/adjective]

| | | | | |
|---|---|---|---|---|
| ass | glass | mass | alas | surpass |
| brass | grass | pass | amass | trespass |
| gas | lass | | harass | |

**CONSORT** [noun/verb]

| | | | | |
|---|---|---|---|---|
| court | sport | deport | import | resort |
| short | thwart | distort | rapport | support |
| sort | | escort | report | transport |
| | | export | | |

**COOL** [adjective]

| | | | | |
|---|---|---|---|---|
| drool | pool | school | stool | overrule |
| fool | rule | spool | tool | ridicule |

**CRAVE** [verb]

| | | | | |
|---|---|---|---|---|
| brave | pave | shave | behave | enslave |
| cave | rave | slave | engrave | forgave |
| gave | save | wave | | |

**CRY** [noun/verb]

| | | | | |
|---|---|---|---|---|
| aye | ply | ally | alibi | mystify |
| buy | pry | apply | amplify | notify |
| by | rye | belie | beautify | nullify |
| die | shy | comply | butterfly | occupy |
| dry | sigh | defy | clarify | pacify |
| eye | sky | deny | crucify | purify |
| fly | sly | good-by | deify | qualify |
| fry | spry | hereby | dignify | rectify |
| guy | spy | imply | edify | sanctify |
| high | thigh | outcry | falsify | satisfy |
| I | thy | rely | fortify | signify |
| lie | tie | reply | glorify | simplify |
| my | try | supply | gratify | specify |
| nigh | vie | thereby | justify | terrify |
| nye | why | untie | magnify | testify |
| pie | fry | whereby | modify | unify |

**CUT** [noun/verb]

| | | | | |
|---|---|---|---|---|
| but | gut | nut | shut | shortcut |
| butt | hut | putt | smut | uncut |
| glut | jut | rut | strut | |

## CUTE [adjective]

| | | | | |
|---|---|---|---|---|
| boot | mute | acute | pollute | absolute |
| brute | root | astute | pursuit | execute |
| chute | route | commute | refute | institute |
| flute | shoot | compute | repute | persecute |
| fruit | suit | dilute | salute | resolute |
| loot | toot | dispute | uproot | |
| lute | | | | |

# D

## DANCE [noun/verb]

| | | | | |
|---|---|---|---|---|
| chance | stance | ants | advance | entrance |
| glance | trance | pants | enhance | romance |
| prance | | plants | expanse | |

## DAWN [noun]

| | | | | |
|---|---|---|---|---|
| brawn | fawn | pawn | begone | whereon |
| con | gone | spawn | hereon | upon |
| don | on | swan | thereon | |
| drawn | lawn | yawn | | |

## DAY [noun]

| | | | | |
|---|---|---|---|---|
| bay | ray | allay | highway | castaway |
| clay | say | astray | mainstay | disarray |
| fray | slay | away | portray | disobey |
| gay | sleigh | betray | obey | holiday |
| grey | spray | bouquet | okay | interplay |
| hay | stay | cafe | outweigh | matinée |
| lay | stray | convey | passé | negligée |
| lei | sway | decay | repay | protegé |
| may | they | delay | replay | resumé |
| pay | tray | display | risqué | runaway |
| play | way | foray | survey | |
| pray | weigh | gourmet | today | |
| prey | | | | |

## DEEP [noun/adjective]

| | | | | |
|---|---|---|---|---|
| cheap | keep | seep | steep | asleep |
| creep | leap | sheep | sweep | outsleep |
| heap | reap | sleep | weep | upkeep |

## DESIRE [noun/verb]

| | | | | |
|---|---|---|---|---|
| choir | briar | buyer | acquire | expire |
| dire | friar | crier | admire | inquire |
| fire | liar | drier | afire | inspire |
| hire | lyre | higher | aspire | require |
| ire | pyre | flier | attire | retire |
| mire | tyre | prior | conspire | sapphire |

**DESIRE** [noun/verb] cont.

| tire | | | enquire | wildfire |
| wire | | | entire | |

**DREAM** [noun/verb]

| beam | scheme | steam | daydream | moonbeam |
| cream | scream | stream | esteem | redeem |
| deem | seam | team | extreme | supreme |
| gleam | seem | theme | | |
| ream | | | | |

**DRINK** [noun/verb]

| blink | ink | mink | shrink | stink |
| brink | kink | pink | sink | think |
| clink | link | rink | slink | wink |

**DWELL** [verb]

| bell | hell | smell | befell | foretell |
| belle | jell | spell | compel | impel |
| cell | knell | swell | dispel | propel |
| dell | quell | tell | excell | rebel |
| ell | sell | well | expel | repel |
| fell | shell | yell | farewell | retell |

# E

**EAR** [noun]

| cheer | here | sphere | adhere | frontier |
| clear | near | steer | appear | revere |
| dear | rear | tear | career | severe |
| fear | sheer | we're | endear | sincere |
| gear | spear | year | | |
| hear | | | | |

**ENCHANT** [verb]

| ant | grant | rant | implant | transplant |
| aunt | pant | scant | supplant | |
| can't | plant | slant | | |
| chant | | | | |

**EXIST** [verb]

| fist | kissed | assist | insist | dismissed |
| list | missed | consist | persist | unkissed |
| mist | | enlist | resist | |
| twist | | | | |

# F

**FACE** [noun/verb]

| | | | | |
|---|---|---|---|---|
| ace | grace | race | disgrace | misplace |
| base | lace | space | displace | replace |
| brace | mace | trace | embrace | retrace |
| case | pace | vase | erase | unlace |
| chase | place | | | |

**FADE** [verb]

| | | | | |
|---|---|---|---|---|
| aid | laid | shade | afraid | invade |
| blade | made | spade | brocade | parade |
| braid | maid | suede | cascade | persuade |
| glade | paid | trade | charade | pervade |
| grade | raid | wade | degrade | repaid |
| jade | | | evade | unpaid |

**FAIL** [verb]

| | | | | |
|---|---|---|---|---|
| frail | nail | stale | assail | impale |
| gale | pail | tail | avail | inhale |
| grail | pale | tale | detail | prevail |
| hail | rail | they'll | entail | unveil |
| jail | sail | trail | exhale | |
| mail | sale | veil | | |
| male | scale | | | |

**FEEL** [noun/verb]

| | | | | |
|---|---|---|---|---|
| deal | keel | reel | steal | appeal |
| eel | kneel | seal | steel | conceal |
| heal | meal | she'll | we'll | reveal |
| he'll | peel | squeal | zeal | unreal |

**FEET** [noun]

| | | | | |
|---|---|---|---|---|
| beat | heat | sheet | compete | discrete |
| cheat | meat | sleet | complete | elite |
| cleat | meet | street | conceit | entreat |
| eat | mete | suite | deceit | mistreat |
| feat | neat | sweet | defeat | receipt |
| fleet | peat | treat | delete | repeat |
| greet | seat | wheat | deplete | retreat |

**FLAME** [noun]

| | | | | |
|---|---|---|---|---|
| aim | frame | name | acclaim | exclaim |
| came | game | same | aflame | inflame |
| claim | lame | shame | ashame | proclaim |
| fame | maim | tame | disclaim | reclaim |

**FLAW** [noun]

| | | | | |
|---|---|---|---|---|
| awe | jaw | saw | foresaw | seesaw |
| claw | law | squaw | in-law | withdraw |
| craw | paw | straw | outlaw | |
| draw | raw | thaw | | |

**FLOAT** [noun/verb]

| | | | | |
|---|---|---|---|---|
| bloat | dote | oat | throat | afloat |
| boat | goat | quote | tote | denote |
| coat | gloat | rote | vote | promote |
| cote | note | smote | wrote | remote |

**FLOWER** [noun/verb]

| | | | | |
|---|---|---|---|---|
| cower | our | scour | sour | devour |
| flour | power | shower | tower | empower |
| hour | | | | |

**FRESHEN** [verb]

| | | | | |
|---|---|---|---|---|
| session | aggression | depression | obsession | profession |
| | compression | digression | oppression | progression |
| | concession | expression | possession | recession |
| | confession | impression | procession | succession |

**FRIEND** [noun]

| | | | | |
|---|---|---|---|---|
| bend | mend | ascend | defend | intend |
| blend | send | attend | depend | offend |
| end | spend | befriend | descend | pretend |
| fend | tend | commend | expend | suspend |
| lend | trend | contend | extend | transcend |

# G

**GAZE** [noun/verb]

| | | | | |
|---|---|---|---|---|
| blaze | maze | days | ablaze | betrays |
| daze | phase | leis | amaze | conveys |
| faze | phrase | plays | appraise | delays |
| glaze | praise | rays | | outweighs |
| graze | raise | sprays | | pathways |
| haze | vase | ways | | repays |

**GIRL** [noun]

| | | | | |
|---|---|---|---|---|
| burl | earl | pearl | twirl | uncurl |
| curl | hurl | swirl | whirl | unfurl |

**GLOW** [noun/verb]

| | | | | |
|---|---|---|---|---|
| beau | low | snow | aglow | forego |
| blow | no | so | although | macho |
| bow | owe | sow | below | 'morrow |
| foe | pro | stow | bestow | outgrow |
| flow | row | throw | borrow | photo |
| go | sew | toe | follow | rainbow |
| grow | show | tow | | |
| know | slow | woe | | |

**GLUM** [adjective]

| bum | hum | slum | become | minimum |
|-----|-----|------|--------|---------|
| chum | numb | some | blossom | overcome |
| come | plum | strum | handsome | premium |
| drum | rum | sum | lonesome | |
| dumb | scum | thumb | winsome | |

**GOOD** [noun/adjective/adverb]

| could | should | wood | withstood | understood |
|-------|--------|------|-----------|------------|
| hood | stood | would | | |

**GRACEFUL** [adjective]

| bull | aweful | faithful | lustful | skillful |
|------|--------|----------|---------|----------|
| full | blissful | fearful | mournful | tactful |
| pull | boastful | fistful | mouthful | tearful |
| wool | cheerful | helpful | peaceful | wishful |
| | doubtful | joyful | restful | wistful |
| | earful | lawful | scournful | woeful |

**GROOM** [noun/verb]

| bloom | gloom | room | assume | heirloom |
|-------|-------|------|--------|----------|
| boom | groom | tomb | consume | perfume |
| doom | loom | whom | costume | presume |
| fume | plume | womb | exhume | resume |

**GRIEVE** [verb]

| eave | sleeve | achieve | deceive | relieve |
|------|--------|---------|---------|---------|
| eve | weave | believe | naive | reprieve |
| heave | we've | bereave | perceive | retrieve |
| leave | vive | conceive | receive | unweave |

# H

**HAND** [noun]

| and | land | banned | command | firsthand |
|-----|------|--------|---------|-----------|
| band | sand | planned | demand | unhand |
| bland | stand | tanned | expand | withstand |
| brand | strand | | | |
| grand | | | | |

**HARD** [adjective/adverb]

| bard | lard | barred | bombard | disregard |
|------|------|--------|---------|-----------|
| card | shard | jarred | discard | boulevard |
| guard | yard | marred | regard | |
| | | scarred | retard | |

**HEAD** [noun/adjective/verb]

| bed | lead | shred | ahead | misled |
|-----|------|-------|-------|--------|
| bread | led | sled | embed | unsaid |
| bred | read | spread | imbed | unwed |

**HEAD** [noun/adjective/verb] cont.

| | | | | |
|---|---|---|---|---|
| dead | red | thread | instead | well-bred |
| dread | said | tread | | |
| fed | shed | wed | | |
| fled | | | | |

**HEALTH** [noun]

| | |
|---|---|
| stealth | wealth |

**HEART** [noun]

| | | | | |
|---|---|---|---|---|
| art | dart | start | apart | restart |
| cart | part | tart | depart | sweetheart |
| chart | smart | | impart | |

**HOLD** [noun/verb]

| | | | | |
|---|---|---|---|---|
| bold | old | behold | unfold | consoled |
| cold | scold | blindfold | untold | controlled |
| fold | sold | enfold | uphold | enrolled |
| gold | told | foretold | withhold | unrolled |

**HOME** [noun]

| | | | | |
|---|---|---|---|---|
| brome | dome | loam | afoam | monochrome |
| chrome | foam | roam | | polychrome |
| comb | gnome | | | |

**HOPE** [noun/verb]

| | | | | |
|---|---|---|---|---|
| cope | grope | rope | slope | elope |
| dope | mope | scope | soap | tightrope |

**HURT** [noun/verb]

| | | | | |
|---|---|---|---|---|
| dirt | shirt | assert | convert | expert |
| flirt | skirt | avert | desert | insert |
| pert | squirt | comfort | divert | revert |
| | | concert | exert | unhurt |

# I - K

**JOY** [noun]

| | | | | |
|---|---|---|---|---|
| boy | ploy | annoy | deploy | employ |
| coy | toy | decoy | destroy | enjoy |

**JUDGE** [noun/verb]

| | | | | |
|---|---|---|---|---|
| budge | grudge | smudge | begrudge | prejudge |
| drudge | nudge | trudge | forejudge | rejudge |
| fudge | sludge | | misjudge | |

**KISS** [noun/verb]

| | | | | |
|---|---|---|---|---|
| bliss | miss | abyss | dismiss | promise |
| hiss | this | amiss | premise | remiss |

# L

**LIFE** [noun]

| | | | |
|---|---|---|---|
| knife | rife | strife | wife |

**LIFT** [noun/verb]

| | | | |
|---|---|---|---|
| drift | rift | sift | thrift | adrift |
| gift | shift | swift | | uplift |

**LIGHT** [noun/verb]

| | | | | |
|---|---|---|---|---|
| bite | knight | sight | delight | moonlight |
| bright | might | site | despite | polite |
| cite | night | slight | excite | relight |
| fight | plight | spite | ignite | starlight |
| flight | quite | tight | incite | tonight |
| fright | right | white | invite | unite |
| height | rite | write | midnight | |

**LIKE** [verb]

| | | | | |
|---|---|---|---|---|
| bike | pike | strike | alike | unlike |
| hike | spike | tyke | dislike | |

**LIPS** [noun]

| | | | | |
|---|---|---|---|---|
| chips | grips | ships | strips | fingertips |
| clips | hips | sips | tips | |
| dips | nips | skips | trips | |
| drips | quips | slips | whips | |
| flips | rips | snips | zips | |

**LIVE** [verb]

| | | | | |
|---|---|---|---|---|
| give | active | misgive | fugitive | relative |
| sieve | festive | native | positive | sensitive |
| | forgive | outlive | | |

**LOAD** [noun/verb]

| | | | | |
|---|---|---|---|---|
| code | road | flowed | showed | abode |
| lode | rode | glowed | snowed | corrode |
| mode | strode | owed | stowed | erode |
| node | toad | sewed | towed | explode |
| ode | | | | unload |

**LOOK** [verb]

| | | | | |
|---|---|---|---|---|
| book | hook | shook | mistook | overlook |
| brook | nook | took | outlook | overtook |
| cook | rook | | partook | undertook |
| crook | | | unhook | |

**LORD** [noun/verb]

| | | | | |
|---|---|---|---|---|
| chord | hoard | aboard | afford | reward |
| board | sword | accord | discord | |
| bored | | | | |

**LOSE** [verb]

| | | | | |
|---|---|---|---|---|
| booze | ooze | blues | enthuse | construes |
| bruise | ruse | dues | peruse | ensues |
| choose | snooze | shoes | | persues |
| cruise | whose | who's | | subdues |

**LOVE** [noun/verb]

| | | | | |
|---|---|---|---|---|
| dove | glove | of | shove | above |

**LOVER** [noun]

| | | | | |
|---|---|---|---|---|
| cover | hover | discover | recover | uncover |

**LURE** [noun/verb]

| | | | | |
|---|---|---|---|---|
| boor | poor | allure | contour | insure |
| doer | sure | amour | endure | mature |
| moor | tour | assure | ensure | unsure |

**LUST** [noun/verb]

| | | | | |
|---|---|---|---|---|
| bust | must | bussed | adjust | mistrust |
| crust | rust | cussed | august | robust |
| dust | thrust | fussed | disgust | stardust |
| gust | trust | mussed | distrust | unjust |
| just | | trussed | entrust | |

# M

**MAN** [noun]

| | | | | |
|---|---|---|---|---|
| an | pan | span | began | caravan |
| ban | plan | tan | outran | overran |
| can | ran | than | suntan | superman |
| clan | scan | van | | |
| fan | | | | |

**MATE** [noun/verb]

| | | | | |
|---|---|---|---|---|
| ate | plate | abate | captivate | saturate |
| bait | rate | await | celebrate | separate |
| date | state | create | cultivate | stimulate |
| fate | straight | debate | dedicate | terminate |
| gate | trait | inflate | fascinate | titillate |
| great | wait | locate | generate | tolerate |
| hate | weight | playmate | permeate | violate |
| late | | relate | radiate | |

**ME** [pronoun]

| | | | | |
|---|---|---|---|---|
| be | agree | happy | saintly | agony |
| bee | balmy | hardy | sassy | disagree |
| fee | beauty | hearty | sexy | ecstacy |
| flea | body | highly | shaky | guarantee |
| flee | city | honey | shapely | honesty |
| free | classy | hungry | silky | poetry |

**ME** [pronoun] cont.

| | | | | |
|---|---|---|---|---|
| glee | cuddly | hurry | slinky | purity |
| he | curvy | lively | spicy | recipe |
| key | cutie | lofty | stately | |
| knee | dainty | lonely | steady | |
| pea | duty | lovely | stormy | |
| plea | deadly | madly | sunny | |
| sea | degree | marry | surely | |
| see | dreamy | merry | sweetie | |
| she | empty | mighty | tingly | |
| ski | fancy | money | trophy | |
| spree | flighty | only | valley | |
| tea | frenzy | pretty | wary | |
| thee | friendly | purely | weary | |
| three | greedy | ready | witty | |
| tree | guilty | risky | worry | |
| we | handy | rosy | zesty | |

**MELT** [verb]

| | | | | |
|---|---|---|---|---|
| belt | dwelt | knelt | pelt | svelte |
| dealt | felt | melt | smelt | welt |

**MIND** [noun/verb]

| | | | | |
|---|---|---|---|---|
| bind | kind | behind | unbind | confined |
| blind | rind | mankind | unkind | refined |
| find | wind | remind | | |

**MINE** [pronoun/noun/verb]

| | | | | |
|---|---|---|---|---|
| dine | sign | align | divine | Valentine |
| fine | spine | combine | entwine | |
| line | thine | confine | malign | |
| nine | twine | consign | outline | |
| pine | vine | decline | outshine | |
| shine | whine | define | refine | |
| shrine | wine | design | resign | |

**MISSION** [noun]

| | | | | |
|---|---|---|---|---|
| addition | edition | position | composition | opposition |
| admission | magician | submission | competition | proposition |
| ambition | musician | suspicion | definition | recognition |
| audition | omission | tactician | disposition | repetition |
| commission | partition | tradition | intuition | |
| condition | permission | transition | | |

**MOOD** [noun]

| | | | | |
|---|---|---|---|---|
| brood | brewed | allude | illude | attitude |
| crude | chewed | conclude | include | fortitude |
| dude | glued | delude | intrude | gratitude |
| food | screwed | denude | preclude | interlude |
| lewd | shrewd | elude | prelude | solitude |
| nude | stewed | exclude | protrude | multitude |
| prude | sued | extrude | seclude | magnitude |
| rude | wooed | exude | | |

**MOON** [noun]

| June | noon | swoon | attune | lagoon |
|------|------|-------|--------|--------|
| Loon | soon | tune | balloon | maroon |

**MOVE** [noun/verb]

| groove | you've | approve | disprove | remove |
|--------|--------|---------|----------|--------|
| prove | | behoove | improve | |

**MUSIC** [noun]

| brick | quick | cosmic | artistic | optimistic |
|-------|-------|--------|----------|------------|
| chick | sick | critic | erotic | pessimistic |
| click | slick | frantic | exotic | realistic |
| flick | stick | heartsick | hypnotic | |
| kick | thick | homesick | neurotic | |
| lick | tic | lipstick | prolific | |
| nick | trick | lovesick | simplistic | |
| pick | wick | mystic | terrific | |

# N

**NATION** [noun]

| citation | notation | accusation | correlation | irritation |
|----------|----------|------------|-------------|------------|
| creation | ovation | admiration | declaration | isolation |
| deflation | probation | adoration | dedication | jubilation |
| donation | pulsation | affirmation | desolation | meditation |
| duration | quotation | agitation | desperation | occupation |
| elation | relation | aggravation | destination | presentation |
| equation | rotation | allegation | excitation | provocation |
| fixation | salvation | alteration | expectation | recreation |
| flirtation | sensation | celebration | explanation | reputation |
| formation | taxation | circulation | exploitation | revelation |
| foundation | temptation | combination | fabrication | separation |
| inflation | translation | consolation | fascination | stimulation |
| location | vacation | consultation | generation | titillation |
| migration | vexation | conversation | innovation | variation |
| mutation | vibration | convocation | inspiration | violation |

**NECK** [noun/verb]

| beck | deck | peck | trek | henpeck |
|------|------|------|------|---------|
| check | fleck | speck | wreck | recheck |

**NEED** [noun/verb]

| bleed | heed | concede | misread | married |
|-------|------|---------|---------|---------|
| breed | lead | exceed | proceed | frenzied |
| deed | plead | impede | recede | |
| feed | read | indeed | succeed | |
| greed | speed | | | |

**NEVER** [adverb]

| | | | | |
|---|---|---|---|---|
| clever | endeavor | whatever | wherever | unsever |
| ever | however | whenever | whoever | whichever |

**NICE** [adjective]

| | | | | |
|---|---|---|---|---|
| dice | spice | advice | entice | paradise |
| ice | twice | concise | precise | sacrifice |
| price | vise | device | suffice | |
| slice | vice | | | |

**NOSE** [noun/verb]

| | | | | |
|---|---|---|---|---|
| chose | blows | arose | impose | bestows |
| clothes | flows | compose | inclose | foregoes |
| doze | foes | depose | oppose | hellos |
| froze | glows | disclose | propose | outgrows |
| pose | goes | dispose | repose | photos |
| prose | knows | enclose | suppose | plateaus |
| Rose | toes | expose | transpose | |
| those | woes | foreclose | Wild Rose | |

**NURSE** [noun/verb]

| | | | | |
|---|---|---|---|---|
| curse | verse | adverse | diverse | perverse |
| purse | worse | coerce | immerse | rehearse |
| terse | | converse | inverse | reverse |

# O - P

**PAIN** [noun]

| | | | | |
|---|---|---|---|---|
| bane | lane | slain | abstain | maintain |
| brain | main | sprain | again | obtain |
| cane | mane | stain | attain | refrain |
| chain | pane | strain | complain | regain |
| crane | plain | train | contain | remain |
| drain | plane | twain | detain | restrain |
| feign | rain | vain | domain | retain |
| gain | reign | vane | explain | sustain |
| grain | sane | vein | insane | unchain |

**PAST** [noun/adjective/preposition]

| | | | | |
|---|---|---|---|---|
| blast | last | passed | contrast | surpassed |
| cast | mast | | downcast | |
| fast | vast | | outlast | |

**PEACE** [noun]

| | | | | |
|---|---|---|---|---|
| cease | geese | neice | decrease | masterpiece |
| crease | grease | piece | increase | |
| fleece | lease | | release | |

**PLEASE** [verb]

| | | | | |
|---|---|---|---|---|
| breeze | squeeze | keys | appease | agrees |
| ease | tease | knees | disease | decrees |
| freeze | these | pleas | displease | degrees |
| seize | | seas | unease | foresees |

**POTION** [noun]

| | | | | |
|---|---|---|---|---|
| lotion | notion | devotion | emotion | promotion |
| motion | ocean | commotion | | |

**PRINCE** [noun]

| | | | |
|---|---|---|---|
| mince | rinse | since | wince |

**PRIZE** [noun/verb]

| | | | | |
|---|---|---|---|---|
| rise | cries | advise | applies | agonize |
| size | dies | arise | complies | compromise |
| wise | eyes | comprise | defies | criticize |
| | guys | devise | denies | harmonize |
| | lies | disguise | good-byes | hypnotize |
| | sighs | revise | implies | idolize |
| | skies | sunrise | outcries | realize |
| | ties | surmise | relies | recognize |
| | tries | surprise | replies | tantalize |
| | vies | unwise | unties | tranquilize |

**PROUD** [adjective]

| | | | | |
|---|---|---|---|---|
| cloud | loud | bowed | aloud | allowed |
| crowd | shroud | vowed | enshroud | endowed |

**PROVOKE** [verb]

| | | | | |
|---|---|---|---|---|
| bloke | croak | smoke | stroke | awoke |
| broke | folk | soak | woke | bespoke |
| choke | joke | spoke | yoke | evoke |
| cloak | oak | stoke | yolk | invoke |
| coke | poke | | | revoke |

**PURE** [adjective]

| | | | | |
|---|---|---|---|---|
| cure | newer | your | figure | procure |
| fewer | truer | you're | obscure | secure |

# Q

**QUEEN** [noun]

| | | | | |
|---|---|---|---|---|
| bean | green | screen | between | pristine |
| been | keen | seen | convene | routine |
| clean | lean | sheen | foreseen | serene |
| dean | mean | 'tween | obscene | unseen |
| glean | scene | wean | | |

**QUENCH** [verb]

| | | | | |
|---|---|---|---|---|
| bench | drench | wench | intrench | unclench |
| clench | trench | wrench | retrench | |

# R

**RARE** [adjective]

| | | | | |
|---|---|---|---|---|
| air | flair | snare | affair | anywhere |
| bare | flare | spare | aware | debonaire |
| bear | glare | stare | beware | millionaire |
| blare | hair | swear | compare | solitaire |
| care | heir | tear | declare | throroughfare |
| chair | lair | their | despair | unaware |
| dare | pair | there | ensnare | |
| ere | prayer | wear | prepare | |
| fair | scare | were | repair | |
| fare | share | where | unfair | |

**REACH** [noun/verb]

| | | | | |
|---|---|---|---|---|
| beach | breach | Peach | speech | beseech |
| bleach | each | screech | teach | impeach |

**REGRET** [noun/verb]

| | | | | |
|---|---|---|---|---|
| bet | let | sweat | asset | offset |
| debt | met | threat | beset | sunset |
| fret | net | wet | duet | upset |
| get | pet | yet | forget | |
| jet | set | | | |

**RESPECT** [noun/verb]

| | | | | |
|---|---|---|---|---|
| affect | defect | expect | object | select |
| collect | detect | infect | protect | subject |
| connect | direct | neglect | reflect | suspect |
| correct | effect | | | |

**RICH** [noun/adjective]

| | | | | |
|---|---|---|---|---|
| ditch | niche | switch | which | bewitch |
| hitch | pitch | twitch | witch | enrich |
| itch | stitch | | | |

**RIPE** [adjective]

| | | | | |
|---|---|---|---|---|
| gripe | snipe | swipe | wipe | unripe |
| pipe | stripe | type | | |

# S

## SAD [adjective]

| | | | | |
|---|---|---|---|---|
| ad | clad | grad | mad | comrade |
| add | Dad | had | pad | forbade |
| bad | fad | lad | plaid | unclad |
| cad | glad | | | |

## SAINT [noun/adjective]

| | | | |
|---|---|---|---|
| faint | paint | acquaint | constraint |
| feint | quaint | complaint | restraint |

## SCENT [noun/verb]

| | | | | |
|---|---|---|---|---|
| bent | advent | repent | argument | eminent |
| cent | assent | resent | compliment | evident |
| dent | augment | torment | confident | imminent |
| gent | cement | unspent | continent | innocent |
| meant | comment | ferment | diligent | sentiment |
| rent | consent | intent | element | turbulent |
| sent | content | invent | eloquent | violent |
| spent | dissent | lament | | |
| tent | event | prevent | | |
| went | extent | present | | |

## SCOOP [noun/verb]

| | | | | |
|---|---|---|---|---|
| coop | hoop | sloop | swoop | recoup |
| droop | loop | soup | troop | |
| group | poop | stoop | whoop | |

## SEDUCE [verb]

| | | | | |
|---|---|---|---|---|
| goose | loose | noose | truce | recluse |
| juice | Moose | Spruce | | unloose |

## SENSE [noun/verb]

| | | | | |
|---|---|---|---|---|
| cense | commence | incense | abstinence | excellence |
| dense | condense | intense | affluence | inference |
| fence | defense | nonsense | confidence | influence |
| hence | dispense | offence | consequence | innocence |
| tense | expense | pretence | difference | permanence |
| thence | immense | suspense | eloquence | preference |

## SHOUT [noun/verb]

| | | | | |
|---|---|---|---|---|
| bout | rout | sprout | about | throughout |
| clout | scout | stout | devout | without |
| doubt | snout | tout | knockout | |
| out | spout | Trout | | |

## SKIN [noun/verb]

| | | | | |
|---|---|---|---|---|
| chin | pin | begin | virgin | discipline |
| gin | sin | chagrin | wherein | genuine |
| grin | spin | herein | within | imagine |

**SKIN** [noun/verb] cont.

| | | | |
|---|---|---|---|
| in | thin | therein | violin |
| inn | twin | | |
| kin | win | | |

**SLIM** [adjective]

| | | | | |
|---|---|---|---|---|
| brim | gym | limb | shim | trim |
| dim | him | prim | skim | vim |
| grim | hymn | rim | swim | whim |

**SMILE** [noun/verb]

| | | | | |
|---|---|---|---|---|
| aisle | pile | awhile | fragile | reconcile |
| file | style | beguile | hostile | versatile |
| isle | while | compile | profile | worthwhile |
| mile | | defile | | |

**SOAR** [verb]

| | | | | |
|---|---|---|---|---|
| bore | more | score | adore | ignore |
| chore | nor | shore | ashore | implore |
| core | oar | store | before | restore |
| door | o'er | swore | deplore | uproar |
| floor | or | war | explore | |
| for | pour | yore | | |
| four | roar | | | |

**SOLVE** [verb]

| | | | | |
|---|---|---|---|---|
| dissolve | evolve | involve | resolve | revolve |

**SOUGHT** [verb past tense]

| | | | | |
|---|---|---|---|---|
| aught | nought | blot | not | a lot |
| bought | ought | cot | plot | besought |
| brought | taught | dot | shot | distraught |
| caught | taut | got | spot | forgot |
| fought | thought | hot | squat | jackpot |
| fraught | wrought | knot | tot | love knot |
| naught | | lot | what | snapshot |

**SOUL** [noun]

| | | | | |
|---|---|---|---|---|
| bowl | knoll | sole | console | parole |
| coal | mole | stole | control | patrol |
| dole | pole | stroll | enroll | unroll |
| droll | role | toll | inscroll | |
| foal | roll | troll | | |
| goal | scroll | whole | | |
| hole | | | | |

**SOUND** [noun/verb]

| | | | | |
|---|---|---|---|---|
| bound | mound | crowned | abound | confound |
| found | pound | drowned | around | profound |
| ground | round | frowned | astound | rebound |
| hound | wound | | compound | surround |

**SPARK** [noun/verb]

| | | | | |
|---|---|---|---|---|
| ark | dark | mark | shark | embark |
| bark | lark | park | stark | remark |

**SPIRIT** [noun/verb]

| | | | | |
|---|---|---|---|---|
| bit | lit | acquit | misfit | definite |
| fit | pit | admit | omit | exquisite |
| hit | quit | commit | outwit | favorite |
| it | sit | emit | permit | infinite |
| kit | split | forfeit | submit | inhabit |
| knit | wit | limit | unfit | opposite |

**SPLENDID** [adjective]

| | | | | |
|---|---|---|---|---|
| bid | mid | amid | placid | invalid |
| did | rid | candid | rigid | overbid |
| grid | skid | forbid | solid | pyramid |
| hid | slid | outbid | undid | underbid |
| kid | squid | outdid | vivid | |
| lid | | | | |

**SPRING** [noun/verb]

| | | | | |
|---|---|---|---|---|
| bring | aging | dreaming | luring | smiling |
| cling | aiding | drowning | lusting | soaring |
| fling | aiming | dulling | mailing | soothing |
| king | backing | earing | melting | spinning |
| ring | beaming | easing | merging | splurging |
| sing | bearing | ending | mounting | stinging |
| sling | being | fading | moving | striking |
| sting | bending | failing | nearing | stunning |
| string | blazing | fasting | outing | surging |
| swing | blending | fearing | packing | swaying |
| thing | bloating | feeling | panting | swelling |
| wing | bolting | filling | pausing | swinging |
| wring | bringing | flaming | playing | swirling |
| alarming | bulging | floating | pleasing | taunting |
| alluring | burning | freeing | pouting | teasing |
| assuring | calming | glancing | prancing | tempting |
| enduring | caring | gleaming | raging | telling |
| maturing | causing | gloating | raising | tending |
| obscuring | charming | glowing | ranting | thrilling |
| opening | chiming | growing | raving | throwing |
| procuring | clearing | harming | reeling | timing |
| reviving | climbing | haunting | rhyming | tingling |
| securing | clowning | heading | ringing | tolling |
| | craving | healing | rising | touting |
| | crowning | jarring | rolling | toting |
| | cunning | jingling | running | tracking |
| | curing | jolting | sailing | turning |
| | dancing | knowing | saying | twirling |
| | daring | lacking | seeing | wearing |
| | darling | lasting | selling | wedding |

**SPRING** [noun/verb] cont.

| | | | |
|---|---|---|---|
| dazzling | lending | sharing | winning |
| dealing | liking | shouting | wishing |
| doubting | longing | showing | whirling |
| doting | loving | singing | yearning |

**STAR** [noun/verb]

| | | | | |
|---|---|---|---|---|
| are | Czar | par | afar | memoir |
| bar | far | scar | ajar | thus far |
| car | jar | spar | boudoir | |
| char | mar | tar | | |

**STIR** [verb]

| | | | | |
|---|---|---|---|---|
| blur | clever | infer | river | deliver |
| burr | concur | leisure | shiver | minister |
| err | confer | manner | suitor | officer |
| fir | defer | measure | teaser | passenger |
| fur | deter | murmur | tempter | prisoner |
| her | dreamer | nature | tender | sinister |
| myrrh | eager | occur | torture | sorcerer |
| per | ferver | picture | transfer | sufferer |
| purr | giver | power | treasure | traveler |
| sir | glamour | prefer | tremor | visitor |
| slur | honor | quiver | vigor | voyager |
| spur | hunger | recur | whisper | wanderer |
| whir | incur | refer | | |

**STOP** [verb]

| | | | | |
|---|---|---|---|---|
| chop | flop | plop | slop | atop |
| cop | hop | pop | swap | eavesdrop |
| crop | lop | prop | top | tiptop |
| drop | mop | shop | | |

**STRONG** [adjective]

| | | | | |
|---|---|---|---|---|
| long | throng | along | headstrong | prolong |
| song | wrong | belong | lifelong | |

**SUN** [noun]

| | | | | |
|---|---|---|---|---|
| done | nun | shun | Sun | begun |
| fun | one | son | ton | outrun |
| gun | pun | spun | won | undone |
| none | run | stun | | woman |

# T

**TALK** [noun/verb]

| | | | | |
|---|---|---|---|---|
| block | hock | rock | stalk | unlock |
| clock | knock | shock | stock | |
| dock | lock | sock | walk | |
| flock | mock | | | |

**TEMPT** [verb]

| | | | | |
|---|---|---|---|---|
| dreamt | attempt | exempt | undreamt | unkempt |
| | contempt | pre-empt | | |

**TENDER** [adjective/verb]

| | | | | |
|---|---|---|---|---|
| fender | lender | sender | splendor | surrender |
| gender | render | slender | vendor | |

**TENSION** [noun]

| | | | | |
|---|---|---|---|---|
| mention | attention | detention | intention | prevention |
| pension | contention | dimension | invention | retention |
| | convention | extension | | |

**THANK** [verb]

| | | | | |
|---|---|---|---|---|
| bank | dank | rank | spank | tank |
| blank | frank | sank | swank | yank |
| crank | prank | shrank | | |

**THIEF** [noun]

| | | | | |
|---|---|---|---|---|
| beef | chief | leaf | reef | belief |
| brief | grief | sheaf | | relief |

**THIRST** [noun/verb]

| | | | | |
|---|---|---|---|---|
| burst | cursed | coerced | immersed | rehearsed |
| first | nursed | disbursed | outburst | reversed |
| worst | versed | dispursed | | |

**THRILL** [noun/verb]

| | | | | |
|---|---|---|---|---|
| bill | kill | spill | distill | refill |
| chill | mill | still | downhill | tranquil |
| drill | pill | till | fulfill | until |
| hill | quill | will | goodwill | uphill |
| ill | skill | | instill | virile |

**THRIVE** [verb]

| | | | | |
|---|---|---|---|---|
| dive | hive | alive | deprive | revive |
| drive | I've | arrive | derive | survive |
| five | live | | | |

**TIME** [noun/verb]

| | | | | |
|---|---|---|---|---|
| chime | dime | mime | lifetime | sometime |
| climb | I'm | prime | pastime | sublime |
| crime | lime | rhyme | | |

**TINGLE** [verb]

| | | | | |
|---|---|---|---|---|
| jingle | mingle | single | comingle | intermingle |

**TORN** [verb past tense]

| | | | | |
|---|---|---|---|---|
| born | mourn | thorn | adorn | love-lorn |
| horn | scorn | worn | forewarn | love-torn |
| morn | | | forlorn | unborn |

**TOUCH** [noun/verb]

| | | | | |
|---|---|---|---|---|
| clutch | crutch | hutch | much | such |

## TOUGH [noun/adjective/adverb]

| | | | | |
|---|---|---|---|---|
| bluff | fluff | puff | slough | enough |
| buff | gruff | rough | snuff | rebuff |
| cuff | huff | scruff | stuff | |
| duff | muff | scuff | | |

## TRAP [noun/verb]

| | | | | |
|---|---|---|---|---|
| cap | map | snap | entrap | handicap |
| chap | nap | strap | mishap | overlap |
| clap | rap | tap | unstrap | |
| flap | sap | trap | unwrap | |
| gap | scrap | wrap | | |
| lap | slap | | | |

## TRUE [adjective]

| | | | | |
|---|---|---|---|---|
| blew | few | spue | accrue | subdue |
| blue | flew | stew | adieu | taboo |
| brew | flue | sue | anew | tattoo |
| chew | glue | threw | askew | undo |
| clue | grew | through | canoe | undue |
| coo | hew | to | construe | unglue |
| coup | hue | too | debut | unscrew |
| crew | knew | two | ensue | untrue |
| cue | lieu | view | imbue | value |
| dew | new | who | outdo | virtue |
| do | pew | woo | pursue | withdrew |
| drew | shoe | you | renew | billet-doux |
| due | slew | zoo | review | rendezvous |

## TRUTH [noun]

| | | | | |
|---|---|---|---|---|
| sleuth | tooth | youth | uncouth | untruth |

# U

## URGE [noun/verb]

| | | | | |
|---|---|---|---|---|
| merge | scourge | surge | converge | emerge |
| purge | splurge | verge | diverge | submerge |

## US [pronoun]

| | | | | |
|---|---|---|---|---|
| fuss | anxious | amorous | glorious | calmness |
| muss | discuss | courteous | marvelous | coldness |
| plus | focus | curious | obvious | gladness |
| thus | gorgeous | chivalrous | perilous | madness |
| | gracious | dangerous | previous | mistress |
| | joyous | dubious | ravenous | sadness |
| | luscious | envious | sensuous | softness |
| | precious | fabulous | serious | toughness |
| | righteous | furious | treacherous | trueness |
| | wondrous | generous | various | weakness |

# V - Z

**VOICE** [noun/verb]

| | | |
|---|---|---|
| choice | invoice | rejoice |

**WARM** [adjective]

| | | | | |
|---|---|---|---|---|
| dorm | storm | conform | inform | reform |
| form | swarm | deform | perform | transform |
| norm | | | | |

**WISH** [noun/verb]

| | | | | |
|---|---|---|---|---|
| dish | anguish | hellish | admonish | feverish |
| fish | cherish | impish | devilish | |
| swish | flourish | | | |

**YEARN** [verb]

| | | | | |
|---|---|---|---|---|
| burn | fern | stern | concern | pattern |
| churn | learn | turn | discern | return |
| earn | spurn | urn | intern | stubborn |

**YEN** [verb]

| | | | | |
|---|---|---|---|---|
| den | men | ten | when | again |
| hen | pen | then | | |

**YIELD** [verb]

| | | | | |
|---|---|---|---|---|
| field | weald | healed | afield | concealed |
| shield | | sealed | | revealed |

# APPENDIX F / WORD LIST

The following list contains over 1,700 words which have been collected to help you increase your vocabulary and spelling ability. In so doing, you will be able to write love letters and love poems with greater confidence.

Each word is categorized as to its part of speech and listed in alphabetical order. Word meanings may be obtained from any dictionary.

## (Example)

### Nouns

| | | |
|---|---|---|
| Advantage | Ally | Argument |
| Adventure | Ambrosia | Arrangement |
| Advice | Animosity | Arrival |
| Affair | Anxiety | Arrogance |
| Affection | Apathy | Assistance |
| Agony | Apology | Attack |
| Agreement | Appeal | Attempt |
| Aim | Appearance | Attention |
| Alarm | Appreciation | Attire |
| Alien | Approval | Attitude |

# WORD LIST

## Nouns
(Words which are names of persons, animals, places or things)
May also refer to a state of mind
Example: Your *attitude* is excellent.

**A**

Advantage
Adventure
Advice
Affair
Affection
Agony
Agreement
Aim
Alarm
Alien
Ally
Ambrosia
Animosity
Anxiety
Apathy
Apology
Appeal
Appearance
Appreciation
Approval
Argument
Arrangement
Arrival
Arrogance
Assistance
Attack
Attempt
Attention
Attire

Attitude
Attraction
Attribute
Authority
Avalanche

**B**

Balance
Barrier
Beginning
Behavior
Blessing
Blindness
Bliss
Blow

**C**

Comfort
Compassion
Complaint
Compliment
Concern
Condition
Conduct
Confession
Confidant
Conflict
Confrontation
Confusion

Connection
Conscience
Consent
Consequence
Consideration
Contact
Contempt
Contention
Contentment
Contest
Contrast
Contribution
Conversation
Convert
Conviction
Cooperation
Correction
Corruption
Courage
Course
Courtesy
Criticism
Curiosity
Cycle

**D**

Debutante
Decency
Deception

Defense
Defiance
Deficiency
Dejection
Delusion
Demand
Demon
Denial
Dependence
Depth
Desolation
Destiny
Destruction
Detachment
Dictator
Difference
Dimension
Disability
Disadvantage
Disagreement
Disapproval
Disarray
Disaster
Disbelief
Discontent
Discord
Discrepancy
Discretion
Discrimination

**D** (cont.)

| | | | |
|---|---|---|---|
| Discussion | Eternity | Fiasco | Haste |
| Disgrace | Etiquette | Finesse | Hate |
| Disguise | Evidence | Finish | Haven |
| Disgust | Evil | Fixation | Headache |
| Dishonesty | Example | Flair | Health |
| Dishonor | Excellence | Flaw | Help |
| Dismay | Exception | Fling | Heredity |
| Disorder | Excitement | Foresight | Heritage |
| Displeasure | Excuse | Formality | Heroism |
| Disposition | Existence | Fortune | Hesitation |
| Disregard | Expectation | Fragrance | Highlight |
| Disrespect | Expense | Frailty | Hindsight |
| Distinction | Experience | Fraud | Home |
| Distortion | Experiment | Freedom | Homecoming |
| Distraction | Expert | Frequency | Honesty |
| Distress | Explosion | Friend | Honor |
| Diversion | Exposure | Frustration | Host |
| Dominance | Expression | Future | Hostess |
| Dream | Extension | | Hostility |
| Drifter | Extravagance | **G** | Humble |
| Duty | | Generation | Humor |
| | **F** | Genius | Hurdle |
| **E** | Façade | Gentleman | Hypocrite |
| Effort | Faith | Gift | Hysteria |
| Egomaniac | Fake | Glory | |
| Elite | Fame | Goal | **I** |
| Eloquence | Familiarity | Gossip | Ice |
| Emotion | Fantasy | Graduation | Idealism |
| Empathy | Fascination | Gratitude | Identity |
| Enchantment | Fashion | Greed | Ignorance |
| Encounter | Fatigue | Grief | Illness |
| Endurance | Fault | Grievance | Illusion |
| Energy | Favor | Guide | Imagination |
| Engagement | Fear | Guilt | Imbalance |
| Enigma | Feast | | Immorality |
| Enjoyment | Feedback | **H** | Immortality |
| Enthusiasm | Feeling | Habit | Impact |
| Environment | Festivity | Handicap | Impatience |
| Error | Feud | Hardship | Imperfection |
| Escort | Fever | Harm | Importance |
| Esteem | Fiancée | Harmony | Imperfection |

**I** (Cont.)

Importance
Imposition
Impostor
Impression
Improvement
Impulse
Inability
Inaction
Inadequacy
Inattention
Incapacity
Incentive
Incidence
Incident
Incompetence
Indecency
Indignation
Inequality
Inexperience
Infection
Infringement
Infusion
Ingenuity
Ingratitude
Injury
Injustice
Innuendo
Insanity
Insight
Insinuation
Instability
Instinct
Insult
Integrity
Intelligence
Intensity
Intent
Intention
Interaction
Interference
Interlude

Introduction
Intrusion
Intuition
Invasion
Invention
Invitation
Isolation

**J**

Jewel
Journey
Judge
Judgment
Justification

**K**

Key
Kindness
Knight
Knowledge

**L**

Lady
Legend
Liability
Limit
Limitation
Loneliness
Luxury

**M**

Mischief
Misconduct
Misdirection
Misery
Misfit
Misfortune
Misgiving
Mistake
Modesty
Moment

Momento
Mood
Morale
Morality
Motivation
Mourning
Mystery

**N**

Necessity
Neglect
Negligence
Neurotic
Nonsense
Nonviolence
Nourishment
Nurture

**O**

Obedience
Object
Objection
Objective
Obligation
Obscenity
Obscurity
Observation
Observer
Obsession
Obstacle
Obstruction
Occasion
Occurrence
Odyssey
Offense
Offer
Offering
Ogre
Oneness
Opening
Opportunity

Opposition
Oppression
Optimum
Option
Ordeal
Order
Origin
Originality
Outburst
Outcast
Outcome
Outlook
Outrage
Outside
Outsider
Oversight

**P**

Partner
Partnership
Past
Patience
Peace
Perception
Performance
Permission
Persecution
Perseverance
Persistence
Personality
Persuasion
Pessimism
Phase
Politician
Politics
Possession
Possibility
Poverty
Power
Praise
Prank

**P** (Cont.)

| P (Cont.) | Q | | S |
|---|---|---|---|
| Prayer | Quarrel | Requirement | Secrecy |
| Preconception | Question | Resemblance | Secret |
| Predicament | Quota | Resentment | Seduction |
| Prediction | Quotation | Resignation | Self-assurance |
| Preference | | Resilience | Self-conception |
| Prejudice | **R** | Resolution | Self-confidence |
| Premonition | Rarity | Resort | Self-defense |
| Preparation | Reaction | Response | Self-denial |
| Present | Reason | Responsibility | Self-destruction |
| Pressure | Reasoning | Result | Self-devotion |
| Prestige | Reassurance | Retirement | Self-discipline |
| Presumption | Recognition | Retreat | Self-doubt |
| Pretense | Reflection | Reunion | Self-image |
| Prevention | Refuge | Revelation | Self-improvement |
| Principle | Regression | Revenge | Self-perception |
| Priority | Regret | Reverence | Self-respect |
| Privacy | Rehabilitation | Reward | Self-restraint |
| Privilege | Reinvestment | Rift | Self-sacrifice |
| Probability | Rejection | Right | Sentiment |
| Proceeding | Rejoicing | Risk | Significance |
| Process | Relapse | Ritual | Situation |
| Proclamation | Relation | Rogue | Skill |
| Production | Relative | Routine | Slave |
| profanity | Relaxation | | Smile |
| Profession | Release | **S** | Soul-searching |
| Proficiency | Relevance | Saturation | Stability |
| Profit | Reliability | Savage | Stain |
| Progress | Reliance | Scandal | Stigma |
| Project | Relief | Scar | Strain |
| Property | Reluctance | Scarcity | Strength |
| Proposal | Remedy | Scenario | Strife |
| Proposition | Remembrance | Scene | Stupidity |
| Prosecution | Remorse | Scent | Subconscious |
| Prospect | Replacement | Scheme | Submission |
| Prosperity | Reply | School | Subsistence |
| Protection | Repression | Schooling | Success |
| Protest | Reprieve | Scolding | Suppression |
| Provision | Reprimand | Scorn | Surprise |
| Punishment | Reprisal | Scream | Survival |
| Purpose | Reputation | Search | Survivor |
| Pushover | Request | Season | Symptom |

## T

| | | | |
|---|---|---|---|
| Tactics | Timing | Trauma | |
| Talent | Tolerance | Treasure | |
| Temperance | Toleration | Treat | |
| Temptation | Tradition | Treatment | |
| Tendency | Tragedy | Trend | |
| Tension | Training | Tribute | |
| Thinking | Tranquilizer | | |
| Time | Transition | | |

## U

Ugliness
Uncertainty
Unity
Usefulness

## V-Z

Vanity
Violation
Violence

# WORD LIST

## Verbs
(Words that express acts, occurrences or states of being)
Example: I will *defend* you if need be.

**A**

Abandon
Abound
Abstain
Abuse
Accept
Access
Accompany
Accuse
Ache
Achieve
Acknowledge
Acquire
Act
Adapt
Adopt
Adjust
Admit
Advance
Advise
Affect
Affirm
Afford
Aggravate
Agitate
Agree
Appeal
Appear
Appreciate
Arrange

Assist
Assume
Assure
Attack
Attain
Attempt

**B**

Believe
Belittle
Betray
Brag
Brighten

**C**

Celebrate
Challenge
Command
Commend
Compete
Complain
Compliment
Concern
Conduct
Confess
Confide
Confirm
Conflict
Confuse

Connect
Consent
Consider
Console
Conspire
Consume
Contact
Contradict
Contrast
Contribute
Control
Converge
Convert
Convey
Convict
Convince
Cooperate
Correct
Corrupt
Criticize
Crumble
Crush
Cultivate

**D**

Decay
Deceive
Declare
Dedicate

Defend
Defy
Degrade
Demand
Demean
Demolish
Denounce
Deplete
Desert
Deserve
Despise
Destroy
Detest
Develop
Devour
Disagree
Disapprove
Disbelieve
Discipline
Disclose
Discontinue
Discourage
Discover
Discriminate
Discuss
Disagree
Disguise
Dishearten
Dishonor

**D** (Cont.)

| | | | |
|---|---|---|---|
| Disinherit | Exaggerate | Grumble | Inflate |
| Disintegrate | Examine | Guard | Infringe |
| Dismantle | Exceed | Guide | Infuriate |
| Disobey | Excel | | Inherit |
| Disperse | Exchange | **H** | Insinuate |
| Displace | Exist | Handle | Instigate |
| Display | Expect | Harass | Instill |
| Displease | Expel | Harm | Insult |
| Dispose | Explain | Harmonize | Intend |
| Disprove | Explode | Hassle | Interfere |
| Dispute | Exploit | Hate | Interrupt |
| Disregard | Explore | Haunt | Introduce |
| Disrupt | Expose | Heal | Intrude |
| Distort | Extend | Help | Invade |
| Disturb | | Hesitate | Invent |
| Divide | **F** | Hide | Invest |
| Divorce | Fabricate | Honor | Investigate |
| Dominate | Fake | Host | Invite |
| Dream | Falter | Humiliate | Involve |
| Drift | Familiarize | | Irritate |
| | Fascinate | **I** | Isolate |
| **E** | Favor | Idealize | |
| Embarrass | Feel | Idle | **J-K** |
| Emerge | Fight | Ignite | Journey |
| Empty | Finalize | Ignore | Judge |
| Emulate | Finish | Imitate | |
| Enable | Flirt | Impair | **L** |
| Encounter | Float | Impart | Lament |
| Encourage | Flood | Impersonate | Limit |
| Endow | Flourish | Implement | |
| Endure | Flow | Implicate | **M** |
| Energize | Force | Implore | Manipulate |
| Enhance | Free | Imply | Minimize |
| Enjoy | Frighten | Impose | Mirror |
| Enlarge | Frustrate | Imprison | Misbehave |
| Enlighten | | Improvise | Miscalculate |
| Enrich | **G** | Incite | Misinterpret |
| Entertain | Generalize | Include | Misjudge |
| Entice | Gloat | Increase | Mislead |
| Entrust | Gossip | Indulge | Misplace |
| Escape | Graduate | Infect | Misrepresent |

**M** (Cont.)
Mistake
Mistreat
Misuse
Mourn

**N**
Neglect
Negotiate
Notice
Notify
Nourish
Nurture

**O**
Object
Oblige
Obscure
Observe
Obstruct
Obtain
Occupy
Offend
Offer
Oppose
Oppress
Order
Organize
Originate
Outmatch
Outreach
Overcome
Overdose
Overflow
Overpower
Overprotect
Overreact
Overrule
Overturn

**P-Q**
Pace

Pain
Panic
Perform
Permit
Persecute
Persuade
Ponder
Praise
Pray
Preach
Predict
Prefer
Prejudge
Prepare
Present
Preserve
Presume
Pretend
Prevail
Prevent
Proceed
Procure
Produce
Profess
Progress
Prohibit
Project
Promote
Propose
Prosecute
Prosper
Protect
Protest
Provide
Provoke
Punish
Question

**R**
Rationalize
Reach

Realize
Reason
Reassure
Rebound
Receive
Reclaim
Recognize
Reconsider
Recover
Rectify
Reduce
Refine
Reflect
Reform
Regress
Regret
Regroup
Regulate
Rehabilitate
Reinforce
Reinvest
Reject
Rejoice
Rejoin
Rejuvenate
Relapse
Relate
Relax
Release
Relieve
Relinquish
Relish
Relive
Relocate
Remain
Remedy
Remember
Remind
Remove
Renege
Re negotiate

Renounce
Reopen
Reorganize
Repair
Repay
Repeat
Replace
Reply
Repossess
Represent
Repress
Reprieve
Reprimand
Request
Require
Rescue
Resemble
Resent
Resign
Respond
Restrain
Restrict
Resume
Retain
Retaliate
Rethink
Retire
Retrace
Retreat
Retrieve
Reverse
Review
Reward
Ridicule
Rise
Risk

**S**
Savor
Scandalize
Scar

**S** (Cont.)

| | | **T** | **U** |
|---|---|---|---|
| Scheme | Spoil | Tame | Understand |
| Scold | Squeeze | Tease | Upset |
| Scream | Stain | Thank | |
| Search | Stifle | Think | **V-Z** |
| Seek | Strain | Threaten | Worry |
| Self-destruct | Succeed | Train | |
| Shock | Surprise | Transform | |
| Smile | Survive | Treat | |
| Smother | Suspect | | |
| Snuggle | Suspend | | |
| Speculate | Sympathize | | |
| Split | | | |

# WORD LIST

## Adjectives

(Words which serve to describe or modify Nouns)
Example: I feel like an *abandoned* person.

**A**

| | | | **D** |
|---|---|---|---|
| Abandoned | Apparent | Casual | Decadent |
| Absent | Appealing | Cheap | Deceitful |
| Absolute | Approachable | Comfortable | Deceptive |
| Abusive | Arbitrary | Compatible | Dedicated |
| Acceptable | Aromatic | Competent | Deep |
| Accepted | Arrogant | Competitive | Defensive |
| Accessible | Ashamed | Complex | Defiant |
| Accidental | Astute | Concerned | Deficient |
| Accustomed | Attached | Confident | Degenerate |
| Active | Available | Confined | Degraded |
| Actual | Awkward | Confused | Degrading |
| Acute | Azure | Conscious | Dejected |
| Adept | | Consistent | Delicate |
| Adequate | **B** | Constant | Delighted |
| Adjacent | Barren | Contemptible | Delinquent |
| Adorable | Bashful | Contented | Dependent |
| Advance | Bearable | Continual | Deplorable |
| Adverse | Beloved | Continuous | Depressed |
| Affective | Beneficial | Controlled | Depressing |
| Affluent | Blessed | Correct | Deserving |
| Aggressive | Blind | Corrupt | Desperate |
| Alert | Blissful | Courteous | Despicable |
| Alien | Boring | Critical | Destitute |
| Amiable | Bright | Crucial | Destructive |
| Amoral | Broken | Crude | Detached |
| Amorous | | Cruel | Detestable |
| Animated | **C** | Curious | Devious |
| Anti-social | Capable | Cynical | Diehard |
| Anxious | Captive | | Different |

**D** (Cont.)

| | | | |
|---|---|---|---|
| Difficult | Eccentric | Exposed | First |
| Diligent | Educated | Expressive | Fitting |
| Diminished | Effective | Extended | Flagrant |
| Disagreeable | Effortless | Extreme | Flexible |
| Disappointed | Egocentric | Exuberant | Floating |
| Disappointing | Eligible | | Forced |
| Disarming | Eloquent | **F** | Forceful |
| Discreet | Elusive | Fabulous | Forgetful |
| Disgraceful | Eminent | Fallible | Forgiving |
| Disgusting | Emotional | False | Formal |
| Dishonest | Emotionless | Familiar | Formidable |
| Dishonorable | Encouraging | Famous | Fragile |
| Disinterested | Enduring | Fanatic | Fraudulent |
| Disloyal | Energetic | Fanciful | Freak |
| Dismal | Engaged | Fantastic | Free |
| Disorderly | Engaging | Farewell | Frequent |
| Disposable | Engrossed | Farfetched | Frigid |
| Distant | Enlightened | Farsighted | Frivolous |
| Distasteful | Enormous | Fascinating | Frugal |
| Distinct | Entertaining | Fashionable | Fruitful |
| Distinctive | Enthusiastic | Fateful | Frustrated |
| Distressful | Erotic | Fatherly | Frustrating |
| Disturbed | Erratic | Faulty | Fugitive |
| Diverse | Essential | Favorable | Fulfilled |
| Divided | Ethical | Favorite | Fulfilling |
| Domestic | Eventful | Fearful | Fundamental |
| Dominant | Evergreen | Fearless | Furious |
| Domineering | Everlasting | Feasible | Future |
| Dreadful | Everyday | Feeble | |
| Driven | Evident | Feisty | **G** |
| Drunken | Evil | Fervent | Genuine |
| Drunk | Excellent | Feverish | Gifted |
| Dubious | Exceptional | Fiendish | Gloomy |
| Durable | Excess | Fierce | Golden |
| Dutiful | Excessive | Fiery | Gradual |
| Dynamic | Excitable | Filthy | Grateful |
| | Excited | Final | Gratifying |
| **E** | Exotic | Financial | Greedy |
| Eager | Expendable | Fine | Gregarious |
| Earthly | Experienced | Finished | Guilty |
| Easygoing | Expert | Firm | |

# H

| | | | |
|---|---|---|---|
| Half-hearted | Identical | Incapable | Inhospitable |
| Handy | Idiotic | Incessant | Inhuman |
| Hard-core | Idle | Inclined | Inhumane |
| Hardheaded | Ignorant | Included | Inoffensive |
| Harmful | Ill | Incoherent | Inquisitive |
| Harmless | Illegal | Incompetent | Insane |
| Harmonious | Ill-fated | Inconceivable | Insensible |
| Harsh | Ill-mannered | Inconclusive | Insidious |
| Hasty | Ill-natured | Inconsiderate | Insightful |
| Hateful | Ill-tempered | Inconspicuous | Insolent |
| Haughty | Imaginary | Inconvenient | Inspired |
| Hazardous | Imaginative | Incorrect | Inspiring |
| Headstrong | Imitation | Incurable | Instinctive |
| Healthful | Immaculate | Indebted | Insufferable |
| Healthy | Immature | Indecent | Insufficient |
| Hectic | Immediate | Indefinite | Intelligent |
| Helpful | Imminent | Independent | Intend |
| Helpless | Immodest | Indestructible | Intense |
| Heroic | Immoral | Indifferent | Intentional |
| Hesitant | Immortal | Indignant | Interested |
| Hidden | Immune | Indirect | Interesting |
| High | Impartial | Indispensable | Intolerant |
| High-spirited | Impatient | Indisputable | Invaluable |
| High-strung | Impeccable | Indistinct | Inventive |
| Homemade | Imperfect | Individual | Invisible |
| Honorable | Impersonal | Indivisible | Inviting |
| Horrendous | Impolite | Ineffective | Involved |
| Horrible | Important | Inept | Invulnerable |
| Hospitable | Imposing | Inescapable | Iron-fisted |
| Hostile | Impossible | Inexcusable | Irrational |
| Huge | Impotent | Infamous | Irreconcilable |
| Humble | Impractical | Infectious | Irregular |
| Humiliating | Impressive | Inferior | Irrelevant |
| Hungry | Improper | Inflammatory | Irresponsible |
| Hung up | Inaccessible | Inflexible | Irreverent |
| Hurtful | Inaccurate | Influential | |
| Hypocritical | Inactive | Infrequent | **J** |
| | Inadequate | Ingenious | Joyous |
| **I** | Inadvertent | Inhabited | Jubilant |
| Idealistic | Inappropriate | Inherent | Justifiable |

**K**
Kind
Kindhearted

**L**
Latent
Legendary
Legitimate
Lenient
Likable
Limited
Logical
Lovesick
Luxurious
Lying

**M**
Malicious
Manly
Meaningful
Mindful
Mischievous
Miserable
Misguided
Moody
Moral
Mournful
Mutual

**N**
Narrow
Nasty
Negative
Negligent
Nervous
Neurotic
Nonviolent
Normal
Noticeable
Nourishing

**O**
Obedient

Objectionable
Objective
Obligatory
Oblivious
Obnoxious
Obscene
Obscure
Observant
Obsessive
Obsolete
Obstinate
Obtrusive
Obvious
Occasional
Ominous
Ongoing
Open-minded
Opposed
Opposite
Oppressive
Orderly
Ordinary
Organized
Original
Outside
Outspoken
Overbearing
Oversensitive

**P**
Painful
Panic
Passive
Past
Patient
Perceptive
Permanent
Permissive
Persistent
Personal
Persuasive

Pessimistic
Petty
Polite
Political
Pompous
Positive
Possessive
Possible
Potent
Potential
Practical
Praiseworthy
Precious
Predatory
Preferable
Premature
Preoccupied
Prepared
Present
Presentable
Pretentious
Pretty
Previous
Primitive
Pristine
Privileged
Probable
Productive
Profane
Professional
Proficient
Profitable
Progressive
Prohibitive
Prominent
Promiscuous
Prompt
Proper
Prosperous
Prudent
Punctual

Purposeful

**Q**
Questionable
Quiet

**R**
Rational
Raving
Reasonable
Receptive
Refined
Regressive
Regrettable
Related
Relative
Relaxed
Relentless
Relevant
Reliable
Relieved
Religious
Reluctant
Remorseful
Remote
Removed
Renewable
Reprehensible
Repressed
Repugnant
Repulsive
Reputable
Resentful
Reserved
Resistant
Resistible
Resourceful
Respectable
Respectful
Responsible
Responsive

**R** (Cont.)

| | | | |
|---|---|---|---|
| Restrained | Self-disciplined | Suppressive | Underlying |
| Restricted | Self-evident | Sure | Undeserved |
| Restrictive | Self-imposed | Sustaining | Undesired |
| Retired | Self-inflicted | Sympathetic | Undiscovered |
| Revengeful | Selfless | | Undivided |
| Reverent | Self-made | **T** | Uneducated |
| Reversible | Self-possessed | Tainted | Unexpected |
| Rewarding | Self-preserving | Tall | Unforgiving |
| Ridiculous | Self-proclaimed | Tame | Unfriendly |
| Righteous | Self-respecting | Tasteless | Unhappy |
| Risky | Self-righteous | Tedious | Unhealthy |
| Risqué | Self-sufficient | Tempestuous | Unkind |
| Rocky | Self-supporting | Tenderhearted | Unlucky |
| Routine | Self-sustaining | Tense | Unnatural |
| Rude | Sensible | Territorial | Unplanned |
| Ruthless | Serious | Thankful | Unpleasant |
| | Serious-minded | Thankless | Unproven |
| **S** | Shameful | Thoughtless | Unpunished |
| Sacred | Significant | Timid | Unreliable |
| Sarcastic | Silent | Tolerable | Unsafe |
| Sassy | Sinful | Tongue-tied | Unsuccessful |
| Satisfactory | Skilled | Touchy | Unsuitable |
| Saturated | Skillful | Tough | Unsuited |
| Savage | Sleazy | Tragic | Unsure |
| Savory | Small-minded | Treacherous | Unwanted |
| Scandalous | Sorrowful | Trivial | Unworthy |
| Scarce | Sorry | Trustworthy | Uptight |
| Scented | Spirited | Trusty | Useful |
| Scornful | Stagnant | Typical | Useless |
| Seasonal | Steady | | |
| Secret | Stingy | **U** | **V** |
| Selective | Stormy | Ugly | Vague |
| Self-appointed | Stressful | Unacceptable | Vain |
| Self-asserting | Strict | Unavoidable | Vicious |
| Self-centered | Strong | Unbecoming | Violent |
| Self-composed | Stupid | Uncaring | |
| Self-confessed | Subliminal | Unclear | **W-Z** |
| Self-conscious | Successful | Uncomfortable | Wasted |
| Self-destructive | Superficial | Uncomplicated | Wasteful |
| Self-determined | Superior | Unconscious | Weary |
| Self-devoted | Supportive | Undecided | Worthless |

# WORD LIST

## Adverbs

(Words which serve to describe or modify Verbs)
Example:   He smiled *sarcastically* and then looked away.

| A-D | H-N | O-Q | R-Z |
|-----|-----|-----|-----|
| Above | Hopefully | Occasionally | Regrettably |
| Across | Ideally | Personally | Rightly |
| Astray | Immediately | | Sarcastically |
| | | | Scarcely |
| **E-G** | | | Surely |
| Extremely | | | |
| Farthest | | | |

# BIBLIOGRAPHY

Barthes, Roland. *A Lover's Discourse*. New York: Hill And Wang, 1978.

Capellanus, Andreas. *The Art Of Courtly Love*. New York: Fredrick Ungar Publishing Co., 1959.

Chapman, Robert L, ed.. *Roget's International Thesaurus, 4th ed.*. New York: Thomas Y. Crowell, Publishers, 1977.

Clark, David; Beaty, John; Bowyer, John; Neu, Jacob. *Form And Style: A Manual Of Composition And Rhetoric*. New York: F.S. Crofts And Co., 1935.

Fraser, Antonia, ed. *Love Letters: An Anthology*. New York: Alfred A. Knopf, Inc., 1977.

Friedman, Norman; McLaughlin, Charles. *Logic, Rhetoric And Style*. Boston: Little, Brown And Company, 1963.

Gilman, E. Ward, ed.. *Merriam-Webster Thesaurus*. New York: Pocket Books, a division of Simon And Schuster, 1978.

Holmes, Richard, ed.. *Shelly On Love*. Berkeley: Univ. Of California Press, 1980.

Lasswell, Marcia; Lobsenz, Norman. *Styles Of Loving*. Garden City, New York: Doubleday And Company, Inc., 1980.

Norman, Charles, ed.. *Come Live With Me*. New York: McKay, 1966.

Perrin, Porter. *Writer's Guide And Index To English, 3rd ed.*. Chicago: Scott, Foresman And Company, 1959.

Roberts, Kate, ed.. *Hoyt's New Cyclopedia Of Practical Quotations*. New York: Funk And Wagnalls Company, 1940.

Semmelmeyer, Madeline; Bolander, Donald. *Instant English Handbook*. Little Falls, N.J.: Career Publishing, Inc., 1981.

Spender, Stephen, ed.. *A Choice Of English Romantic Poetry*. New York: The Dial Press, 1947.

Strunk; White. *Elements Of Style, 3rd ed.*. New York: Macmillan, 1979.

**Sullerot, Evelyne.** *Women On Love.* Garden City, New York: Doubleday And Company, Inc., 1979.

**Trefethen, Florence.** *Writing A Poem.* Boston: The Writer, Inc., 1970.

**Untermeyer, Louis.** *An Uninhibited Treasury Of Erotic Poetry.* New York: The Dial Press, 1963.

**Walsh, Chad.** *Doors Into Poetry.* Englewood Cliffs, N.J.: Prentice-Hall, Inc., 1962.

**Walsh, William, ed..** *Encyclopedia Of Prose And Poetical Quotations.* Philadelphia: The John C. Winston Company, 1959.

**Wilkinson, Bonaro.** *The Poetic Way Of Release.* New York: Alfred A. Knopf, Inc., 1931.

**Wyse, Lois.** *Lovetalk.* Garden City, N.J.: Doubleday And Company, Inc., 1973.

# INDEX

## A

Abandoned, 102,111
Absence, 89
Actuality, 89
Adjective Love Terms, 215-229
Adjectives, 191-192
Admiration, 89
Admire, 111
Admit, 111
Adorable, 102
Adoration, 89
Adore, 111
Adverb Love Terms, 237-240
Adverbs, 195-196
Affection, 74-89
Affectionate, 102
Affectionately, 116
Affirm, 111
Agony, 89
Alliteration, 133
Allusion, 138
Alone, 102
Anacreon, 20
Anapest, 127
Angelic, 102
Anguish, 67, 89
Anniversaries, 68
Answer, 89
Anticipation, 90
Anxiety, 90
Assonance, 133
Attachment, 90
Attraction, 37
Attractive, 102
Attributive Adjectives, 192

## B

Ballad Stanza, 136
Basic Poetic Unit, 134
Beauty, 90
Belated Reply, 38
Biblical Characters, 246
Biblical Places, 246
Biblical Terms, 246
Birds, 251
Body, 90
Bonaparte, Napoleon, 7-9
Bond, 90
Bourdillon, Francis W., 16
Bracket Rhyme, 133
Brawne, Fanny, 10
Browning, Elizabeth Barrett, 15, 20
Build, 90

## C

Caress, 90, 111
Caring, 102
Charm, 91
Charming, 102
Cheeks, 91
Cherish, 111
Christmas, 69
Cities, 254-255
Clauses, 198-199
Closed Couplet, 134
Closeness, 91
Closings, 85
Coates, Florence E., 15
Coleridge, Samuel T., 19
Colon, 201
Comma, 199-200
Commitment, 91
Common Nouns, 187
Compassionate, 102
Confidence, 91
Conjugation, 192-193
Consonance, 133
Constancy, 91
Constellations, 245
Couplet, 134, 167-184
Credibility, 91

## D

Dad, 55, 58, 93
Dactyl, 127
D'Agoult, Marie, 12
Darkness, 91
Dash, 201
De Beauharnais, Josephine, 7-9
Declarations, 39
Dedication, 91
Delight, 91
Delightful, 102
Delirious, 103
Departure, 92
Depend, 111
Depression, 92
Deprived, 111
Descriptive Adjectives, 191
Deserted, 112
Deserts of the World, 252
Desirable, 103
Desire, 40, 80, 92, 112
Desolate, 103
Despair, 67, 92
Desperation, 92
Destiny, 41

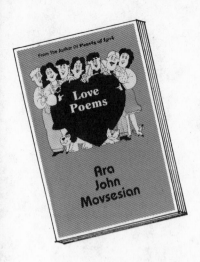

# Order Form
(May be Photocopied - Please Do Not Tear Out)

Name _____

Address _____

City _____ State _____ Zip _____-_____

Purchase Order No. (Governmental/Institutional Only) _____

Telephone ( ) _____-_____ Ordered By _____

Ship To _____

Address _____

City _____ State _____ Zip _____-_____

Attention _____

Please send me/us the following book(s):

| Qty | Description | Each | Total |
|---|---|---|---|
|  | Pearls of Love (0-916919-00-5) | $12.95 |  |
|  | Love Poems  (0-916919-60-9) | $ 6.95 |  |
|  | **Subtotal** | | |
|  | State Sales Tax (Calif. Residents Only) | | |
|  | Postage & Handling ($3.50 or 20% of Subtotal, Whichever is Greater) | | |
|  | **Total Order Amount** | | |

❑ Check  ❑ Money Order  in the amount of $_____ is enclosed to cover the total cost of the order.

## The Electric Press
*Mail-Order Department*
P.O. Box 6025 • Fresno, CA  93703

# About The Author

Kalinian

Ara John Movsesian was born on June 16, 1949, in Troy, New York. In 1955, he and his parents moved to California and settled in Fresno where he spent his childhood and adolescence. While still in his teens, he began to write songs for personal enjoyment, and a love of poetry grew out of this passtime. In 1969, Ara entered the University of California at Berkeley from where, in 1974, he graduated with a Masters Degree in Architecture. Today, he is a licensed architect and a published poet whose works have won several awards. To him, his vocation and avocation are interrelated endeavors. "One cannot separate Writing - a romantic and creative process from Architecture - a visionary profession. They both require inspiration, technical ability, and discipline." **Pearls of Love** is his first major literary work in which he combines poetry and prose to create a comprehensive and valuable "How-To" book on Love Letters and Love Poems.